The American Legal System and Civic Engagement

The American Legal System and Civic Engagement

Why We All Should Think Like Lawyers

Kenneth A. Manaster

palgrave
macmillan

THE AMERICAN LEGAL SYSTEM AND CIVIC ENGAGEMENT

First published in 2013 by
PALGRAVE MACMILLAN®
in the United States—a division of St. Martin's Press LLC,
175 Fifth Avenue, New York, NY 10010.

Where this book is distributed in the UK, Europe and the rest of the world, this is by Palgrave Macmillan, a division of Macmillan Publishers Limited, registered in England, company number 785998, of Houndmills, Basingstoke, Hampshire RG21 6XS.

Palgrave Macmillan is the global academic imprint of the above companies and has companies and representatives throughout the world.

ISBN: 978–1–137–34481–6

Library of Congress Cataloging-in-Publication Data

Manaster, Kenneth A.
The American legal system and civic engagement : why we all should think like lawyers / By Kenneth A. Manaster.
pages cm
Includes index.
ISBN 978–1–137–34481–6 (alk. paper)
1. Justice, Administration of—United States—Citizen participation.
I. Title.

KF384.M26 2013
349.73—dc23 2013008556

A catalogue record of the book is available from the British Library.

Design by Newgen Knowledge Works (P) Ltd., Chennai, India.

First edition: September 2013

10 9 8 7 6 5 4 3 2 1

To Guy Manaster, My Brother

"To communicate the spirit of the judges to the minds of all the citizens..."

Alexis de Tocqueville
Democracy in America

Contents

Acknowledgments

As I wrote this book, I benefited tremendously from ideas, assistance, and encouragement from many people. I am grateful to them all.

Central to the effort were colleagues at Santa Clara University. Under the auspices of the University's Markkula Center for Applied Ethics, workshops in 2011 and 2012 brought together faculty members from multiple disciplines to discuss this project. My thanks go to Brian Buckley, David DeCosse, Janet Flammang, Kirk Hanson, Sally Lehrman, Lawrence Nelson, Terri Peretti, and Chad Raphael. Their insights were invaluable, and their kindness is deeply appreciated.

At the School of Law, Dean Donald J. Polden's sustained interest and support helped me keep moving forward with this work. A law faculty workshop provided helpful reactions from many of my fellow law teachers. The thorough and enthusiastic research assistance of the following extraordinarily talented Santa Clara law students nourished the project in many ways: Amber D'Ercole, Michael Foy, Carrie Macintosh, Tijana Martinovic, and Ahan Kim Morris. The faculty support services of Hayley Redburn and Kristen Whyte masterfully managed the logistics of bringing the manuscript to fruition.

Beyond Santa Clara, Alicia Oberman generously and thoughtfully responded to the evolving manuscript. Kevin Esterling and other participants in a panel discussion at the 2012 Midwest Political Science Association conference also provided helpful comments.

At Palgrave Macmillan, the initial interest and guidance of Matthew Kopel, and the later skillful and kind assistance of Scarlet Neath, Brian O'Connor, Deepa John, and Ciara Vincent, were this book's lifeline.

My deepest gratitude is to my beloved wife, Ann Brandewie, for her unfailing support and so much more, for which I am thankful beyond words.

1

The Citizen's Task

Everybody has an opinion. Each of us has a point of view on at least one issue of public concern. Around election time, and at most other times too, we somehow reach our individual conclusions on topics of the day, big and small. Most of us find frequent opportunities to express those opinions as well. This is obviously just as it should be in a democracy, especially one that so highly values free speech. We share and test our ideas through "the eternal arguing that is the essence of American democracy."[1]

The premise of this book is that the ordinary citizen could form his opinions on public issues—and fulfill his civic responsibility—more intelligently and confidently if he had more guidance on how to do it. More specifically, he could benefit from perspectives on how to evaluate the information and arguments swirling around him, seek out additional information if he thinks he needs it, and reach conclusions about what makes sense and what does not. The individual who is better oriented and equipped in these ways can contribute much more effectively to a rational and civil discussion of these issues. As is widely recognized, in recent years there has been a serious and disheartening paucity of such public discussion. This book, drawing from the tools and traditions of the American legal system, offers guidance to aid the citizen in understanding public issues and participating in the type of responsible public debate these challenging issues deserve.

Our democracy has been aptly described as "an engine for producing a diverse menu of conversation about public affairs, largely carried on in public."[2] John Locke, too, spoke of "the variety of opinions and contrariety of interest which happen in all collections of men."[3] Through the noisy, chaotic expression of our opinions, we create the evolving character, values, and concerns of our society. More concretely, we choose the leadership and shape the policy directions of our government. Alexander Hamilton, in *The Federalist No. 71*, emphasized "that the deliberate sense of the community should govern the conduct of those to whom they intrust the management of their affairs."[4] This "deliberate sense" is the combined result of the opinions, and ultimately the voices and votes, of individual men and women. A bedrock principle of modern American democracy—"today's most honored notion of citizenship, the ideal of the 'informed citizen'"—is that we each have this opportunity to think for ourselves and express our own conclusions on public issues.[5]

This opportunity is sometimes described as a *privilege* the citizen enjoys. California voters, for example, are officially advised, "It is a wonderful privilege in a democracy to have a choice and the right to voice your opinion."[6] At other times, we speak of the citizen as having a *duty* to make up his mind about public issues and give voice to his conclusions. From this perspective, at a minimum, each of us should express our views through voting. More frequently, the formation and expression of our opinions take place through other means: private conversations with friends, relatives, and coworkers; classroom discussions with fellow students and teachers; participation in political campaigns and community groups; letters to the editor, Internet blogs, emails and other writings; calls to radio and television talk shows; and in many other settings.

Although this individual responsibility is not a legally enforceable duty, its importance has long been emphasized by political leaders and commentators. Justice Louis Brandeis of the Supreme Court believed "that public discussion is a political duty."[7] President Truman reportedly said, "The highest office in a democracy is that of a citizen."[8] More sharply, Thomas Jefferson observed that "people who expect to be ignorant and free expect what never was and never will be."[9]

A modern scholar has acknowledged, albeit skeptically, "the widespread conviction that it is the responsibility of a citizen in a democracy to have opinions about everything, or at least everything that pertains to the conduct of this country's affairs."[10] Similar doubts about this expectation were well expressed by the central character in a leading British novel:

> People may indeed have a certain duty to think about great affairs and form their opinions. But life being what it is, how can ordinary people truly be expected to have "strong opinions" on all manner of things...? There is, after all, a real limit to how much ordinary people can learn and know, and to demand that each and every one of them contribute "strong opinions" to the great debates of the nation cannot, surely, be wise.[11]

Other commentators over recent decades have described the citizen's duty more positively, even eloquently:

> Universal suffrage, by giving all a share in the control of the government, makes it mandatory for every man to become a statesman."[12]
>
> Democracy offers more but also requires more from the individual than any other form of society... In a democracy... it is [the individual's] personal responsibility and that of educational institutions to prepare him for participation in community affairs... The individual must be independent and informed and conscious of the choices before him. He must develop the capacity to weigh values and know the implications and consequences of his decisions.[13]
>
> There is a fundamental difference between shouldering the rights and responsibilities that come with citizenship—engagement, participation, debate—and merely inhabiting the land.[14]
>
> Democracy is only effective to the extent that the public are well informed about issues and can think independently and critically about those issues.[15]
>
> The claim of democracy is that every man decides for himself. The use of one's natural faculties to determine for oneself what is true and false and good and bad is the American philosophic method.[16]

However this responsibility may be phrased, meeting it is not easy for anyone. It is difficult to understand the ever-changing issues confronting us in twenty-first-century America, and perhaps it always has been. Public issues are usually complicated, and we are often barraged with arguments and asserted "facts" thrust before us by those who want to persuade us to share their views. Again, this is as it should be. In a society that cherishes freedom of speech, we should welcome the incessant contest of information and argument, even though it often seems confusing and overwhelming.

Unfortunately, when we try to discern how to meet our individual civic responsibility, we find very little guidance available to us, either as children in the educational system or as adults in the working, and voting, worlds. "In the schools, the young have been exposed to an education which has been far more effective in preparing for academic learning and vocation than for an understanding of the processes and problems of democratic society."[17] This obviously is a serious failing, especially in light of the importance of education in a democracy. The critical role of American education was emphasized by Justice Thurgood Marshall:

> Education serves the essential function of instilling in our young an understanding of and appreciation for the principles and operation of our governmental processes. Education may instill the interest and provide the tools necessary for political discourse and debate. Indeed, it

has frequently been suggested that education is the dominant factor affecting political consciousness and participation.[18]

There is no substitute for the kind of education Justice Marshall describes. There is, however, an additional area of our public life in which guidance can be found for enhancing individual capability to meet our civic duty. This guidance comes from the American legal system, which prides itself on using structured processes for reaching decisions based on solid evidence and purposeful policy. Every day judges and jurors rely on these processes to help guide them toward decisions in complex disputes. Lawyers perform a central role in these processes, as they marshal evidence and arguments both to highlight the facts and reasoning behind the positions they want judges and juries to accept, and also to challenge opposing positions.

This book will explain the core tools and traditions of the law that are used by lawyers, judges, and jurors. As should be obvious, these three categories of participants in the legal system do not all use the law's methods in exactly the same ways or for the same purposes. Nonetheless, the tools and traditions explained here characterize in a variety of ways the work people do in all three of these roles. These methods of the law are, in other words, the foundation and common denominator of the work of lawyers, judges, and jurors. This book's guidance for the citizen builds on this foundation.

Occasionally, we speak of "the court of public opinion" to describe the ongoing discussion of controversial issues. Certainly, any comparison would be imperfect between a court of law, with its established procedures and decorum, and the diverse, everyday arenas in which people try to inform and persuade each other about public issues. Nevertheless, the law's well-established methods for reaching decisions can be drawn from to help citizens reach their decisions on public issues.

When we speak of "public issues," the governance and welfare of our society are our most prominent concerns, and they will be the most frequent reference point here. They are the issues found in "each day's serious reported news, the iron core of information that is at the center of a functioning democracy," as distinguished from merely "pleasant and diverting stories."[19] Our purpose here, however, is not to evaluate the relative importance of some kinds of issues as compared to others. Lots of people focus frequently on matters that virtually everyone knows do not raise any broad, serious concerns. Public debates—at times, really, just widespread gossip or tabloid publicity—regularly dissect, for example, the steps and missteps of established or newly minted celebrities. These topics, too, probably can be included within the broad scope of public issues in this exploration of guidance on how to understand and evaluate them.[20]

This book rests on four important assumptions. First, it assumes that the individual citizen is likely to be interested at some times in some issues. It conversely assumes that he or she is not, nor even should be, interested at all times in all issues. In a society as complex and contentious as ours, with so many people so busy with so many obligations and pastimes, it would be unrealistic in the extreme to assume otherwise.

Second, it is assumed here that the function of public opinion is not for voters, individually or collectively, to constantly convey to their representatives exactly what positions those officials should adopt on specific issues. Certainly citizens often should and do express their preferences on issues to both their elected leaders and other government officials. In doing so, they are pursuing what political scientists view as a "delegate" model of democracy, in which citizens' expressed preferences guide the actions of the government. To a considerable degree, however, a "trustee" model characterizes our society. In that view, officials are charged to exercise their own best judgment on behalf of the citizenry, even if messages from the voters are absent, ambiguous, or contrary.[21] Regardless of which model or combination of models best describes American democracy,[22] the need remains for informed, thoughtful citizens to understand various issues. They then are able to apply their understanding to the selection of their leaders, and to the communication of their ideas to those leaders and other government functionaries.

A third assumption, grounded in the many kinds of differences that characterize the American people, is that not all individuals or communities are equally well positioned to delve into and understand public issues and to express their views effectively. By virtue of many factors—education, economic status, life experiences, regional needs and interests, and many other circumstances—our inclinations, opportunities, and abilities to grapple with specific issues are not evenly distributed among us. "Indeed, greatly unequal citizen contributions to any ongoing dialogue about public matters seems an irreducible fact of our public life."[23] A major, recent study of political participation described the situation this way:

> One of the hallmarks of democracy is that the concerns and interests of each citizen be given equal consideration in the process of making decisions that are binding on a political community. Nevertheless, . . . the

> disparities in political voice across various segments of society are so substantial and so persistent as to preclude equal consideration.[24]

In particular, that study documents "the association between socioeconomic status and political voice."[25] It confirms the serious reality that "economic inequality undercuts the possibility for political equality."[26]

With this reality in mind, the guidance to be offered here is not simply intended to benefit intellectual or economic elites who might be broadly advantaged in these respects, at least regarding some types of national issues. Instead, it is hoped that different aspects of what is suggested here will be of potential utility to all citizens. Not all of the ideas offered will be equally accessible and comfortable for everyone, of course, but the intention is that at least some of them, sometimes, can be beneficial to anyone.

A final assumption is that it is worthwhile to focus on the ideal operation of the legal system, even though in reality it often falls short. It is no secret that on a daily basis, the law, and the work of lawyers and others within it, are far from perfect. Not all lawyers always honor their ethical and professional responsibilities. Indeed, not all lawyers unfailingly employ the methods often capsulized as "thinking like a lawyer." Nevertheless, it is assumed here that most of what is done by lawyers, judges, and jurors comes close to the ideal, at least close enough to provide a solid model to extrapolate from, in developing guidance for the ordinary citizen.

This inquiry will begin by summarizing, in chapter 2, some of the major obstacles citizens face in trying to understand issues and reach sound conclusions on them. Chapter 3 will summarize sources of guidance conventionally available to help us form our opinions. This will be followed by the pivotal portion, chapter 4, a survey of the tools and traditions of legal analysis and decision making. The discussion will turn next, in chapter 5, to the embodiment of those tools and traditions in our expectations for how jurors perform their role. Since our society expects so much of ordinary citizens when they are called to serve as jurors, it is worthwhile to ask whether similarly high expectations can be applied to all of us in our everyday roles as voices and voters in our democracy.

Chapter 6 will summarize some of the inescapable differences between the ways in which the law's tools aid decision making in legal contexts and the ways in which opinions are formed and decisions made in broader, much less structured public arenas. After acknowledging these differences, the discussion will turn, in chapter 7, to the applicability of the law's methods to the citizen's task. The analysis will demonstrate how the methods of the law can help guide Americans in forming their opinions and conclusions on public issues. For the reader's convenience and assistance, main points of that guidance will be reviewed in the brief Appendix as well.

Hopefully, as chapter 8 will summarize, it will be shown that there is something useful to be borrowed from the legal arena—something to help the confused, overwhelmed, ordinary American who aims to be a responsible citizen.

2

THE CITIZEN'S OBSTACLES

Even under the best of circumstances, the citizen's task is not easy. By definition, public issues involve matters bigger than the immediate, private concerns of the individual. A person who wants to make intelligent contributions to discussion of public issues must find the time and energy to think and learn about them. Many people are disinclined to do so. Leo Tolstoy pointed this out in *War and Peace* long ago:

> Personal interests of the moment are always so much more significant than the general issues that because of them the latter are never felt—not even noticed, in fact. The majority of the people paid no attention to the general course of events but were influenced only by their immediate personal interests.[1]

Alexis De Tocqueville did so as well, in *Democracy in America*:

> It is difficult to draw a man out of his own circle to interest him in the destiny of the state because he does not clearly understand what influence the destiny of the state can have upon his own lot.[2]

Political scientists debate whether modern technology makes the citizen's job easier or more difficult. The greater flow of information, especially through electronic means, would seem to make it easier to know what is going on, what is at stake, and what needs to be decided in the public realm. "It seems there are fewer and fewer excuses for citizens to claim ignorance and sit democracy out."[3] Some scholars posit that the electronic media's capacity to provide information quickly, conveniently, and comprehensively, including widespread dissemination of political analysis, will produce a significant increase in political participation.[4] In particular, the possibilities opened up by the Internet are unprecedented:

> The Internet can convey everything that television, magazines, radio, and newspapers do, and in a more timely manner with an easily accessible interface. The Internet can convey every type of visual and audio information on demand. Yet, beyond being simply a compilation of the previous mass media, the Internet presents the first two-way mass conversation . . . One can discover an issue, research that issue and respond to it, and then respond to the responses or even chat about it, and distribute it to networks of other people from any of a multitude of mobile or fixed computing devices.[5]

Many observers, however, see a bleaker picture. In the words of a journalism professor,

> It is hard to reconcile the students' lack of knowledge [of critical public issues] with the notion that they are a part of the celebrated information age, creatures of the Internet who arguably have at their disposal more information than all the preceding generations combined. Despite their BlackBerrys, cellphones, and Wi-Fi, they are, in their own way, as isolated as the remote tribes of New Guinea. They disprove the notion that technology fosters engagement, that connectivity and community are synonymous.[6]

Another study of the Internet's impact observed, "People are using the Internet to gather information in increasing numbers with a clear upward trend, though whether this is resulting in actual learning is unclear."[7]

Regardless of which perspective is most accurate, it is undeniable that the American citizen faces great obstacles to the discharge of her civic duty. The obstacles seem to fall into four overlapping categories, which will be discussed next:

A. The issues are more complex than ever.
B. The volume of information the citizen encounters is greater than ever.
C. The distortion and bias embodied in the information barrage, and its resulting untrustworthiness, are great, perhaps greater than ever.
D. The opportunities, both of time and place, available to the individual for careful, reflective study of the issues seem smaller than ever.

Each of these obstacles has been studied in depth by scholars in various fields. They will only be summarized here, however, as what matters now is the combined effect of these obstacles—discouragement. Citizens increasingly feel confused, distrustful, overwhelmed, and resigned when considering their ability to understand issues and express opinions on them with confidence and clarity. This trend was confirmed in the recent finding "that people under thirty today are less likely than they were fifty years ago to read books or newspapers, watch the news on television, or have interest in and factual knowledge about politics."[8]

A. Complexity

Considering the complexity obstacle, we find an array of daunting issues. Speaking even of the early years of the twentieth century, one scholar observed, "The sea of modern life threatened to engulf everything before it. Everywhere observers recognized a growing complexity of human affairs."[9] Certainly life has not gotten any simpler in the succeeding decades and on into the twenty-first century.

To name some of the most prominent recent issues, we confront global economic interdependence and recession, climate change, international terrorism, diminishing quality in public education, the health care crisis, abortion, stem cell research, medical marijuana, political campaign financing, same-sex marriage, and the futures of Iraq and Afghanistan.[10] Under most of these broad topics, there also are more specific questions and subtopics, which often are difficult to understand separately and which cumulatively make the broader issue seem way beyond our ken. For example, how much of global climate change is caused by human influences? What is the future for climate temperatures if we do nothing? Who is the pertinent "we"? What are the most promising technological, economic, and legal steps to take to diminish the rate of global warming? What are their benefits and costs, particularly as related to economic growth and jobs? Can we do better than just slow the rate of warming and instead actually reverse warming trends?[11]

Similar batches of subsidiary questions could be identified for most of these high-profile, much-talked-about issues. There undoubtedly are experts who can offer informed answers to many of the questions. But can the nonexpert, the ordinary citizen, hope to understand the questions and evaluate possible answers to any of them? Again, it is not easy, as we face "staggeringly complex issues of war and social justice" and more.[12] Nevertheless, we talk about these issues, float our ideas about what should be done, and try to make the best choices we can among political candidates who claim to have good answers and to be well equipped to lead us toward good solutions.

In other words, we try to cope, and sometimes even try just to deny how complicated things are:

> You and I exist in an extraordinarily complicated environment, easily the most rapidly moving and complex that has ever existed on this

> planet. To deal with it, we *need* shortcuts. We can't be expected to recognize and analyze all the aspects in each person, event, and situation we encounter in even one day. We haven't the time, energy or capacity for it. Instead, we must very often use our stereotypes, our rules of thumb, to classify things according to a few key features and then to respond without thinking when one or another of these trigger features is present.[13]

Facing the complexity problem, we understandably attempt to simplify issues or ignore them. "People turn away from news that confuses them."[14] Even the Internet, with the vast variety of information it makes readily available, does not overcome this tendency: "While the Internet is freer and more accessible than any media or medium in history, users can use it to avoid anything with which they may disagree or simply choose not [to] see."[15]

Attempting to find "shortcuts" to simplify our cognitive processes, at times we do thoughtfully seek reliable sources of helpful information on issues. However, we often instead just retreat and do not even try to find added knowledge or sources of guidance to help us function as well-informed citizens. It thus has been suggested that voter turnout in America "may be low because people are called on to vote so often and on so many things...The number and complexity of items on the typical American ballot adds to the information costs; the fact that there always is another election just around the corner makes it easier to rationalize not doing one's civic duty."[16]

"Because of the increasing tendency for cognitive overload in our society, the prevalence of shortcut decision making is likely to increase proportionately."[17] One shortcut is loyalty to a political party that appears generally to favor issue positions the individual finds appealing. When such loyalty rests on the individual's own continuing effort to understand the issues and to confirm that the party's values correspond with his own, then reliance on the party is a constructive shortcut. It is a practical and sensible substitute for a more intensive, personal comprehension of issues. It is a form of "rational ignorance," a choice to "leave the political information gathering to others" as "our jobs, families, hobbies, and other interests leave us little time for in-depth study of political issues."[18]

In contrast, if adherence to party positions lacks such personal inquiry and a readiness to occasionally stray from the party line, and instead becomes merely blind loyalty, then this shortcut is nothing more than a default. It is an abdication of personal engagement with the issues. Growth in the numbers of so-called independent voters, who shun unwavering party loyalty, would seem to be encouraging in this respect.[19]

Nevertheless, the challenge of grappling with complex issues, and the temptation to oversimplify or ignore them, persist. If the challenge is not met and the temptation not resisted, a thoughtful, informed citizenry diminishes, as the following two statements rather harshly assert:

> Too often in the great debates of our time . . . each side envisions a particular characterization of the opposition. In reality, the positions on either side of these debates are often well argued. The debates exist because the issues in question are complex. To ignore this complexity is to become a characterization yourself.[20]
>
> But closing one's mind to complexity isn't mere intellectual laziness; it's a fundamental evasion of freedom.[21]

Further aggravating our difficulty is the tendency of news media, especially television, to blur the line between information and entertainment, at the expense of the former. This tendency has been criticized, but remains strong:

> Today's news is pseudo-news, entertaining bits of fluff that lead viewers and citizens away from the really important information that truly affects our lives . . . There is a real conflict in the news business between news that is useful and necessary—news that news directors think people *need* to know about, even if it is unpleasant or difficult—and news that news directors think that people *want* to know about and will watch—no matter now inane or pointless.[22]
>
> As Dan Rather put it, television news has been "dumbed down and tarted up." The purpose of television news now seems primarily to be to "glue eyeballs to the screen" in order to build ratings and sell advertising. This was a point made by Jon Stewart, the brilliant host of *The Daily Show with Jon Stewart*, when he visited CNN's *Crossfire*: There should be a distinction between news and entertainment. It really matters. The subjugation of news by entertainment seriously harms our democracy: It leads to dysfunctional journalism that fails to inform the people. And when the people are not informed, they cannot hold government accountable when it is incompetent, corrupt, or both.[23]
>
> For their part, the news media do little to provide a model of public discourse. Media commentary, attuned to the standards of spectacle and diversion, is typically confrontational and ideological, consisting of exchanges among people who have already made up their minds. Media accounts tend to focus on personalities rather than issues.[24]

These inclinations of the news media to distract and amuse, rather than to engage and inform, only make it even more difficult for the citizen to come to grips with the complexity of the issues of the day.

B. Flood of Information

There are lots of available nouns to describe the flow of information nowadays: Flood, barrage, and avalanche readily come to mind. The flow simply cannot be avoided. Perhaps an individual who never turns on a television or radio, who never boots up a computer, or never reads a magazine or newspaper would appear to be safely on a bank of this river of information—safely on the bank with his back turned. Even for that unlikely American, however, the torrent sooner or later will spill over and soak him with information on at least some issues. "And due to the sheer volume of news today, even very young kids are exposed to far more information than we ever were at their age."[25]

At many moments during an ordinary day, we are at risk of being inundated with information. "Radio, the Internet, movies, cell phones, iPods, computers, instant messaging, video games, and personal digital assistants all now vie for our attention—but it is television that still dominates the flow of information in modern America."[26] In multitudes of public places around the clock, there are radios and televisions blaring the latest news developments, opinions, and debates. In offices and homes, and while we are on the go, computers and mobile devices keep us informed. "In this era of twenty-four-hour, instantaneous, satellite-transmitted news, it seems like everywhere you turn there is new information to be processed and absorbed, a new crisis to be followed, another health hazard to be on the lookout for, or a new trend to be aware of. With so much news, it's difficult to know what to focus on, and for children of all ages it is mind-boggling."[27]

Especially for young people and students, the information just keeps on coming:

> We follow links sent by our friends. We catch news on apps we read while riding the bus to school or work. We check out blogs or Twitter feeds from folks we know have a good track record of identifying news content which matters to us. We are constantly checking news because news comes to us through every conversation we have throughout the day.[28]

Information on public issues, in other words, is there for us all the time—when we want it and even when we do not. We can choose to find it in broadcast or print journalism, or on the infinite array of sites available on the Internet. Even if we do not look for information, some of it will still find us—in the bus station or airport, pizza shop or coffee shop, hair salon or hospital waiting room, automobile show-room or university cafeteria.

C. Trust

An additional obstacle to engaging with public issues is the sense that so much information in the public arena is not trustworthy. We sometimes can discern that a particular source of information, such as a magazine, cable channel, or website, expressly identifies itself as having a particular point of view on many issues. "Political advertising, many blogs, and most commercial talk radio shows make no claim or pretense of being unbiased."[29] This is not necessarily a bad thing:

> From a positive perspective...the Balkanization of the media—the proliferation of information sources that stretch from foreign TV networks to Weblogs—is a high-tech bonanza of diverse expression...In some cases, the most distinctive characteristic of [modern electronic] journalism is its personalism or unabashed subjectiveness, with gut instinct, rumor or ideology substituted for evidence, deduction or expertise. But while that is at sharp counterpoint to old-school journalism's ideals of objective reporting, it carries the imprimatur of added candor and up-front disclosure.[30]

During the 2008 presidential election campaign period, for example, some news outlets' predilections were evident:

> On any given night, there are two distinctly, even extremely, different views of the presidential campaign offered on two of the three big cable news networks, Fox News Channel and MSNBC, a dual reality that is reflected on the Internet as well.[31]

It had become possible and even easy "to go through the day and watch only networks that agreed with your point of view, Internet shows that filtered out anything you found dull or objectionable."[32] In this way the Internet arguably widens political differences, rather than promoting serious consideration of competing viewpoints. It has been observed that the "Internet provides more opportunity than traditional media sources for people to acquire one-sided information...Unlike television or even newspapers, the content of information on the Internet is entirely at the discretion of the user."[33] "Each of us can select a free-speech package that suits our interests" by consulting only websites that confirm our preexisting inclinations.[34]

Polarization in our politics is thus reflected in, and probably exacerbated by, the electronic media's appeal to niche audiences defined by partisan ideology. "As people acquire less conflicting information by relying on news sources and blogs that share their point of view, they have less cognitive conflict, less ambivalence, and the nation as a whole may become more polarized."[35]

In contrast to obviously partisan voices, it is quite another thing to suspect that supposedly objective, disinterested sources of information are not what they seem. More corrosive to public engagement with the issues are supposedly neutral sources that are not neutral, yet whose hidden agendas and biases cannot readily be discerned:

> The assertions by the established media that it's [*sic*] impartial or balanced in its coverage of news are received by cynical consumers with "a wink and a nod." The concerns of those consumers are not only about the quality of news coverage, but the hidden and undeclared biases that determine what's selected for any coverage at all.[36]

If the citizen cannot tell whether the source of the information is as advertised—knowledgeable, unbiased, and objective—his entirely appropriate response is a frequently heard lament: "I don't know what to believe."[37]

His predicament is most severe when disagreements are based on contradictory statements of what purport to be facts. It has been said that "each of us is entitled to his own opinion, but not to his own facts."[38] Unfortunately, it is not unusual for "the poisoned character of our politics"[39] to produce "lies, distortions, and racist fearmongering."[40] Less sinister, but probably equally problematic, is the frequency of the subject of Princeton philosophy professor Harry Frankfurt's book entitled *On Bullshit*. Frankfurt writes:

> Bullshit is unavoidable whenever circumstances require someone to talk without knowing what he is talking about. Thus the production of bullshit is stimulated whenever a person's obligations or opportunities to speak about some topic exceed his knowledge of the facts that are relevant to that topic. This discrepancy is common in public life, where people are frequently impelled—whether by their own propensities or by the demands of others—to speak extensively about matters of which they are to some degree ignorant.[41]

Streams of ignorant, erroneous, incomplete, or overstated assertions combine to pollute the flow of information. For example, the simple, verifiable detail of where and when President Barack Obama was born has been noisily disputed in some circles, despite the existence of multiple, normal documents establishing the event. At the opposite end of the political spectrum, and without supporting evidence, "somewhere out there, somebody still thinks George W. Bush had the Pentagon bombed on September 11."[42]

There is undoubtedly an abundance of incorrect information in the public arena, and much of it gets visibility and wide circulation. In this climate, it is not surprising that people get confused about facts.[43] A striking example occurred during a meeting between a Member of Congress and a group of his constituents on the issue of health care reform:

> An activist turned to his fellow attendees and asked if "they oppose any form of socialized or government-run health care." Nearly all did. Then [Congressman] Green asked how many of those present were on Medicare. Almost half raised their hands. Now, people who don't know that Medicare is a government program ... may believe some of the disinformation opponents of health care reform are spreading.[44]

There are some places an enterprising citizen can look in order to make better sense of facts, statistics, and claims that are bombarding him. These places include a few relatively new, nonpartisan Internet sites dedicated to fact-checking information in the public arena. Some of the leading examples are:

> www.politifact.com: "A feature of the *Tampa Bay Times* (formerly the *St. Petersburg Times*), is an impartial site that helps you sort out the truth in American politics. We rate the accuracy of statements by elected officials, special interest groups, pundits and talk show hosts.";
>
> www.newstrust.net: "NewsTrust.net provides a wide range of tools that enable users to separate fact from fiction on important public issues. We promote good journalism, news literacy and civic engagement ... In May 2012, NewsTrust.net was acquired by the Poynter Institute, a non-profit journalism training organization.";
>
> www.factcheck.org: "A project of the Annenberg Public Policy Center of the University of Pennsylvania";
>
> http://voices.washingtonpost.com/fact-checker/: "The purpose of this website, and an accompanying column in the [Washington] Post, is to 'truth squad' the statements of political figures regarding issues of great importance, be they national, international, or local."; and

> http://newsbound.com: "A young company experimenting with how to make ongoing news stories more accessible and manageable."

Unfortunately, most Americans are unaware of these sites and might well approach them initially, if at all, with the mistrust that has come to affect so much public perception of information sources.

D. Time and Space

The mixed blessing of massive information flow becomes even more of an obstacle when the citizen has diminished opportunities to digest information. A common observation, as in Tolstoy's statement quoted above, is that most people are so busy with work, family, health concerns, and other personal obligations that they do not have time to study the issues. The sense that a great deal of time is needed for this task is heightened by the three preceding factors—the complexity of the issues, the tremendous volume of available information, and the dubious accuracy and objectivity of that information.

Some scholars assert that opportunities have diminished for interaction among citizens in forums for thoughtful discussion of community concerns. They believe we are more atomized in our daily pursuits, spending less time engaged in the life of our communities. In the words of Robert Putnam, author of *Bowling Alone*, "Without at first noticing, we have been pulled apart from one another and from our communities over the last third of the [twentieth] century."[45]

However, observations about a lack of opportunities to be informed, and its significance, are debatable.[46] It is plausible that "by far the most common explanation" Americans offer for not participating in community affairs is "pervasive busyness," the claim that "I don't have enough time."[47] Nevertheless, the large amounts of time Americans spend in recreational pursuits, including watching television and surfing the Internet, arguably could be diverted, at least in part, to more vital civic concerns.

From a historical perspective, a prominent scholar wrote:

> As Western nations became more prosperous, leisure, which had been put off for several centuries in favor of the pursuit of property, the means to leisure, finally began to be of primary concern. But, in the meantime, any notion of the serious life of leisure, as well as men's taste and capacity to live it, had disappeared. Leisure became entertainment. The end for which they had labored for so long has turned out to be amusement.[48]

Recent studies also suggest that Americans perhaps have "*more* leisure time now than several decades ago...but there is surely no evidence that we have *less*."[49]

The question, simply stated, is not whether people have free time but how they choose to spend it. For example, large numbers of Americans continue to be actively engaged with churches and other religious groups on a regular basis. This suggests the availability of both forums for discussion of issues and personal time for discourse. Additionally, the explosion of content and participation in the Internet opens up entirely new ways—new "spaces"—in which Americans can communicate with each other, as well as with people in other parts of the world. Scholars have examined this transformation resulting from the Internet and have reached striking conclusions:

> It changes how conversations are held and who gets to speak. It changes the location of the public sphere and brings it into homes and offices...There is little argument that the Internet is altering the fundamental nature of how ideas are communicated in society.[50]

> The Internet has made possible a new generation of deliberative discussions...Thousands of chat rooms, listservs, moderated discussions, and other on-line processes bring together people from across the country (and, in some cases, across the globe) to discuss public issues with one another in a way that was not possible before the widespread adoption of the Internet.[51]

Although there is reason to believe that most of us have neither the time to study and discuss public issues, nor available forums in which to do so, this simply may not be as true as some observers fear. Citizens' readiness to grapple with the issues also may be underestimated. President Obama, for one, claims that Americans "not only have a toleration but also a hunger for explanation and complexity, and a willingness to acknowledge hard problems. I think one of the biggest mistakes that is made in Washington is this notion you have to dumb things down for the public."[52]

3

Conventional Guidance

Facing these obstacles, what is a citizen to do? Where can one find guidance on how to understand the issues and develop opinions and conclusions on them? A few conventional sources of guidance are available. Each type mostly operates separately from the others, as they do not have clearly shared objectives, much less shared or coordinated approaches. In other words, individually or in combination, they have only limited and varying degrees of helpfulness.

A. Civics Education

The most logical source of instruction is the educational system. Preparation for participation in the democratic process should be part of an American's education, beginning in the early years and extending at least through secondary school. The importance of also continuing this preparation through undergraduate education has been emphasized in the recommendations of the Political Engagement Project, an initiative of the American Association of State Colleges and Universities.

The Project's 2007 report, entitled *Educating for Democracy: Preparing Undergraduates for Responsible Political Engagement*, states, "Ideally, preparation for active, capable citizenship begins much earlier than during the college years." The report then affirms that this preparation "for the complex demands of informed and active citizenship" should continue on into college. This assertion rests on the premise that "formal education is a powerful predictor of political knowledge, civic values, and active engagement in the political realm."[1] The report urges that college students should be expected to "gain the understanding and skills to be engaged citizens of their communities" and that the "curriculum, the cocurriculum, and the campus culture all hold great potential" for such learning.[2]

High school curricula traditionally included a course in "civics." The course commonly was an introduction to the structure of American government.[3] It has been said that "a basic knowledge of the nation's constitution and legal system, of its political history and institutions, and of its culture and political practice is obviously indispensable to democracy in any form."[4] It is not clear, however, whether the traditional civics course ever even purported to have such breadth. What is even less clear is whether this course, with any consistency or consensus, has ever aimed to strengthen skills in personal information gathering and critical analysis to foster thoughtful development of opinions on public issues. One observer described the deficiency as follows:

> Many school systems have no standards for civic knowledge, much less guidelines for the acquisition of citizen skills that might aid participation in later life... There is little or no attention to student civic orientations, engagement levels, or skills that might enable the discussion of real political issues.[5]

Modern civics education originated early in the twentieth century with the goal of "Americanizing" the country's growing population of immigrants. By the 1960s, however, there was a backlash against civics education, prompted in part by the concern that such instruction could dissuade students from questioning established political norms.[6] Even now, "some faculty worry about whether efforts to promote political development might, even if only inadvertently, bias students in favor of or against particular perspectives or ideologies. And some believe that steering clear of all political issues is the only way to avoid being suspected or accused of political bias."[7] The impacts of these attitudes are still evident in the decreased emphasis on civics, "the withering away of civic education in schools."[8] A similar decline at the college level has also been lamented, as another report of the Political Engagement Project observed:

> The segregation of moral and civic education from the main concerns of the [academic] disciplines put this aspect of undergraduate education very much at risk as curricular flexibility and specialization among both students and faculty continued to grow, as it did throughout the twentieth century.[9]

In high schools, "most formal civic education today comprises only a single semester course on government."[10] The relative unimportance of civics has been acknowledged even in some civics textbooks.

"Americans do most of their political learning without teachers or classes," says one textbook. It also concludes that, for many students, civics education makes virtually no difference in their political attitudes and beliefs.[11]

In the face of this negative assessment—recognition that "educationally, society has put democracy on autopilot and hoped for the best"[12]—there are signs of possible renewal. "Many foundations and progressive educators are experimenting with creative alternatives."[13] These efforts are quite different from traditional classroom civics. The We the People program, for example, applies a hands-on approach to civics education by immersing students in "simulated legislative hearings on constitutional issues."[14]

Similarly, the Close Up Foundation aims to engage students in intensive issue analysis so they may learn how "widely disparate views are ultimately reconciled into public policy."[15] Supreme Court Justice David Souter has spoken about the importance of revitalizing civics education, and has noted President Obama's "support for the legislation and the administrative action needed state by state to ensure that a rising generation will not duplicate the dangerous state of civic knowledge today."[16]

In January 2012, the National Task Force on Civic Learning and Democratic Engagement issued an extensive report on the current state of higher education for democracy. The Task Force's work included participation by the US Department of Education and the Association of American Colleges and Universities. Its report, entitled *A Crucible Moment: College Learning & Democracy's Future*, recommended "four defined areas of endeavor (ethos, literacy, inquiry, and action) to ensure all students and the public benefit from higher education's civic investment."[17] More generally, at the college level "the knowledge, skills, and experiences students need for responsible citizenship should be part of each student's general education program."

The Task Force report concluded, "Civic learning needs to be an integral component of every level of education, from grade school through graduate school, across all fields of study."[18] Similarly, two college professors who have written about "the concern with declining levels of civic engagement" have observed that the increased attention it is receiving "is focused primarily on three levels: The content and curriculum of social studies in high schools, teaching and engaging students in civic engagement in the higher education context, and on the role of service learning."[19]

Some commentators have suggested that civics education would benefit from an injection of some elements of the study of law, such as the intensive study of specific cases and the use of mock trials. These components, at a minimum, could foster greater appreciation for America's legal system.[20] Similarly, organizations led by prominent judges and lawyers are developing educational programs to enhance civic understanding and participation, rather than just knowledge of governmental structure.[21] Supreme Court Justice Sandra Day O'Connor has created the iCivics organization (formerly called Our Courts), "a web-based education project designed to teach students civics and inspire them to be active participants in our democracy."[22] This project's website, www.iCivics.org, describes its development of teaching tools, including a game in which "students will choose, investigate, and argue cases," and a game called "Argument Wars" in which the student is invited to "try out your persuasive abilities by arguing a real Supreme Court case."

Apart from civics classes, the most prominent area of secondary and undergraduate education in which citizen skills are promoted, for at least a relatively small group of students, is debate.[23] School debate programs foster development of important abilities, including "the capacity for critical thinking, increasing the comprehension of substantive information," and "how to think and respond quickly, but carefully, to unexpected arguments, as well as to evolving events in a changing world."[24] The relationship of debate activities to the work of lawyers, as well as to civic engagement, has also been recognized:

> Debate, perhaps better than any other academic training, teaches students how to "think like a lawyer" long before they ever set foot in a law school... Participation in debate... teaches students much of what lawyers do in daily practice. But these skills are also important for every student we hope and expect to become an effective and engaged citizen.[25]

Debate programs enable students to "engage in issues of civic importance." This involvement in turn encourages political participation because "people who have some confidence in analyzing public affairs are much more likely to engage in them."[26] These programs are usually an elective course or extracurricular activity, so the vast majority of students are not involved in them. Nonetheless, there does appear to be a recent growth in participation, as well as an increase in accessibility of debate programs for students of diverse socioeconomic backgrounds.[27]

An additional educational area of possible utility in developing the citizen's analytic strength is science. The scientific method—with its heavy reliance on proof of facts, a questioning and objective mindset, and a readiness to modify conclusions based on new evidence and sound reasoning—might provide a useful model for discharge of at least some aspects of the citizen's responsibilities. Although the scientific method can be described in different ways, its key steps are usually identified more or less as follows:

> Induction: Forming a hypothesis by drawing general conclusions from existing data.
>
> Deduction: Making specific predictions based on the hypothesis.
>
> Observation: Gathering data, driven by hypotheses that tell us what to look for in nature.
>
> Verification: Testing the predictions against further observations to confirm or falsify the initial hypotheses.
>
> Science, of course, is not this rigid; and no scientist consciously goes through "steps." The process is a constant interaction of making observations, drawing conclusions, making predictions, and checking them against evidence.[28]

With this type of methodical approach to scientific inquiry in mind, one scholar has traced a close historical connection between the advancement of science and the growth of democracy. He observes:

> Whereas prior systems dealt in claims of certitude, such as philosophers' allegedly airtight reasoning and monarchs' god-given right to rule, science and democracy are steeped in doubt. Both start with tentative ideas, go through agonies of experimentation, and arrive at merely probabilistic conclusions that remain vulnerable to disproof. Both are bottom-up systems, constructed more from individual actions in laboratories and legislatures than from a few allegedly impervious precepts.[29]

The author aptly could also have alluded to the formation of individual citizens' opinions, and not just actions of their legislatures, as powerful forces in the construction of democracy.

Science's emphasis on experimentation and doubt might well be applied to citizens' approach to their own opinion development and discharge of civic duties. Nonetheless, it is a tall order to expect teachers of science to make this extrapolation, and there is little evidence that it has been attempted. Perhaps, at best, the inculcation of habits of careful, fact-based analysis of scientific issues can have some beneficial carryover effect when science students and scientists approach public issues. A more promising path, however, would be the reinvigoration of civics education, both at precollege and college levels, along the lines of the recent efforts described above. Civics programs such as these could more directly aim to prepare young citizens for thoughtful engagement with the issues.

B. THE MEDIA

As discussed in chapter 2, the ordinary citizen is bombarded with information through the news and information media. Historically, newspapers were his primary source. More recently, television and the Internet have taken the dominant positions.[30] As a recent poll of voters concluded, "Even as online news sources make inroads, voters still rely on local television for their daily news more than any other news source." The survey found "older Americans far more likely than younger voters to rely on television for their news." It also stated that "younger voters were most likely to rely on Facebook for their news," though for more than half of those voters "it was mostly news they had already seen or heard about."[31]

The combination of modern media sources provides an easily accessible mass of information, though it is not always clear what is presented as fact and what as opinion. The obvious importance of the news media has been well stated by the Supreme Court:

> Without the information provided by the press, most of us and many of our representatives would be unable to vote intelligently or to register opinions on the administration of government generally.[32]

As noted earlier, there is debate about the extent to which the news media inform the public or just entertain it. Either way, citizens get a lot of information from the media about current, hot issues, even if it is difficult to sort through it to grasp the complexities. However this flood of information may be assessed, the question remains: Do the media offer any guidance to the reader/listener/viewer/surfer about how to make sense of it all?

It is easy to find media sources to tell us what issues are controversial. Newspapers, websites, blogs, television, and other sources are constantly trumpeting the latest public disputes. One might fairly ask whether in all instances what the media deem important is so because of broader, real public concerns or just seems so because the media say so. Scholars have reached varying answers to the question of "whether there was a link between what was being emphasized by the media and what the voters considered important." What seems to be widely agreed, however, is that "the press 'may not be successful much of the time in telling people what to think, but it is stunningly successful in telling its readers what to think *about*.'"[33]

It is not easy to find media sources with advice on how to go about reaching our own conclusions. One pertinent effort can be found on the NewsTrust website, already mentioned earlier in chapter 2. It seeks "to promote quality journalism in the Internet age, a formidable task as millions of news-related posts, blogs and sites are created each day."

Extrapolating from the journalism profession, NewsTrust encourages individual citizens to evaluate news stories critically. It states, "Remember to think like a journalist—so you can make more informed decisions as a citizen." The site emphasizes "news literacy," including four aspects of thinking like a journalist:

> Doubt—a healthy skepticism that questions everything;
>
> Detect—a 'nose for news' and relentless pursuit of the truth;
>
> Discern—a priority for fairness, balance and objectivity in reporting;
>
> Demand—a focus on free access to information and freedom of speech.[34]

Guidance of this sort is useful, particularly when integrated into educational programs such as reinvigorated civics programs as discussed above. In this vein, one college text used in political science courses advocates "thinking like a political scientist" as a helpful approach. It suggests the acronym "CLUES" as an aid to memory of the following "five major steps of critical thinking" about politics:

> Consider the source and the audience.
>
> Lay out the argument and the underlying values and assumptions.
>
> Uncover the evidence.
>
> Evaluate the conclusion.
>
> Sort out the political implications.[35]

The pervasiveness and easy accessibility of media information in our lives make the media, and the Internet in particular, especially fertile ground for communicating this type of guidance. At present, however, even the modest perspective offered on the NewsTrust website is a rare example of what is possible. For the foreseeable future, almost all the citizen can expect from the media is lots of dramatic calls for *what to think about*, and quite a bit of persistent exhortation of *what to think* on specific issues, but very little guidance on *how to think* in trying to reach her own conclusions.

C. Citizens Group Guides

In addition to the cacophony of media voices urging specific conclusions on issues and candidates, there are many types of organizations—especially the two major political parties—pleading for our agreement and support. Few organizations, however, step back from the fray long enough to suggest ways of understanding the issues, sorting through the competing information and arguments, and forming our own opinions. The need for guidance of this sort is especially acute in states, most notably California, in which voters not only select government leaders but also make laws themselves, and even change state constitutions, through ballot initiatives and other forms of direct democracy.[36]

Fortunately, there are some sources of such advice. One of the best known is the League of Women Voters, a long-standing national organization that works through local branches "to influence public policy through education and advocacy." The California League, for example, in conjunction with the California State Library, publishes an "Easy Voter Guide" for each statewide election and maintains a related website under the heading "easyvoter.org."[37] It also distributes documents with titles such as "Pros and Cons: State Ballot Measures" to help voters understand the many ballot propositions they are asked to address. The League thus advises voters on "how to evaluate ballot propositions," listing a number of considerations voters should try to resolve, such as the following:

- Who are the real sponsors and opponents of the measure?
- Does the measure deal with one issue that can be easily decided by a "yes" or "no," or is it a complex issue that should be thoroughly examined in the legislative arena?
- Is it written well?
- If the measure amends the Constitution, consider whether it really belongs in the Constitution.
- Does the measure create its own revenue source? Does it earmark, restrict, or obligate a specific percentage of General Fund revenues?
- Consider the effect on the overall flexibility of the budget.
- Examine the measure by its merits. During the campaign, be wary of distortion tactics and commercials that rely on image but tell nothing of substance about the measure.[38]

More broadly, the Easy Voter Guide has urged:

- Talk with your family and friends to see what you think should be done.
- You don't have to vote on everything on your ballot. Choose the things that matter to you and learn more about them.[39]

The League also maintains the nationally oriented "Smart Voter" website, which includes, among other types of information about elections, advice called "Debate Watching 101" and a suggested multiple-step approach for "How to Judge a Candidate."[40] The approach forthrightly describes "examples of distortion techniques that you should watch for as you review candidates' campaign materials."

Another unofficial source of guidance is academic institutions. To aid voters in responding to California ballot measures, for example, the website of the Institute of Governmental Studies at the University of California at Berkeley presents not only summaries of the propositions, but also an extensive chart that lists the positions—yes or no—that organizations have taken on them.[41] The chart does not make suggestions on how the voter should go about reaching his or her voting decision, but the implicit message is that voters will be, and should be, influenced by knowledge of the stands various groups are taking on ballot measures.

A similar online guide was recently launched under the name TransparentDemocracy.org, a website that chronicles the positions advocacy groups have taken on issues before the voters in each state.[42] Another online source is ProCon.org, which seeks to present "controversial issues in a straightforward, nonpartisan, primarily pro-con format." As of early 2013, that website explained opposing positions on 47 controversial issues under 11 categories, including education, health and medicine, politics, religion, sex and gender, and world/international.[43]

Collecting and publicizing positions others have taken on issues is an undoubtedly useful function, giving the voter at least indirect clues about the implications of an issue from various perspectives. Is such information, as well as ubiquitous campaign advertisements and endorsements, also any sort of catalyst for individual analysis and opinion formation? This is harder to assess, as suggested in a statement emanating from the law school at Berkeley:

> As lawyers and responsible citizens, how should we go about deciding how to vote on these measures?...So what is a lawyer voter to

> do? What should any voter do? For many, the traditional approach is to read the ballot arguments, and see who has taken a stand on which side of the issue. The hope is that trusted people who are closer to the issues at hand can vouch for their positions. We look at editorials and endorsements, read letters to the editor, and wait for slate cards to arrive...We are presented with television, radio, and print advertisements. It is usually the ads that merit the greatest caution. To make a case in 30 seconds, the complex must be drastically simplified, and shades of grey are often expressed in terms of black and white. In considering those ads, one should apply more than a grain of salt. A pinch of more careful analysis may be in order.[44]

There is nothing wrong in urging voters to apply "a pinch of more careful analysis" or to "choose the things that matter to you and learn more about them." But platitudes such as these certainly do not give the citizen much, if anything, in the nature of direction signs on a path toward clearer understanding and more confident formation of opinions.

D. State and Local Voter Guides

It has become common for state voting officials, and occasionally local governments, to prepare booklets of information about candidates and ballot measures. For example, for a 2008 election in Massachusetts, which included three state-wide ballot questions, "the 2008 Information for Voters booklet list[ed] each question with the text of the proposed law, statements describing the effect of a yes or no vote, a summary and brief argument for and against each question." The booklet also cautioned that the state "does not endorse...and does not certify the truth or accuracy of any statements made" in the booklet by proponents and opponents of each question.[45]

Often these ostensibly helpful publications, whether available in hard copy or electronically, make for difficult reading, especially with regard to ballot propositions. Legal requirements aimed at ensuring that candidates are accurately listed and that ballot measures are set forth in full detail can be useful, but they also can be counterproductive. They can produce intimidating batches of material, including texts of proposed laws and summaries of opposing viewpoints, which leave the voter struggling to understand the main points.

Scholars have commented on the frequent combination of an official election booklet with cleverly crafted opposing arguments, the actual ballot's misleadingly "short and simple description of each proposal's legal complexities," the multiplicity of ballot propositions presented, the simultaneous presentation of candidates for elective office, and the surrounding "swirl of media hype." They have aptly summarized the impact: "The resulting cacophony simply overwhelms the cognitive capacities of the most conscientious citizens."[46]

In addition to trying to explain the election choices to be made, these official publications occasionally offer brief advice on how to study the choices and reach decisions. For example, the California Secretary of State's Official Voter Information Guide observes:

> You can help educate other voters about the candidates and issues by organizing discussion groups or participating in debates with friends, family, and community leaders.
>
> It is a wonderful privilege in a democracy to have a choice and the right to voice your opinion... Thank you for taking your civic responsibility seriously and making your voice heard![47]

Florida's official list of "Voter Responsibilities" urges each voter to "familiarize himself or herself with the candidates and issues" and to "ask questions, if needed." Ironically, to avoid overstating individual responsibilities, and with a nod to reality, the Florida guidance adds a "Note to Voter": "Failure to perform any of these responsibilities does not prohibit a voter from voting."[48]

Guidance at the local level may take a different tack. One California city urges voters to "make ethics part of your candidate choice criteria." The city suggests a "voter checklist for evaluating the candidates," emphasizing questions such as these about whether the candidates have:

- Told the truth about themselves?
- Told truths about opponents that are important for voters to know?
- Pointed out differences between themselves and opponents that are relevant to the political office?
- Never tried to confuse or mislead voters?
- Clearly identified who supported any candidate-controlled committee?[49]

Once again, as with the citizens group guides, the guidance offered by voter guides is general, noncontroversial, and not very useful.

E. DELIBERATION PROJECTS

Recently an academic and political effort labeled "deliberative democracy" has emerged. It has been described as "a nascent movement to make deliberation a central feature of our political culture and, perhaps, our institutions."[50] Its key concept is "conversation: the exercise of political power, according to deliberative democrats, is only legitimate when it is justified by conversation and (ideally) agreement with other citizens, based on reasons that they can all understand."[51] Deliberative democracy's key process, "political deliberation," is "a particular kind of political dialogue in which people engage in reasoned consideration of multiple sides of an issue under conditions of mutual respect and equal inclusion in the conversation."[52]

The movement's advocates urge that moral and political disagreements can be bridged through deliberation-fueled compromise, a more productive approach than adversarial politics in which there are clear winners and losers on difficult issues.[53] There is considerable scholarly and political agreement that the deliberation experiments are worthwhile attempts to rescue political discourse and opinion formation from the discouraging context and obstacles described in chapter 2.

Even among scholars who generally applaud these efforts, however, there is some criticism and skepticism. Among the comments is the argument that the emphasis on opinion formation through external deliberation renders deliberative democracy susceptible to various ills and pressures of group decision making. Professor Cass Sunstein, for example, has expressed skepticism as to whether deliberation succeeds at producing "wiser judgments and better outcomes," in light of informational influences and social pressures that, respectively, cause group members to fail to disclose pertinent knowledge and "lead people to silence themselves in order to avoid reputational sanctions."[54] He also has emphasized the detrimental effects of group polarization, or "groupthink," in which "like-minded people insulated from others move in extreme directions simply because of limited argument pools and parochial influences." Sunstein urges that "an obvious response to the dangers of group polarization is to ensure that members of deliberating groups, whether small or large, will not isolate themselves from competing views" and to expose "group members, at one point or another, to arguments to which they are not antecedently inclined."[55]

One particularly creative manifestation of this movement is the proposal for "deliberation day," a national holiday to be observed two weeks before major national elections.[56] Its premise is that one historic strength of democracy is face-to-face, reasoned, respectful discussion of issues, leading to mutual understanding and increased agreement. The loss of habits, opportunities, and incentives for such thoughtful interaction is the problem that deliberation day advocates hope to redress.[57] Their suggested solution hinges on the creation of group discussions, focused on specific pending issues, on a designated day in advance of elections which raise those issues.

Proponents point to the deliberative process as assisting and motivating people to reach reasoned conclusions:

> DDay alerts each private citizen that the collective failure of deliberation seriously threatens the enterprise of self-government. This signal, in turn, can provoke private citizens to change their behavior as part of their ongoing process of reappraisal and adaptation.[58]

Specifically, the winter Presidents Day holiday would be transformed into a two-day autumn holiday about two weeks before Presidential or Congressional elections. Registered voters in communities across the country would congregate in groups—as large as 500 but including small breakout groups of about 15—and would be paid from public funds to watch a nationally televised debate on the central issues of the election and then to discuss them, to get down to the tough business at hand:[59]

> The real work at DDay begins after small-group members watch the initial television debate. As they define unanswered questions, and ponder the responses of local party representatives, they move beyond top-down communication and engage in the serious bottom-up enterprise of self-government. Question and answer, back and forth, hour after hour. The exercise of public reason is a social activity on Deliberation Day.[60]

The opinions, and possible consensus, arising from this process can then be communicated to appropriate government officials, either orally if the officials are present at the event or through other subsequent paths, including, of course, voting. The authors of the deliberation day concept, Professors Bruce Ackerman and James Fishkin, emphasize this ultimate route: "We are not seeking a return to the imaginary glories of the city-state. We are trying to strengthen the modern system of representative democracy."[61]

Although the professors offer a detailed framework for the organization and conduct of these meetings, they also acknowledge some of their proposal's limits. They state, for example:

> Although it makes good sense to hold DDays on referenda of extraordinary importance, it is absurd to take a couple of days off to debate

> each one of the large number of citizen initiatives that get on the ballot in California or other states.[62]

Even with its limitations, however, the proposal attempts to induce the ordinary voter to actively participate in opinion formation through careful deliberation with others, following the ideal model that has long been applied to legislative bodies. As Fishkin has observed:

> On many issues, the elites may deliberate to a high degree and the public hardly at all... At bottom, a major part of the problem of democratic reform is how to promote *mass deliberation*—how to bring the people into the process under conditions where they can be engaged and think seriously about public issues.[63]

Deliberation day is based on a related tool earlier devised by Fishkin. It is called "deliberative polling" and is already in occasional use in Britain, the United States, and some other nations.[64] In a deliberative poll, a randomly chosen group of people, who earlier have been polled for their views on selected public issues, gather for a day or two "under conditions facilitating sustained deliberation" to discuss information and diverse viewpoints on issues.[65] First in Britain, and then in the United States, these polls at times have been televised to provide at least some of their benefits to a broader segment of the public.[66] At the end of each gathering, having become better informed and having had their opinions tested and refined through the scrutiny of other participants, the group members again are polled on their views.[67] The salutary effects of these exercises, in advancing thoughtful opinion formation for the participants, have been documented.[68]

Whatever the ultimate verdict on these and other deliberative democracy tools may be,[69] and while recognizing that inclinations toward more critical thought are surely positive results of participation, it still does not appear that these tools address the need for guidance to assist the individual citizen on a continuous, day-to-day basis. In other words, the focus on *deliberation among many citizens* does not directly address *deliberation within each citizen*.

The latter phrase would be an oxymoron if "deliberation" always is defined to include conversation among various people. As used here and elsewhere, however, the phrase often refers more broadly to thoughtful consideration of a matter, either by a group of people or by an individual not actively in dialogue with others. In discussing "*deliberation*, a term that is often used quite loosely," it has been said that "to deliberate is not just to 'talk about' problems... To deliberate means to weigh carefully both the consequences of various options for action and the views of others."[70]

Dictionary definitions also vary, with some emphasizing interpersonal communication and others emphasizing intrapersonal consideration.[71] The relationship between deliberation in its group "external-collective" aspect and its individual "internal-reflective" aspect, and the importance of the relationship, has been commented on as follows:

> My suggestion is that we ease the burdens of deliberative democracy in mass society by altering our focus from the 'external-collective' to the 'internal-reflective' mode, shifting much of the work of democratic deliberation back inside the head of each individual... Internal-reflective deliberations are not a substitute for, but rather an input into, external-collective decision procedures.[72]

In short, the deliberative individual is better prepared to contribute to group deliberation.

Fishkin contrasts "the ideal of face-to-face democracy" with the reality of "a democracy of atomized, individual voters who have no effective motivation to think through the issues or discuss them with other citizens." Nonetheless, he and other deliberative democracy advocates strive to enhance "social conditions... that facilitate everyone's thinking through the issues together."[73] In pursuing this goal, even Fishkin and Ackerman acknowledge that their deliberation day initiative to get people talking with their neighbors "on *one* day every *four* years" is of "modest dimensions."[74]

Alongside these modest but worthy efforts to enhance what we do *together*, it should be recognized that what we do and think *alone*—as members of communities but also simultaneously as "atomized individuals"—can also be advanced.[75] Alongside the deliberation projects, it remains important to assist the individual with the ongoing, personal challenge of being able somewhat systematically to gather and evaluate information and reach conclusions, while preparing to be a constructive participant in opportunities for deliberation with others when they arise.

F. OTHER TIPS

The last category is a hodge podge, in which random nuggets of advice are offered to the public, usually through the news and entertainment media. These random tips often surface as quotations from celebrities. Consider the following portion of an interview with veteran broadcaster Walter Cronkite, who often was referred to as "the most trusted man in America":

> Interviewer: Who does the public know to trust then, when we've got the Internet, we've got radio, we've got television and newspaper, and everyone has an opinion, everyone's a sudden expert, it seems, in this day and age? Who does the public trust?
>
> Cronkite: I think they're most likely to trust that source which they have learned is fair and impartial in gathering the facts and presenting the facts. That can be tested as to whether the source is constantly on one side of the political spectrum or another. That opinion which I think is fair and worth listening to is that which you can't predict is going to take a stand one way or the other on any particular issue, but bases the position upon the facts of that issue alone [and] does not approach subjects in a doctrinaire fashion and judge everything according to a doctrine, but on the basis of the facts.[76]

Other, more concise observations come from a broad spectrum of public personalities. The young actress Natalie Portman, when asked whether celebrities should use their "stardom" to influence voters, said:

> Sure. People can listen to a host of influences and still make their own decisions. I'm always interested to hear who the people I respect are voting for.[77]

Another broadcast journalist, Tim Russert, was asked how a "regular person" can get to the underlying truth of candidates' claims. His reply:

> I think it's imperative that you try. The best way is to watch programs like *Meet the Press* and the other Sunday programs. I'm a great believer of watching C-SPAN. The more information you can learn, the more complete your judgment will be.[78]

This type of advice on how individuals can form their own opinions is rare, when compared to the more common type of advice from celebrities. They usually either just endorse in general the virtues of voting,[79] or they specifically endorse a candidate or viewpoint while leaving the voter uninformed as to how that belief was developed and why the speaker considers it the preferred stance.[80]

This last category of guidance is obviously just a conglomeration of random voices, and not a source the citizen can consistently expect to rely on. Looking back at the other conventional sources discussed above, they too are somewhat random and unreliable. That is, with the exception of civics education, all of the other sources—the media, citizens group guides, state and local voter guides, deliberation projects, and other tips—are a largely unpredictable hodgepodge, too. The citizen cannot be sure they will always be available, nor can she anticipate just how much depth, if any, their guidance will have. Although some of these conventional sources may be helpful at times, they cannot be consistently counted on to aid the citizen's effort to understand the issues.

Civics education, in contrast, ought to be a reliable, even systematic source of instruction for civic engagement. As discussed above, however, its recent track record and immediate prospects are not encouraging, despite some worthy experiments now under way. Unless and until those efforts are proven successful and are more widely employed, the citizen must look elsewhere for reliable, cohesive guidance. As will be explored in the following chapters, lessons to be drawn from the legal system can provide such guidance as a more methodical supplement to the various, separate types of conventional guidance.

4

The Law's Tools and Traditions

Before determining whether the legal system's approach to decisions can provide guidance for the citizen, we need to identify the particular legal tools and traditions that might be helpful. Twelve such methods will be explained here. They will be roughly grouped into the following four categories, each of which declares a broad goal for how legal work should be done:

A: Focusing on the task
  1. Defining the issue
  2. Separating facts from standards and evaluations

B: Taking an organized approach
  1. Respecting procedure
  2. Taking time

C: Finding reliable information
  1. Gathering the facts
  2. Recognizing incomplete facts
  3. Dividing labor
  4. Using expertise
  5. Identifying bias

D: Keeping an open mind
  1. Arguing and persuading
  2. Listening and negotiating
  3. Making hard choices in gray areas

Some of these approaches to legal work are often labeled as "thinking like a lawyer." This phrase is used, however, with many different meanings. One professor has even written, "Many law professors and lawyers argue that you cannot *explain* what it means to think like a lawyer, that you can only *experience* it."[1] Another scholar, taking a quite different perspective, states:

> Thinking like a lawyer is thinking like a human being, a human being who is tolerant, sophisticated, pragmatic, critical, and engaged. It means combining passion and principle, reason and judgment.[2]

In light of these and other definitions, it might not be universally agreed that all of the tools and traditions discussed here are components of thinking like a lawyer, but undoubtedly many of them are.

Although the "thinking like a lawyer" label is popular, it might be equally apt to speak of "thinking like a judge," for many of the tools used by practicing lawyers are also used by them when they become judges.[3] Furthermore, to think like a lawyer often requires, in a very literal sense, thinking like a judge. Whether in tasks arising from litigation, or in planning functions to reduce risks of later conflict, lawyers often must try to anticipate how a judge would understand and evaluate the legal aspects of specific actions or circumstances. In litigation, this kind of thinking sooner or later leads to development of strategy to try to persuade the judge—or at times a jury—to think about the issue in the same way the lawyer and her client do.

Many of the strengths of the legal system described here are also important features of other areas of thought and practice, such as science, journalism, economics, ethics, and even religion.[4] The legal system certainly can claim no monopoly on purposeful, civil, reasoned investigation and analysis of problems. Some of the types of conventional guidance discussed earlier in chapter 3—scientific method, traditional journalism practices, voter guidance, and deliberative democracy—advance approaches similar to those to be discussed here. Indeed some of the law's methods are not much more than the practices followed by responsible, thinking people in many aspects of their daily life.

Nevertheless, the law combines these practices and methods in a distinctive way. "The fact that law's methods are not unique to law does not mean that law is no different from anything else, and . . . it is a mistake to fail to recognize how decision-making within the legal system is, at the very least, a little bit different."[5] The law offers a distinctive, comprehensive, structured, realistic, and functional set of tools and traditions for decision making on social concerns and disputes. It is, in other words and as it is commonly called, the legal "system."[6] As such, it offers a complete and coherent resource from which to draw in this search for citizen guidance.

These tools of the legal system promote the four central goals listed above for effective performance of legal work. That is, persons working in the law should consistently be focusing on the task, taking an organized approach, finding reliable information, and keeping an open mind. Of course, readers who have even minimal familiarity with the legal system may react with skepticism as to whether in daily practice these goals are achieved and whether the tools and traditions always operate as advertised. They do not. Ideally they should, and in practice they often do, but it would be incorrect to suggest that these critical features of legal work and decision making are never ignored, compromised, or corrupted. They also may be obstructed by serious inequalities in the resources and abilities of the participants. The purpose of this chapter is not to evaluate the frequency or degree of such departures from the ideal, but rather to explain the way these features are intended to work and presumably do, at least most of the time.

A. FOCUSING ON THE TASK

At the outset of any legal work, it is necessary for the lawyer, judge, or juror to understand the task at hand as fully and clearly as possible. What is the problem or question to be addressed, and what are its component parts? It is critical to try to begin with a clear focus, and then to remember to adapt it as new information and perspectives emerge. At least two of the law's methods address this goal.

1. Defining the Issue

One of the first things the beginning law student hears from the professor in class discussion is "What's the issue in this case?" This is commonly asked when the student is studying a past decision in a dispute that has gone to court. The result reached by the court cannot be understood unless the student is able to identify the particular points of disagreement the court had to resolve—those are the "issues" in the case.

Similarly, in the daily practice of law, effort is constantly exerted to understand the issues raised by a present or anticipated dispute. Even in legal work that precedes an actual controversy, and that is intended to prevent disputes from arising, it is necessary to anticipate and understand potential legal issues. In writing a contract, lawyers look ahead and imagine what problems might develop, that is, what points of conflict could result as activities are to be performed under the terms of the contract. Once the lawyers have identified the potential pitfalls, their work focuses on drafting and redrafting the contract to prevent them.

The word "issue" has many different meanings in popular usage and is used in two different ways here. Beginning in chapter 1, we are speaking of "public issues," questions and concerns of broad public significance and interest. In this vein, "issue" has a broad definition as "an important topic or problem for debate or discussion," or "a subject or problem which people are thinking and talking about."[7] The discussion of the complexity obstacle in chapter 2 listed many such current public issues, such as global climate change, health care reform, terrorism, abortion, and campaign financing.[8]

In contrast, when we speak of "legal issues" or the "issues in a case," we are focusing on specific points of disagreement that must be resolved in order to decide the case.

> When writing opinions, judges use the word "issue" as shorthand for "a question we must answer in order to decide this case"...It is useful to think of issues as "forks in the road" of your analysis of the dispute. Like a "fork" you encounter in a real road, an issue presents you with a choice between two (and sometimes more) paths leading in different directions.[9]

For present purposes, we can think of a "public issue" as, in effect, a broad problem or "case" to be resolved. "Legal issues" are then the more focused points of dispute that bear on resolution of the case and on which the parties present their contending, alternative positions. Each party, in other words, is trying to show what really matters, what should be the controlling information and considerations, for reaching the best decision. Lawyers are trained from the outset to sharpen their thinking so they can identify and stay focused on the issues raised by cases or problems before them. The lawyer who is unclear about the issues—like the law student who does not have a clear answer to that professor's question—will not be effective in grappling with the work at hand.

Flowing from the clarification of issues are some additional features of the legal system. Lawyers and judges talk a lot about "relevance." Once the issues in a legal matter are identified, the only evidence and argument that should be considered are the evidence and argument that have logical bearing on resolution of those issues, that is, evidence and argument "of consequence to the determination" of the case.[10] If the issue is whether the car ran into the pedestrian because of the way the car was driven, then the year the car was made is probably irrelevant, unless there is something about the design features of that model year car that could affect the way it was driven. In contrast, the speed of the car and intoxication of the driver at the time of the collision are certainly relevant. The middle name of the driver, his religion, and the particular scent of the air freshener in the car that day probably are not. Lawyers and judges in courtroom trials are constantly assessing the relevance or irrelevance of the evidence presented. Jurors, too, are supposed to restrict their consideration of the evidence to what is relevant to the issues.

Another aspect of relevance concerns information that appears to be connected to the points in dispute but which, on further examination, is of no significance. If the name of the driver is George—and there is evidence that just before the accident someone nearby yelled out "George!"—that evidence at first would seem relevant because the driver might have become distracted upon hearing his name. However, if other evidence shows that the windows of George's car were fully closed, and he was playing loud music on the car radio at the time, evidence of the yelling of his name becomes irrelevant because he could not possibly have heard the yell. What at first seems relevant is transformed by other overriding information into an irrelevancy.

Lawyers' fixation on identification of the issues keeps the legal process focused on what really matters. Extraneous information, though possibly interesting as background, history, or for other tangential reasons, is to be disregarded because it fails to tell us anything truly helpful about the issues we need to resolve.

2. Separating Facts from Standards and Evaluations

All legal issues are based on facts, that is, some actual events or conditions people have experienced or observed.[11] An important aspect of legal work, as will be discussed later, is the gathering of facts in an effort to decide what happened previously or is happening now, or to predict what will happen. Occasionally the facts are so clear and indisputable that they "speak for themselves" and, when similarly unambiguous legal rules are applied to them, compel a particular legal outcome. Much more often, however, disagreement about the facts persists. Either way, whether or not the facts are in dispute, the ultimate question is not merely what happened but how are the facts to be evaluated under the pertinent legal rules.

Participants in the legal process understand these distinctions among the facts, the applicable rules or standards of the law,[12] and the application of those standards to the facts.[13] The issue is not just what the automobile driver did, but also whether his conduct meets the legal standard of carelessness—negligence. This dispute cannot be concluded until there is an evaluation of the facts under that test. In an ordinary trial, it is commonly said that the jury's job is to decide what happened, what the true facts are; the judge's job includes the identification and explanation of the pertinent legal criteria; and the jury's ultimate role is to apply those criteria, those standards, to the facts. For this process to work fairly for everyone concerned, the distinctions among facts, legal standards, and the evaluation of facts under law must be respected.

B. Taking an Organized Approach

Many distinctive aspects of the legal system are designed to promote orderly, deliberate decision making. Instead of random and hurried processes, an organized approach is taken, aimed at following a careful, step-by-step pattern. This pattern often is slow, but hopefully for good reasons and with sound results.

1. Respecting Procedure

In the American legal system, what matters is not just *what* decisions are reached but also *how* they are reached. "The law's great concern with the procedure of decision making is one of its more basic and important characteristics. Any discussion of the law that did not note the importance of procedure would be inadequate."[14] Lawyers and judges pay lots of attention to following prescribed procedures. In the constitutional law realm, this attention often is stated in terms of the US Constitution's phrase "due process of law."[15]

Even apart from constitutional mandates, tremendous emphasis is placed on following correct procedures. There are instances in which a seemingly incorrect result is tolerated simply because it was reached through prescribed—albeit not infallible—procedures. A criminal defendant may be absolved of guilt after a well-conducted trial, despite available information to the contrary. If, for example, some of that information on its face is damning but has been found inadmissible under the governing rules of evidence, the acquittal must stand.

The law's perspective in this regard has been aptly summarized as follows:

> Legal standards are often phrased not in terms of results but in terms of procedure. For example, it is not unlawful to convict the innocent if the right procedures are used (and it *is* unlawful to convict the guilty if the wrong procedures are followed.) The law feels that it cannot

> guarantee that the right result will always be reached and that only the guilty will be caught, so it minimizes the risk of reaching the wrong result or convicting the innocent by specifying procedural steps to be followed. Lawyers, more than most people, are satisfied if the right procedures are followed even if there is something disturbing about the outcome.[16]

Two law professors, Henry Hart and Albert Sacks, emphasized the overriding importance of procedure:

> Implicit in every...system of procedures is the central idea of law—an idea which can be described as *the principle of institutional settlement*...The alternative to disintegrating resort to violence [to resolve questions of common concern in society] is the establishment of regularized and peaceable methods of decision. The principle of institutional settlement expresses the judgment that decisions which are the duly arrived at result of duly established procedures of this kind ought to be accepted as binding upon the whole society unless and until they are duly changed.[17]

These scholars and others have identified many reasons for the prominent place lawyers and judges give to correct procedure. In general, procedure is instrumental, as it serves to facilitate other important goals. "For the most part, procedure is a means to an end—the accomplishment of social purposes—but to a certain extent procedural forms in themselves may create or destroy important human values."[18] Describing a basic objective of legal procedures, Hart wrote:

> The first recourse of law, in dealing with intractable questions, is to seek not final answers but an agreeable procedure for getting acceptable answers...Philosophers and ordinary men alike can agree that if some answer is better than no answer at all a way must be found to get an answer.
>
> Implicit in the problems of settling and carrying out the terms of collaboration in a society, in other words, is the need for deciding who shall decide the various questions which arise in the process, and how they shall be decided.[19]

Another value that procedures should enhance is consistency of outcomes in similar cases—"equal justice under law." If the same methods are used for evaluating and deciding analogous cases, the likelihood of the results being similar will increase, or at least the extent to which they differ will be logically understandable. Respect for the interests and needs of individuals is thus promoted, and public confidence in the stability, fairness, and integrity of the legal system is also enhanced.

Also, the gathering of facts can be accomplished in a more orderly, reliable, and thorough manner if established procedures for procuring and presenting information are followed. Strategies and substantive decisions then are more likely to be based on adequate, relevant information. "Experience is replete with proof of the vitally important relation between procedure and substance. A procedure which is soundly adapted to the type of power to be exercised is conducive to well-informed and wise decisions."[20]

Additionally, procedural ground rules facilitate predictability and planning in the interaction of lawyers and their clients with the law. Sometimes, of course, legal procedures seem to be inefficient because they take lots of time. Surely there is often more delay than necessary, but, for the reasons to be discussed later, taking the time necessary for careful, orderly fact gathering and decision making fundamentally makes good sense.

Another simple but important aspect of legal procedure, particularly in courtroom settings, is the practice of only allowing one party at a time to speak. In the presentation of legal arguments and testimony, one party goes first, the other responds, the first replies, and so on. This, too, takes time, and sometimes is frustrating for the party who has something important to say but remains obliged to wait its turn. Without an orderly pattern of alternating statements, however, lawsuits and other types of hearings could readily degenerate into chaotic shouting matches, thereby decreasing the prospects for a clear understanding of the legal merits of the dispute.

An inflexible commitment to following procedural rules and traditions admittedly has potential to cause unwise delay and inhibit intelligent decision making.[21] Fortunately, to mitigate this risk, there are some safety valves in legal processes. For example, as is well known, the requirement to wait your turn before speaking is subject to an exception that objections may be raised immediately if inadmissible evidence or highly prejudicial, irrelevant arguments are presented. Also, not all procedural missteps ultimately must make a difference in the outcome. Frequently, an appellate court will find that a procedural error was made at the trial court level but that the error made no difference because the same result would have been reached even without the error. This "harmless error" in procedure, as opposed to a "prejudicial error," will not require the result to be overturned or the proceeding redone.

The list of values that procedural requirements aim to advance is long, and perhaps ultimately has no limit. At a minimum, apart from the above-mentioned practical considerations such as efficiency, predictability, and orderliness, it is foundational in American law that personal interests in "life, liberty, and property" are always to be protected from infringement by government unless the constitutional requirements of "due process" are observed.[22] "Major instruments of control of the exercise of official powers [include] the arrangements which prescribe the procedure to be followed in exercising the power."[23] In cases involving the exercise of official powers affecting constitutionally protected interests, as in virtually all types of legal proceedings, lawyers know that the legitimacy of the result is inextricably bound to the sufficiency of the procedure.

2. Taking Time

The American legal system is often criticized for moving slowly. Business deals seem to be slowed up by the lawyers' work on them, litigation languishes before even getting to the courtroom phase, and trials themselves often are subject to tedious procedural steps and postponements. Some of these delays result from an overload of demands on judges and juries, and some result from dilatory tactics.

More respectably and importantly, legal processes often take time for very good reasons. Complicated issues need time for careful collection of facts, weighing of competing opinions, and thoughtful deliberation on the best outcome. When judges or government agencies make decisions, "haste breeds arbitrary decisions that are no more than edicts, or 'absolute' principles that soon collide with other principles, fail to resolve conflicting interests, or collapse in the face of experience."[24]

For example, with respect to requirements in environmental law, criticism is often leveled at the time-consuming processes of environmental impact review to which many proposed government actions, such as the licensing of nuclear power plants, are subject under the National Environmental Policy Act.[25] A cogent response to this criticism was expressed by a federal judge who understood what these environmental laws were intended to accomplish:

> For no action which might minimize environmental damage may be dismissed out of hand. Of course, final operation of the facility may be delayed thereby. But some delay is inherent whenever [environmental impact] consideration is conducted—whether before or at the [nuclear

> power plant] license proceedings. It is far more consistent with the purposes of the Act to delay operation at a stage where real environmental protection may come about than at a stage where corrective action may be so costly as to be impossible.[26]

Another judge who found good reason for the delays in an environmental conflict found perspective from the Founding Fathers: "As Thomas Jefferson said in a letter to George Washington on May 16, 1792, 'Delay is preferable to error.'"[27] For legal processes to avoid error and reach sound results, it often just takes time.

C. Finding Reliable Information

For the results reached by the legal system to be worthy of public respect and confidence, they must be based on the most honest, complete, solid information available. Many of the law's tools and traditions are designed to promote this objective.

1. Gathering the Facts

Lawyers, judges, and jurors spend lots of time collecting evidence, that is, gathering the facts on which decisions ultimately will rest. "In the law, as well as in life itself, judging is the act of selecting and weighing facts and suggestions as they present themselves, as well as deciding whether the alleged facts are really facts."[28] Some of the fact gathering by lawyers is done through informal methods. They read through documents and records of many different types, interview clients and other people who may have relevant information, and occasionally hire outside investigators or expert consultants to dig into the details.

The discussion here of the gathering and presentation of facts is mostly set in the context of a typical lawsuit. The facts at issue in such cases usually concern "the questions of who did what, where, when, how, why, with what motive or intent." Scholars have called such facts "adjudicative facts," emphasizing that they are the type of information needed to paint a full picture of individual conduct and usually provided in large part by the concerned individual himself. "An individual knows more about the facts concerning herself and her activities than anyone else is likely to know."

In contrast, other types of legal proceedings, such as the passage of legislation or the adoption of regulations by government agencies, depend on different types of information, sometimes called "legislative facts." Those are "the general facts that help a government institution decide questions of law, policy, and discretion... The most useful sources of data for resolution of disputes concerning legislative facts often are contained in the published literature of the social or natural science disciplines relevant to the legislative fact at issue."[29]

In preparation for a courtroom trial, the lawyer's gathering of facts usually takes on considerable structure and formality. Interviews of potential witnesses become "depositions," questioning conducted with representatives of all litigants present and with the witness speaking under oath as a court reporter or electronic equipment creates a permanent record of what is said. In the actual trial, of course, witnesses also testify under oath, and their statements are subject to a variety of official rules concerning evidence.

Testimony under Oath

The witness's oath or affirmation—to tell "the truth, the whole truth, and nothing but the truth"—has the obvious purpose of promoting divulgence of only what is honestly believed to be true, reflecting what some commentators have labeled "sincerity."[30] This purpose is promoted by the possibility that the witness who lies under oath—commits perjury—will be subject to serious penalties imposed by a court, even imprisonment. The requirement that testimony be under oath thus underscores the seriousness of the legal system's search for true facts. "That a witness will raise his hand, swear to tell the truth, and then do so is a breathtakingly simple proposition on which the entire American legal system rests."[31] Perjury not only undermines this search for truth, but also wastes the time, money, and energy of all the participants.

Direct Evidence and Circumstantial Evidence

The rules of evidence are complex, covering many types of information and many potential problems arising from the oral testimony of witnesses and the presentation of evidence in other forms, such as through documents, observation of the sites of specific events, or demonstrations of the physical characteristics of people, products, or mechanical processes. One of the most important concepts in the law of evidence is the distinction between direct evidence and circumstantial evidence. Direct evidence is just what it sounds like: An individual's statement of what he or she did, saw, heard, or otherwise perceived through close personal contact with the facts in question.

In contrast, circumstantial evidence is only indirectly connected to the facts being pursued. Was the driver of the car drinking liquor? The witness who testifies that he saw the driver doing so is offering direct evidence of that fact. The witness who did not see the driver, but did see the car weaving back and forth, is describing circumstances which suggest that the driver was intoxicated. Circumstantial evidence of that sort is said to "raise an inference" of the fact in question.

This witness's statement standing alone may or may not be enough to convince the decision maker, the "trier of fact," that drunk driving has been proven. However, when added to other evidence raising the same inference, the "corroborating evidence" of other people who also saw the erratic movement of the vehicle, that conclusion can more confidently be reached. A federal court explained the logic behind the legal system's treatment of circumstantial evidence:

> Inferred factual conclusions based on circumstantial evidence are permitted only when, and to the extent that, human experience indicates a probability that certain consequences can and do follow from the basic circumstantial facts. The inferences that the court permits the jury to educe in a courtroom do not differ significantly from inferences that rational beings reach daily in informally accepting a probability or arriving at a conclusion when presented with some hard, or basic evidence. A court permits the jury to draw inferences because of this shared experience in human endeavors.[32]

Hearsay Evidence and Cross-Examination

The well-known phrase "hearsay evidence" similarly represents the legal system's effort to recognize that some kinds of witness statements have greater bearing on the issues in dispute and thus deserve greater weight in the ultimate decision, while other kinds of statement are of more dubious import and should have little or no impact. Hearsay evidence essentially is a statement allegedly made by a person who is not in court but whose statement is presented there through someone else's oral testimony or a document brought in by someone other than the original speaker. When that type of out-of-court statement is offered in court in an attempt to help prove the truth of the statement's content, it is objectionable. Either the judge will refuse to allow the statement to be heard and considered by the decision maker—such as a jury—or, in some situations, the statement will be allowed into evidence but with the caveat that it is to be given little weight, or perhaps no weight at all, unless there is other, non–hearsay evidence that supports it, that corroborates it.

The most problematic aspect of hearsay evidence is linked to another crucial tool in the law's search for the true facts—cross-examination. In American legal processes, a witness is first asked questions by one party to offer evidence helpful to that party's position. That questioning is called "direct examination." It is followed in turn by the opposing party's opportunity to test the strength and veracity of the witness's statements through an additional round of questioning, known as "cross-examination." This reliance on alternating rounds of questioning of the witness by the various parties—direct examination, cross-examination, redirect examination, recross, etc.—is one of the most important ways in which many legal proceedings are conducted.

Cross-examination is allowed to probe more aggressively in order to help bring out the truth. Whereas the witness's oath underlines the importance of honesty, cross-examination provides for "challenging *accuracy* through stringent investigations that question the truth in a witness" as to both honesty and accuracy.[33] Courts have often emphasized this purpose, as in the following statement:

> The acid test of truth in judicial proceedings is cross-examination. It is admittedly the most efficacious agency which the law devised for the discovery of truth. The ordinary rule is, by cross-examination, the situation of the witness with respect to the parties in interest, and to the subject of litigation, his interest, his motives, his inclination and prejudices, may all be fully investigated and ascertained, and submitted to the consideration of the jury before whom he has testified, and who have had the opportunity of observing and determining the just weight and value of his testimony.[34]

The obvious problem with a hearsay statement is that no cross-examination is possible when the person who originally made the statement is not in court. "The theory of the hearsay rule . . . is that the many possible sources of inaccuracy and untrustworthiness which may lie underneath the bare untested assertion of a witness can be best brought to light and exposed, if they exist, by the test of cross-examination."[35] The truth of the absent witness's out-of-court statement cannot be tested, thus putting the party who would like to probe or challenge the statement at a serious disadvantage. The evidentiary rules restricting hearsay evidence are designed to avoid that unfairness.

Standard of Proof and Burden of Proof

The final fact-gathering tools worth noting here are the concepts of standard of proof and burden of proof. A standard of proof functions to "instruct the fact-finder concerning the degree of confidence our society thinks he should have in the correctness of factual conclusions for a particular type of adjudication."[36] This concept is well known through the frequently heard statement that a criminal defendant's guilt must be proven "beyond a reasonable doubt." That phrase embodies a very demanding standard of proof because in criminal cases jurors usually have "a very serious task before them: determining a fellow citizen's guilt or innocence of a heinous act, to which we attach the most severe of possible penalties, loss of liberty and even life."[37]

In the ordinary noncriminal case—known as a "civil case"—the standard is different and less demanding. It usually is said that the critical conclusions in the civil case, such as whether the defendant acted negligently and caused the plaintiff's harm, must be proven by a preponderance of the evidence. The same thought is expressed by saying that the evidence must add up to a showing that it is more probable than not that those conclusions—those applications of legal principles to facts—are correct. The divergent outcomes in the two trials of football star O. J. Simpson—not guilty in the criminal case but liable in the civil case—are often cited to illustrate both the difference between the two standards and "anecdotal evidence that juries can competently differentiate between the standards."[38]

These are the two principal standards of proof legal proceedings use, though variations arise in some contexts. Lawyers understand that these different verbal formulations can be also be viewed roughly in terms of the percentage of likelihood that something has been proven. In the criminal case, in such terms, the defendant's guilt must be shown by the evidence as highly probable, well over 90 percent. In a civil case, the defendant's legal responsibility must be shown as more likely than not, that is, over 50 percent probable, based on the evidence. Courts seldom attach such numerical percentages because numbers suggest an illusory precision, thus creating more trouble and confusion for lawyers and juries than the verbal standards create. In the back of their minds, however, regular participants in legal proceedings often think of such percentages as another way of grasping the standards of proof.

The other key concept is burden of proof. The party who is assigned the burden of proof must persuade the decision maker that the totality of evidence presented in the case by all the parties satisfies the applicable standard of proof. If the standard is not met, that party loses. In criminal cases the burden of proof is on the prosecution, the government officer who initiates the case. If the "beyond a reasonable doubt" standard is not met, the government has not carried the burden of proving its case. In a civil case, the burden of proof ordinarily is on the party initiating the case, the plaintiff. If the evidence weighs equally between the plaintiff and the defendant, or weighs more heavily toward the defendant, the plaintiff has not demonstrated a favorable preponderance of facts and therefore loses. These interrelated concepts—standard of proof and burden of proof—reflect the usual necessity for legal disputes to be resolved one way or another, even though the evidence available may be frustratingly, but unavoidably, incomplete or ambiguous.[39]

2. Recognizing Incomplete Facts

Very often in law, as in life generally, we simply do not know as much as we wish we did. This is especially true with regard to facts that provide important foundations for decisions the legal system must produce. Despite all the effort that goes into gathering facts, as discussed above, frequently there are information gaps that cannot be filled. "Law navigates through a fog of uncertainty. In attempting to figure out what happened in the past, the legal system must deal with faulty recollections, lost documents, missing witnesses, inattentive jurors, and countless other impediments to knowing with very much confidence what actually took place months or years earlier."[40] At times, the public becomes quite frustrated when legal processes produce only incomplete information. This happened, for example, in 2011, in a highly publicized murder trial in Florida:

> Many of the thousands who followed the Casey Anthony trial did not get the guilty verdict they wanted, nor did they learn the truth about what happened to the 2-year-old daughter she was accused of killing. And for the public, that may be one of the most frustrating parts of the case: Despite all the speculation and theories, they will never know how or why Caylee Anthony died... "Watching all of these crime shows has spoiled all of us. In TV shows, the coroner always has the answer."[41]

To take a less dramatic example, a merger of two companies may be in the works, and potential liabilities for environmental cleanup of contaminated properties may need to be quantified as part of the deal. However, the clock for completion of the transaction is ticking away, and technical evaluation of cleanup needs and costs is a lengthy process that cannot be finished in time. The deal will have to close without the parties having the hard information they ideally would like.

Frequently, with regard to legal issues on which technical expertise is needed, decision makers do not have all the information they could use. Perhaps the data could be gathered if more time were available, or perhaps the state of scientific knowledge just has not yet progressed to the point where all the pertinent data can be obtained in the foreseeable future, much less clearly understood in all its implications. In government policy decisions on the risks posed by various chemicals or environmental pollutants, for example, it is not unusual for the science to be incomplete even though a legal mandate and public expectations for regulatory action are looming. "Decision making must in that circumstance depend to a greater extent upon policy judgments and less upon purely factual analysis."[42]

Even in an ordinary civil trial of a tort claim—that is, a suit for monetary compensation for harm allegedly caused by the defendant's conduct or product—the jury may not receive full information about what caused the plaintiff's harm. Were the plaintiff's lungs impaired by working with chemicals the defendant manufactured, or was the harm caused wholly or partially by the plaintiff's prior working conditions, cigarette smoking, genetic predisposition, or exposure to chemicals in the home? Whatever the reason for the uncertainty and incompleteness of information may be, a verdict has to be reached and the legal system remains willing not infrequently "to make decisions on the basis of less than all of the best or available information."[43]

As already mentioned, the law has developed tools for helping in these situations, although methods for improving decision making under uncertainty are also found, of course, in fields other than law.[44] The standard of proof and burden of proof concepts are such tools, embodying policy choices to place the legal effect of incomplete or ambiguous information on one party rather than another.

Regulation of environmental and health dangers often is governed by a legislative requirement to take protective measures on the basis of levels of risk, or estimated probabilities of harm, if hard information about dangers is unknown or unknowable.[45] Environmental law thus relies at times on a concept labeled "the precautionary principle," which calls for making very conservative assumptions about how bad things ultimately could get.[46] These assumptions support protective policies and actions even before all relevant evidence is obtained.[47] For example, an important court decision on climate change in 2012, upholding the Environmental Protection Agency's greenhouse gas regulations, stated:

> If a statute is "precautionary in nature" and "designed to protect the public health," and the relevant evidence is "difficult to come by, uncertain, or conflicting because it is on the frontiers of scientific knowledge," EPA need not provide "rigorous step-by-step proof of

> cause and effect" to support [its regulations]. As we have stated before, "Awaiting certainty will often allow for only reactive, not preventive, regulation."[48]

In sum, in a variety of ways the legal system has adapted to the reality that even though often we do not know all that we would like to know, we still have a responsibility to make prompt and sensible decisions.

3. Dividing Labor

As already discussed, the gathering of information about a legal matter is often a complicated, lengthy process. Much of the time this work is not done by one person, even if the lawyer is a sole practitioner. Investigators, consultants, paralegals, law clerks, and even additional lawyers are commonly brought in to develop and organize relevant facts. Similarly, in researching the relevant law—whether statutes, regulations, prior court decisions, or other pronouncements—lawyers increasingly rely on work that others do for them. "Task sharing among lawyers is not only increasingly common but increasingly important; what was once done with little conscious planning is becoming a common mode of operation, perhaps the standard building block in the larger organizational constructs within which lawyers operate."[49]

It used to be said, and occasionally still is, that the lawyer's main research tool is the telephone. Lawyers often call each other—or now send emails—inquiring of their colleagues about whether others are familiar with, or have researched, a particular question. The reason for dividing up the workload through quick and easy communication like this is obvious: Results can be obtained more quickly and cheaply.

Judges also divide their labor, relying on law clerks and staff research attorneys to digest the factual records in court proceedings, to do research regarding applicable law, and often to prepare initial drafts of decisions. Ultimately, of course, the task of deciding the case, or of instructing the jury on the applicable law, is the judge's own responsibility. Dividing the labor as the case unfolds and the groundwork for decision is laid does not include delegating the responsibility for decision to others.

Division of labor is not a unique feature of the legal system, of course, as this common and useful practice is found in many types of work and other endeavors. By the same token, legal work is often enhanced by a team effort, with different members assigned different tasks to help get the whole job done intelligently and efficiently.

4. Using Expertise

One aspect of the division of labor is the use of expertise. Again, the point is obvious: Because so many legal disputes raise complex issues in specialized areas of knowledge—medicine, construction, technology, financial transactions, environmental impacts, and the list goes on and on—the parties to legal controversies, and decision makers with the responsibility to resolve them, somehow must get information from people familiar with the intricacies of the particular subject.

Sometimes reliance on expert witnesses is not a matter of choice or convenience, but is legally required. This is true, for example, in cases claiming physical harm caused by careless treatment by a doctor, that is, cases of alleged medical malpractice:

> The reason for the requirement of expert opinion testimony in most medical malpractice cases is obvious: matters relating to medical diagnosis and treatment ordinarily involve a level of technical knowledge and skill beyond the realm of lay knowledge and experience. Without expert opinion testimony in such cases, the trier of fact would be left with no standard at all against which to evaluate the defendant's conduct.[50]

We often hear of "battles of experts" in high-profile disputes involving allegations of medical malpractice, defective products, or product designs infringing the intellectual property rights of others. Experts in a particular field obviously do not always agree. Nevertheless, there seems to be no good alternative to hearing their information and opinions, even if the ultimate decision maker who evaluates the experts' views—a judge, jury, or arbitrator, for example—has no prior expertise or familiarity with the subject.[51]

One way of thinking about the experts used in legal processes is as "staff," as employees who support and assist the lawyer or decision maker. A common forum in which staff is relied on is legislatures. Legislative committees usually employ full-time staff members charged with gathering information about possible new laws or about the operation and impacts of existing laws. These staff members may have prior specialized expertise or they may develop it over time through sustained work on a particular topic. The information they gather, and recommendations they then can make to the elected legislators, help to make the lawmaking process more sophisticated, focused, and informed.

Legislators themselves also frequently develop expertise over the course of time in specific subjects. Other legislators may gravitate toward those more experienced "specialists" in their ranks for advice on legislative matters within the specialized areas. These legislators recognize—as do government and business executives and ordinary people in many aspects of their lives—that nobody can be an expert in everything. Nevertheless, intelligent decisions often require the input of someone who is an expert in something.

5. Identifying Bias

In legal disputes, it is often not difficult to identify the interests—the self-interests—being pursued by the parties. Perhaps not all the motivations for an individual to enter into a contract or file a lawsuit may be evident, but usually some will be. People normally enter into commercial agreements simply and obviously to enhance their own financial or other circumstances. In most litigation, it is required that the plaintiff have a real, personal stake in the matter, rather than just filing suit out of broad intellectual curiosity or some generalized concern. Federal courts, for example, insist that the plaintiff demonstrate such a stake, called "standing," in order to make sure that a real case or controversy exists, as required by the US Constitution before the judicial machinery can be set in motion.[52] "At bottom, 'the gist of the question of standing' is whether petitioners have 'such a personal stake in the outcome of the controversy as to assure that concrete adverseness which sharpens the presentation of issues upon which the court so largely depends for illumination.'"[53]

Self-interest, broadly defined, is thus a prerequisite to most legal proceedings. It does not taint the proceedings but rather gives rise to them. There is no hiding the fact that the parties are in the case to achieve some personal benefit, or avoid personal loss. They are not expected, much less required, to be serving higher purposes, even though at times they may be. The merits of the legal dispute can be addressed and resolved on the basis of the evidence and arguments each side presents in order to protect its own interests. There is, in short, nothing wrong with bias in favor of oneself in that context. Usually there is no secret about the self-interested motivations of the parties, and their positions in the case can be understood and evaluated in light of them.

When it comes to the decision maker—the judge, jury, arbitrator, hearing officer, or other officials—bias has entirely different significance. A core expectation in our legal system is that the decision maker is unbiased, open-minded, and lacking any self-interest in the outcome. The decision maker with those traits, and a certain modicum of intelligence, is well positioned to resolve the matter on the basis of the facts and law. It is thus fundamental that the decision maker must have no personal agendas or interests that might lead to a decision on other bases. Accordingly, the Supreme Court has declared:

> Not only is a biased decisionmaker constitutionally unacceptable but "our system of law has always endeavored to prevent even the probability of unfairness." In pursuit of this end, various situations have been identified in which experience teaches that the probability of actual bias on the part of the judge or decisionmaker is too high to be constitutionally tolerable. Among these cases are those in which the adjudicator has a pecuniary interest in the outcome and in which he has been the target of personal abuse or criticism from the party before him.[54]

This concern is reflected in the difficult, often tedious process of questioning potential jurors about their possible associations with the parties, in addition to their ability to listen to the evidence, grasp the judge's explanation of the pertinent legal rules, and render a fair-minded verdict.

In the selection of judges, too, objectivity is usually touted as one of the most important virtues to be sought in candidates. However, many legal scholars have observed that differing philosophical and political—broadly defined[55]—perspectives on the judiciary's role, and on methods of interpretation of the law, frequently come into play in a judge's work. The prior professional and life experiences of the individual do, too. The following are good examples of such observations:

> In making judgments, triers of fact inevitably act with predispositions that may affect how they evaluate the evidence. The psychological literature has documented a variety of cognitive biases that affect judges and juries.[56]
>
> Judges are people too. Judges... "are shaped not only by our learning but by our varied engagements with life, by experiences both inside and outside the law."[57]
>
> Democracy must, indeed, fail unless our courts try cases fairly, and there can be no fair trial before a judge lacking in impartiality and disinterestedness. If, however, "bias" and "partiality" be defined to mean the total absence of preconceptions in the mind of the judge, then no one has ever had a fair trial and no one ever will... We are born with predispositions; and the process of education, formal and informal, creates attitudes in all men which affect them in judging situations, attitudes which precede reasoning in particular instances and which therefore, by definition, are prejudices... Many of them represent the community's most cherished values and ideals. Such social preconceptions,

> the "value judgments" which members of any given society take for granted and use as the unspoken axioms of thinking, find their way into that society's legal system, become what has been termed "the valuation system of the law." The judge in our society owes a duty to act in accordance with those basic predilections inhering in our legal system (although, of course, he has the right, at times, to urge that some of them be modified or abandoned.) The standard of dispassionateness obviously does not require the judge to rid himself of the unconscious influence of such social attitudes.[58]

These and many similar observations on judicial behavior confirm the obvious fact that judges are diverse human beings and are not mechanical, or fungible, in the performance of their duties. Practical confirmation is shown by lawyers' common practice of "forum shopping," that is, trying to have a case heard by one judge rather than another because of perceived differences between them.

Even though complete objectivity and a tabula rasa are thus impossible and probably undesirable, it is understood that in any given case the judge at least should not have a personal interest at stake or bring a personal or political agenda to bear on the conduct of the proceedings or the ultimate decision. As with so many other things in law, however, often there are close questions to be answered regarding the presence or appearance of bias in the decision maker.

The judge may have formerly owned stock in one of the companies appearing in the case. The juror's cousin may be a police officer in the department that arrested the criminal defendant. The judge, in her prior status as a state legislator, may have given a speech critical of the commercial practices of a company similar to one of the parties. If at all possible, that decision maker in these situations—most certainly in those in which biases are clear cut—should be eliminated from the proceeding and another, who does not have the taint of bias or self-interest, substituted in.

Sometimes it is considered sufficient to disclose the bias but let the decision maker stay on the job. This can be done when the taint is less clear, giving rise only to a potential or appearance of bias, or when there is absolutely no substitute available and a decision must be reached. In those situations, even though the decision maker may not meet the ideal level of disinterestedness, her participation is allowed. The assumption is that the parties and the public now know who is deciding the matter, and are aware of the possibility that bias may influence the outcome. The decision then can be evaluated in light of this information, and conclusions can be reached as to whether the matter was fairly resolved. This approach is reflected in the federal statute pertaining to disqualification of federal trial judges in proceedings in which "impartiality might reasonably be questioned." The parties to the case may waive the disqualification if there has been "a full disclosure on the record of the basis for disqualification."[59]

For integrity of results in the legal system, bias in the parties is business as usual but bias in decision makers must be avoided whenever possible, and ambiguous or unavoidable bias in decision makers should, at the very least, be brought into the public spotlight.

D. Keeping an Open Mind

For a variety of reasons, and in a variety of ways, the legal system operates at its best when the people who work within it are open-minded as they do so. This means that lawyers, judges, and jurors have to consistently accept that the problems they are dealing with are complicated and susceptible to a variety of perspectives. New angles, implications, and information may arise at just about any time. The individual who is not open to seeing them, and to fairly evaluating their merits and significance, is unlikely to be effective in his work.

1. Arguing and Persuading

Lawyers argue a lot. They are supposed to. What "argument" means for lawyers, however, is not the kind of heated, personal disagreement the word usually connotes. Instead, it refers to lawyers' attempts, orally and in writing, to persuade others that their views on a particular legal issue are the better views and the ones that should be followed. Those attempts, of course, rest on the assumption that the target audience is open to being persuaded.

Like anyone else, lawyers sometimes get angry with their opponents, and then legal arguments, for better or worse, may be accompanied by the venting of hostile sentiments. More often, lawyers air their disagreements with a high degree of civility—even formality—and mutual respect. There are many reasons for this tradition, starting with lawyers' shared recognition that legal issues are usually complex, subtle, and riddled with competing considerations. Supreme Court Justice John Paul Stevens described "the inevitability of disagreement among independent and thoughtful judges charged with the task of interpreting broad language in the constitution." He continued:

> Students of [Supreme Court] opinions sometimes infer that such disagreements are partly due to personal friction or disrespect. Nothing

> could be further from the truth. Indeed, I have often thought that Tranio's reference to litigating advocates applies with equally full force to members of our Court: "[A]s adversaries do in law—[we] [s]trive mightily, but eat and drink as friends."[60]

Judges' responsibilities extend not only to respect among members of the bench, but to civil treatment of others as well:

> A judge shall be patient, dignified, and courteous to litigants, jurors, witnesses, lawyers, court staff, court officials, and others with whom the judge deals in an official capacity, and shall require similar conduct of lawyers, court staff, court officials, and others subject to the judge's direction and control.[61]

Unfortunately, viewers of television entertainment programs that purport to show courtroom proceedings are usually treated to a very different and unrealistic view of judicial behavior, with heavy doses of "sarcasm, verbosity, and aggression . . . Many individuals are not aware that television brethren are not acting in the role as true judges or that some are not judges at all . . . As one sitting judge discovered, behavior that would garner applause in the television courtroom renders official sanctioning when occurring in the 'real' courtroom."[62]

Lawyers have an unusually keen understanding that on many legal questions, there is seldom an indisputably "right" answer. More often there are multiple, sensible perspectives, based on different understandings of the significance of particular facts in the dispute, varying interpretations of prior law, and competing views of good social policy. Lawyers know that there are usually at least two sides to the story, and ordinarily there is at least some merit to them all. "Even when the plaintiff and defendant agree on the applicable law, and even on a particular interpretation of that law, plenty remains for the parties to argue about. A significant number—indeed, we would guess a majority—of actual legal disputes turn not on questions of what the law is, but on questions of how the law actually *applies* to a particular case."[63]

Similarly, even if there is agreement on what the facts are, the rhetorical characterization of them may vary widely. One, perhaps apocryphal, illustration of this phenomenon is the so-called whiskey speech, allegedly delivered by a member of the Mississippi legislature in about 1952. The speaker powerfully stated his opposition to whiskey, if the term meant "the devil's brew, the poison scourge, the bloody monster that dethrones reason, destroys the home," etc. At the same time, the same speaker asserted that he was unequivocally in favor of whiskey if the term meant "the oil of conversation, the philosophic wine, the elixir of life... Christmas cheer," etc.[64]

The legal system thus accepts disagreement, and nuanced expressions of it, as a normal condition. Again, this is not because lawyers are supposed to stir up conflict, but rather because so many issues invite, or at least are readily susceptible to, honest differences of interpretation and opinion. In his classic lectures on the study of law in America, Karl Llewellyn wrote:

> If we are to watch law's relation to civilization we must... watch law's development in civilization—and what we watch will be a different thing from time to time and place to place. The sole inescapable common element is dealing with disputes. The sole inescapable common focus is the relation between the *ways* of dealing with dispute and the other ways of living.[65]

In this context, lawyers and judges not only expect disagreement but enjoy a tradition of disagreeing without being disagreeable.

Clients are sometimes shocked to discover that their lawyers are actually friendly with opposing counsel. Hollywood took this scenario a step further in the classic 1949 film "Adam's Rib." Spencer Tracy and Katherine Hepburn portrayed a married couple, both lawyers but on opposing sides in a criminal case.[66] Probably the best known example of this tradition of amicability among lawyers is Abraham Lincoln's participation in "riding the circuit" in mid-nineteenth-century Illinois. He and a group of other lawyers travelled from one small town to another with a judge for about ten weeks twice a year, litigating cases arising in those locales.

> The members of the bar formed a bright, congenial company who strove mightily with each other in the court-rooms, but ate and drank as friends... Every man knew every other man, and the close, daily contact in the court-rooms and on the road created a spirit of comradeship which no mere professional interest could supply.[67]

Lincoln "relished the convivial life he shared with the lawyers who battled one another fiercely during the day, only to gather as friends in the taverns at night."[68]

Friendly relationships among lawyers, even when they are on opposite sides of a transaction or lawsuit, should not be surprising, once it is understood that their arguments and disagreements concern, above all, the merits of the matter. The client may urge the lawyer, as his "mouthpiece," to make sure that opposing parties are forcefully informed of the depth of the client's low esteem for them. Lawyers usually resist such urging, for that type of communication is unlikely to advance dialogue on the merits toward a constructive outcome.

For the same reason, to keep legal decision making focused on the real issues at stake, there are well-established constraints on legal arguments, rooted in both procedural rules and long-standing traditions. In court proceedings, especially in front of juries, lawyers are admonished to restrain themselves from appealing heavily to the decision makers' prejudices and emotions. Such appeals are likely to distract from the identified issues, proven facts, and applicable rules. In short, if cases are to be decided on their merits, rather than on tangential or extraneous considerations, legal argument must remain focused on the merits.

Similarly, the rules of evidence have great bearing on the proper bounds of legal argument. A lawyer should not try to make hay out of irrelevant information, nor should she try to obscure the applicable standard of proof or burden of proof. If there is evidence of little or no probative significance, such as hearsay, arguments should be correspondingly calibrated to give that evidence only the weight, if any, to which it is properly entitled. As recognized in the rules of evidence for federal court cases, even relevant evidence can be excluded from consideration "if its probative value is substantially outweighed by the danger of unfair prejudice, confusion of the issues, or misleading the jury."[69]

Although lawyers spend a lot of time, in both formal and informal settings, trying to persuade others, their arguments are supposed to be focused constantly on the issues at hand. Lawyers are obligated to avoid the distortions and distractions that angry, unfocused arguments and harassing tactics can create. Unfortunately, lawyers do not always abide by this constraint:

> In recent years, a number of legal representatives—especially in large urban areas—have decided to employ highly offensive tactics to advance client interests. They may be rude, sarcastic, or nasty. These individuals erroneously equate discourteous actions with effective advocacy. They use these techniques as a substitute for lawyering skill. Proficient practitioners recognize that impolite behavior is the antithesis of competent representation.[70]

The adversary structure of legal disputes can transform the lawyer's duty to forcefully represent his client into an invitation to depart from professionally responsible conduct and to try instead to win at any cost. In a discussion of civility and professionalism of lawyers, one trial lawyer observed, "I do not think the problem is that lawyers do not know how to act in a civil manner. Rather, I think some lawyers will simply do that with which they can get away."[71] Lawyers may succumb to the temptation to obscure the truth, rather than help search for it, and to distract from the issues, rather than illuminate them. Civil, honest legal argument can then be overcome by inflammatory or deceptive tactics.

Although it does not always happen, such unprofessional conduct can be penalized by the courts. In a federal court case in Florida, the judge reduced by over $350,000 the amount of attorneys fees to be paid to a lawyer who had persistently engaged in uncivil, unprofessional conduct during the litigation.[72] In a California divorce case, uncivil conduct by a young lawyer resulted in a court order requiring him and his client to pay a $100,000 penalty and over $300,000 of the opposing party's attorneys fees. The court aptly concluded:

> We close this discussion with a reminder to counsel—all counsel, regardless of practice, regardless of age—that zealous advocacy does not equate with "attack dog" or "scorched earth"; nor does it mean lack of civility.... Zeal and vigor in the representation of clients are commendable. So are civility, courtesy, and cooperation. They are not mutually exclusive.[73]

Sometimes lawyers' improper conduct does seem to successfully promote clients' objectives, but usually it does not. Instead, it "guarantees the offensive actors far more nonsettlements than are experienced by their more cooperative cohorts."[74] It also tarnishes the reputation of the lawyer who chooses this unprofessional path. Lincoln himself recognized "the vague popular belief that lawyers are necessarily dishonest." His pithy response emphasized the individual's power to choose both a line of work and a path of honesty:

> Let no young man, choosing the law for a calling, for a moment yield to this popular belief. Resolve to be honest at all events; and if, in your own judgment, you can not be an honest lawyer, resolve to be honest without being a lawyer. Choose some other occupation.[75]

2. Listening and Negotiating

It is well known that lawyers are expected to be forceful and articulate speakers. If they are, then the legal arguments they make may be persuasive not just because of the content but also because of the manner of presentation. What is perhaps not so obvious is that lawyers also have to be extremely good listeners. For starters, a lawyer has to be able to listen closely to what his client is saying about his experiences, concerns, and goals. If the lawyer does not understand what the client is trying to accomplish, the lawyer's chances of helping the client are not good.

Good listening obviously is an important capability and habit for everyone, not just people working in the law. At an early age, children are admonished to listen to their parents and teachers, and relationships of many sorts can founder if the participants do not hear one another well. Listening thus may be one of the least distinctive tools of the legal system, and yet it is one of the most important.

Because of the complexity of most legal issues and the variety of available perspectives on them, the lawyer needs to attend carefully to others' viewpoints. By doing so, he will be able to develop and express the position that best serves his client's interests. He especially will need to hear what opposing parties are saying so that he can formulate the best response. His attentive listening must not just focus on what is said but also on how it is said. Some researchers have even found that "more than half of a person's feelings and attitudes are communicated via channels other than the literal meanings of the words being used."[76]

If the lawyer brings good listening and an open mind to the dialogue with opposing parties, she also increases the likelihood of discovering points of agreement. By adapting her position accordingly, she can help lead the way to a speedier and hopefully less contentious resolution. "Learning how to make arguments on different sides of a question is learning that there are arguments on both sides, and learning how to hear them. That is the core of the liberal value of tolerance, but also the precondition for order in a society that chooses to engage in conflict with words rather than guns."[77]

The lawyer who listens well may learn, among other things, of new facts, new perspectives on facts already known, unexpected concerns or implications for other parties or even his own client, or legal rules or precedents he had not yet realized were pertinent. A laudatory remembrance of how Thurgood Marshall practiced law before ascending to the Supreme Court emphasizes the point:

> "That was one of his great virtues, seeing things from the other guy's side. He was a good tough advocate who functioned without having to feel that his opponents were either knaves or fools."[78]

Lawyers also must listen closely in order to be able to identify weakness or illogic in others' views. Law students are often admonished by their professors for offering observations that are "conclusionary." What they are being told is that they are asserting a conclusion on an issue without having explained the evidence and reasoning to justify it. In common parlance, they have "leaped to a conclusion." A conclusion may ultimately be a solid one, but the lawyer who cannot explain how it was reached will be sorely hindered in defending it. In contrast, the opposing lawyer who listens closely, is unswayed by oratorical flourishes alone, and realizes that the statement is simply conclusionary will be well positioned to undermine its persuasive force.

Probably the most active and important realm in which good listening is essential in the law is negotiation. As with listening generally, negotiation is not something unique to the legal system:

> Everyone negotiates something every day...Negotiation is a basic means of getting what you want from others. It is back-and-forth communication designed to reach an agreement when you and the other side have some interests that are shared and others that are opposed (as well as some that may simply be different).[79]

Although negotiation is not distinctive to the law, it is of central importance. One legal scholar asserts that negotiation is the "single most prevalent and important" process within the legal system,[80] while another claims, "Most legal practitioners use their negotiating skills more frequently than their other lawyering talents."[81]

Whether or not these statements are correct, they emphasize that there is a plethora of situations in which lawyers regularly engage in negotiation to accomplish their work and promote their clients' interests:

> Everyone negotiates, and lawyers negotiate for a living. Acting as agents, lawyers work on behalf of other people to reach a mutually agreeable resolution—a sale, a settlement, a development deal—for the parties involved. Even those lawyers who specialize in litigation are primarily negotiators, since fewer than 10% of lawsuits are actually tried to verdict. Lawyers negotiate the details of their professional daily life—when depositions and meetings will take place; whether and when a particular motion will be filed or set for hearing; which documents will be produced without a judge's order—as well as the large and small elements of a long-term supply contract or of a settlement in a major case.[82]

In the settlement of litigation, the conclusion of a contractual agreement, or the resolution of some other legal dispute, mutual agreement is not possible unless the parties have heard each other's concerns and found ways to compromise to resolve their differences. "It is hard to overstate the importance of listening skills in bargaining" in the law, as well as in other aspects of our lives.[83]

Although lawyers must be good listeners for all of the reasons discussed above, the most obvious listeners in the legal process are judges and jurors. If they do not pay close attention to the evidence and arguments, and keep their minds open to new information and perspectives, they simply will be unable to do the jobs society expects them to perform. They must listen and learn before they can intelligently and fairly decide. It has been stated that a key "criterion for determining judicial greatness is the nature of a judge's temperament, including... his or her open-mindedness, patience, even-handedness, [and] disposition to listen to all sides of an issue."[84]

One federal judge even has described the fact-finding aspect of litigation as a type of listening with, among other things, a spiritual dimension:

> When we are given the responsibility of listening to disputants, who are often locked in a moral crisis with each other, and trying to determine where truth and justice lie in a dispute, we are called on, to the best of our ability, to pay attention. Paying attention... is more than simply trying not to be distracted. It is trying to ascertain the truth, unobstructed by our own biases, prejudices, self-interest and resentments, as well as by the blinding limitations of our own experience. I suggest that to the extent that the work of judging has a spiritual dimension, it inheres in this: that we are charged with paying close attention to our fellow human beings and trying, by listening to them, to find the truth. Listening to others, hearing them, and reaching a fair assessment where both sides have been heard and feel that they have been heard, is what justice in its full significance is about.[85]

3. Making Hard Choices in Gray Areas

Lawyers are sometimes said to be congenitally lacking in firm beliefs about anything. They often hedge their views with qualifications and limiting conditions. They frequently answer a question with a question, or state an opinion and then promptly state another, prefacing the second with, "On the other hand..." In *To Kill a Mockingbird*, a lawyer's child says, "First thing you learn when you're in a lawin' family is that there ain't any definite answers to anything."[86]

It is undeniable that these tendencies can be annoying to others, and that sometimes lawyers are much more equivocal in conversations than they ought to be. "People who have learned to think like lawyers usually also talk like lawyers, often to the considerable annoyance of their families and friends."[87] Nevertheless, there are good reasons for lawyers' inclination to see issues as gray, rather than black or white. As has been emphasized repeatedly here, the legal system deals with complex issues, and it values the ability to see a problem from more than one viewpoint. Lawyers sometimes express more than one side on an issue because their training, and the demands of their work, require them to be able to see more than one. As already explained, an effective legal argument demands an ability to hear and understand the opposing argument.

Lawyers realize, in other words, that legal issues often pose hard choices between competing interests and values. Judges especially face this challenge, since they are called on to make and articulate those choices. In making them, they often have to compare the policy significance and impact of the adoption of one legal position against the adoption of another. Seldom are those choices cost-free, for to strike a balance in favor of one goal or value may well impinge on another.[88]

Judges thus often must choose between the horns of a dilemma, and they may have to do so despite the inescapable uncertainty or incompleteness of relevant information.[89] Judicial explanation of such a decision candidly should acknowledge that even though the choice being made is hoped to lead to a better result than an available alternative, something else is being sacrificed through rejection of the alternative.

Lawyers and judges do not enjoy the luxury of pretending that society's problems are easy to understand and solve. They understand that good social policies frequently compete or conflict with one another. Even though the parties to a legal dispute may each be promoting respectable concerns, hard choices among them still may have to be made. This inevitable need is often and strongly emphasized:

> Judges constantly strive to seek an accommodation between competing sets of principles. There are times, however, when the scales seem evenly balanced, and it is difficult to determine exactly where the weight does lie. It is here when the judge makes a value judgment. At these times, the jural philosophy of the individual judge comes into play, consciously or otherwise, by means of a value judgment that places a greater weight on one competing principle than another.[90]

> Legal reasoning is impossible without reference to the policies, that is, the values, underlying the law... These policies are in conflict, and thus legal reasoning requires one to make judgments about which policies are to prevail in particular circumstances.[91]

> In most cases, judges must reconcile the competing pulls of constitutional values, the actual wording of legal provisions, prior judicial opinions, and their own views of the facts and values—the social realities—of the cases before them. Judges must make difficult choices.[92]
>
> Debates about justice and rights are often, unavoidably, debates about the purpose of social institutions, the goods they allocate, and the virtues they honor and reward.[93]

Supreme Court Justice David Souter made similar observations when discussing interpretation of the Constitution, and the First Amendment in particular:

> Even the First Amendment, then, expressing the value of speech and publication in the terms of a right as paramount as any fundamental right can be, does not quite get to the point of an absolute guarantee. It fails because the Constitution has to be read as a whole, and when it is, other values crop up in potential conflict with an unfettered right to publish, the value of security for the nation and the value of the President's authority in matters foreign and military. The explicit terms of the Constitution, in other words, can create *a conflict of approved values*, and the explicit terms of the Constitution do not resolve that conflict when it arises...A choice may have to be made, not because language is vague but because the Constitution embodies the desire of the American people, like most people, to have things both ways. We want order and security, and we want liberty. And we want not only liberty but equality as well. These paired desires of ours can clash, and when they do a court is forced to choose between them, between one constitutional good and another one. The court has to decide which of our approved desires has the better claim, right here, right now...Choices...make up much of what we call law.[94]

Another commentary on essentially the same point put it quite simply:

> The Constitution...contains language protecting the freedom of the press. It also contains language insuring the fairness of criminal trials. But an unrestrained press can do much to prejudice the fairness of a trial.[95]

Jurors also may face hard decisions, although they are not expected or required to explain them as judges are, nor generally are jurors even supposed to make—at least not explicitly—the kinds of policy choices embodied in the law.[96] The broader implications of jurors' verdicts, however, may at times be evident to them. As an example, considering the O. J. Simpson murder trial and his acquittal in 1995, had he been convicted, justice presumably would have been served. That is, the evidence would have satisfied the standard of proof beyond a reasonable doubt that he committed the crimes charged.

However, in view of the strong evidence of misconduct by the police and prosecutors in the investigation of the case, a conviction implicitly would have validated dangerous government practices. Therefore, the acquittal could be seen in part as a rejection of those practices, as a law professor who worked on Simpson's defense team explained:

> Inevitably, the verdict delivers a message to the parties who are in court. An appeal to "send a message" to the prosecutors who tried the case, or to the police who investigated it, is *not* an appeal to decide the case on the basis of extraneous factors apart from the evidence. The "message" [Simpson's lawyers] asked jurors to deliver is that "we don't trust the messengers you sent into this courtroom. They lied to us." For the Los Angeles Police Department, that's a fair reading of the verdict.[97]

Nevertheless, many people believe the acquittal disserved the fundamental notion that criminal conduct should be stigmatized as such and punished. In short, either outcome—conviction or acquittal—would have been both a win and a loss for important public concerns.

Reasoning from Precedents, Examples, and Analogies

When judges face these types of challenges, they often seek comfort in prior decisions. If a judge can find a relevant precedent—"an earlier case in which the facts resemble the current conflict a judge has to resolve"[98]—reliance on that precedent makes sense. Another court has already thought through the problem and reached, and explained, a conclusion. Some important homework has already been done. Respect for precedent also promotes stability and predictability in the law, and, most importantly, consistent and equal treatment of people in similar cases.

It is common while looking for precedents to come across prior cases that have only a few similarities to the current dispute but not enough to make it evident that the precedent provides a full, solid answer for the new case. Lawyers and judges then engage in a process of analyzing the prior cases to see whether they are analogous in ways that can help resolve the case at hand. "If the comparison yields a perfect fit, if both the law and its application are clear, the task is simple. If the law is unclear, it is necessary to 'extract from the precedents the underlying principle [and] then determine the path or direction along which the principle is to move and develop'"[99] "Rules of law often turn out to be ambiguous but... judges must make legal choices anyway."[100]

Sometimes there are multiple precedents that seem to be relevant, but which do not all point in the same direction. The task then becomes more challenging, because it now requires "choice from among competing analogies."[101] These are not easy choices to make:

> Judges make choices because no two cases are identical, and judges are imperfect human beings prone to inject into decisions their views of how society should work. Because no two cases are identical, a judge, in order to resolve the current case, must sometimes select a guiding principle... from among "competing legal principles of equal validity."[102]

As an example, consider a lawsuit for false imprisonment based on the plaintiff's allegation that a room he was in was locked by the defendant for a number of hours. The plaintiff concedes, however, that he was sleeping during the entire time and did not know until later, after the door was unlocked, that he had been locked in. If he had tried to leave the room during his confinement, he would not have been able to do so, but in fact he did not know about the confinement or try to leave. Should this case be treated as a false imprisonment for which the plaintiff successfully can sue?

If the case is compared to the law of battery, plaintiff should win, but if it is compared to the law of assault, he should lose. That is because a battery—an intentional and unconsented contact with the plaintiff's body—is committed even if the plaintiff was not aware of the contact at the time it occurred, but only found out later. In contrast, an assault is conduct that causes the plaintiff to perceive that a battery is about to occur, but there is no assault unless the plaintiff was aware of the threat at the time it occurred. Is false imprisonment more like battery or more like assault? Those are the competing analogies from which the judge must choose. Presumably, the choice will be made on a principled basis, in order to promote what the judge believes is the best social policy.

People working in the law thus commonly reason and argue by drawing lessons from similar problems and their resolutions in the past. It has even been asserted that "analogies can be considered the most important aspect of the study and practice of law."[103] In this analytical process, there is room for interpretation and creativity as lawyers in argument, and judges in decision, rely on the precedential analogies they find most pertinent and helpful.[104] The process, even at the highest judicial level, is not without constraints, however. One scholar emphasized the point with respect to decisions of the Supreme Court:

> The cases the [Supreme Court] hears are all very hard, almost by definition, with excellent legal arguments (not just ideological ones) on both sides...More than one interpretation [of the pertinent law] is possible in hard cases, of course, but constraining interpretive traditions make some readings more persuasive than others...Any good lawyer can argue the plausibility of competing precedents and interpretations, the plasticity of legal doctrines and different ways of viewing the same facts—and these arguments create openings that judges can and do exploit to reach a preferred outcome...[Nonetheless,] these constraints significantly limit justices' discretion, and the justices take them seriously.[105]

The greatest constraint is that ideally court decisions, whether at the Supreme Court or any other level, are to be "entirely principled," which means that they are to rest on "reasons with respect to all the issues in the case, reasons that in their generality and their neutrality transcend any immediate result that is involved."[106]

In a discussion of recent, sharp differences among Supreme Court justices' approaches to interpretation of the Constitution, it was charged that "we've gotten in a box where each side is constantly accusing the other of deciding cases based on their personal views." Rejecting that type of accusation, one Supreme Court lawyer has responded, "These are complicated questions. In fact, they're hard questions. It doesn't mean people are reaching bankrupt results. It just means they're hard questions."[107] The subjects the law addresses, and the way lawyers and judges do their work, remind us—more often than we might wish—that life in our society, and the disputes that emerge from it, are just not simple.

As we recognize this reality, we see more clearly how important it is that lawyers, judges, and jurors keep an open mind as they perform their challenging work. Additionally, the other broad goals discussed above—focusing on the task, taking an organized approach, and finding reliable information—are crucial as well if the legal system is to reach wise and fair conclusions on the matters it addresses, whether big or small. As we shall see in subsequent chapters, these goals also would be beneficial for the individual citizen to pursue. Adaptation of the 12 legal tools and traditions to the citizen's ongoing task should help greatly in that pursuit.

5

The Citizen as Juror

Chapter 4 emphasized the work of lawyers and judges. Now the focus shifts to jurors. Jury duty most clearly connects the legal system's methods to the ordinary citizen. On virtually every weekday, American citizens find themselves serving as jurors in criminal or civil cases. They become an integral part of the legal system's approach to dispute resolution. In doing so, they are expected to apply and observe the law's tools and traditions, even though they do not possess the expertise of lawyers and judges.

Jury service offers a model to which we can look for guidance on the citizen's broader civic responsibilities. This connection is reflected in a popular author's comment that "a trial... is just a microcosm of the entire political system." He explained:

> When a democratic government decides to raise taxes or wage war or write child safety laws, it is essentially saying to an enormous jury, "This is our theory of how the world works, and this is our proposal for dealing with it. If our theory makes sense to you, vote for us in the next election. If it doesn't, throw us out." If ordinary citizens can't coolly and rationally evaluate a prosecutor's summation in a criminal trial, they won't have a chance at calling to task a deceitful government.[1]

There are at least two reasons to emphasize our society's expectations for jurors. First, we cannot have much confidence in our system of justice unless we believe that jurors generally perform their duties intelligently and fairly. Second, and more pertinently, jury service rests on the assumption that any citizen—at least any citizen technically qualified for jury service by being a registered voter, a licensed driver, or otherwise included by jury eligibility laws—is capable of performing this duty as it should be performed. As one court's guide to jury duty puts it:

> This is an awesome responsibility, but we do not require any particular skills, expertise or education level of our jurors; in fact, just the opposite

> is true—we strive to offer to litigants, or parties before the Court, the opportunity to select a jury which represents all cross-sections of our community. Remember, the jury's task is to make a determination of the truth, and all of our citizens are equipped with the ability to undertake that responsibility.[2]

A recent book on the importance of jury service emphasized, "Jury service elevates regular people to the task of contributing to the government."[3] The Supreme Court has made essentially the same point:

> Recognition must be given to the fact that those eligible for jury service are to be found in every stratum of society. Jury competence is an individual rather than a group or class matter. That fact lies at the heart of the jury system. To disregard it is to open the door to class distinctions and discriminations which are abhorrent to the democratic ideals of trial by jury.[4]

Another court has even said that "no other country has placed so much faith in the ability of ordinary citizens directly to participate in the function of the justice system."[5]

Since we assume that virtually every adult has the capability to think and act responsibly as a juror, should we not also assume that each person can act similarly in his broader participation in democratic discourse on public issues? The contexts for these two different types of civic duties are obviously different, as will be highlighted in chapter 6. Nonetheless, if the ordinary citizen is capable of being a thoughtful and fair-minded juror, he should be capable of thoughtful and fair-minded participation in other facets of civic life as well. Guidance to help him develop and apply these capabilities may be enhanced by understanding what we expect citizens to do as jurors.

A. JURY SERVICE AS EDUCATION

As early as Tocqueville's *Democracy in America*, and continuing in the observations of modern scholars, jury service has been seen as having dual benefits. Most obviously, jurors participate in the administration of civil and criminal justice. Less obvious are the ways in which jurors themselves benefit through the time they spend in that role. "Jury duty is not only a way of resolving cases. It is also a form of civic education, and an expression of democratic citizenship."[6] Tocqueville expressed it this way:

> The jury contributes powerfully to form the judgment and to increase the natural intelligence of a people; and this, in my opinion, is its greatest advantage. It may be regarded as a gratuitous public school, ever open, in which every juror learns his rights…and becomes practically acquainted with the laws, which are brought within the reach of his capacity by the efforts of the bar, the advice of the judge, and even the passions of the parties. I think that the practical intelligence and political good sense of the Americans are mainly attributable to the long use that they have made of the jury in civil causes.
>
> I do not know whether the jury is useful to those who have lawsuits, but I am certain it is highly beneficial to those who judge them; and I look upon it as one of the most efficacious means for the education of the people which society can employ.[7]

He grandly described jury service as a means "to communicate the spirit of the judges to the minds of all the citizens."[8]

Confirmation of Tocqueville's insight has been recently provided in modern studies of jurors. "Not only does the jury allow the people to contribute to the legal system, but the legal system, through the jury, contributes to the education of the people. De Tocqueville saw this very clearly."[9] One recent study, *The Jury and Democracy: How Jury Deliberation Promotes Civic Engagement and Political Participation*, offered an intensive analysis of individuals' actual jury service and its impact on their subsequent attitudes and activities.[10] It documented ways in which service on a jury "can be an invigorating experience for jurors that changes their understanding of themselves and their sense of political power and broader civic responsibilities."[11] The study examined "the unique position of the jury, through which a state institution brings private citizens together to deliberate on a public problem."[12]

The Jury and Democracy presented a variety of important findings, including these:

- Deliberation on a jury causes previously infrequent voters to become more likely to vote in future elections.
- Serving on a jury can change many aspects of an individual's political and community life… This investigation reveals general patterns, such as increased attention to news media and more frequent participation in conversations with neighbors about community issues.
- Jurors can develop stronger faith in government and their fellow citizens, and they come to see themselves as more politically capable and virtuous.[13]

The study also included this strong statement by a former juror on the educational value of his experience:

> I truly felt that Jury Duty was the best civics lesson I've ever had. In no other way that I can think of are citizens so equally involved in the state's affairs. In daily life, our conversations and opinions rarely have serious consequences...In the trial, our sphere of concern overlaps our sphere of influence and our involvement produces very real consequences. Thus, as Jurors and as citizens, we become more aware of the weight and responsibility of our decisions. Ultimately, this is a lesson in civics that a high school social studies class could never replicate.[14]

Although many Americans will serve as jurors at some point, most of us will not[15] and so will not experience firsthand this important type of "lesson in civics." Even for those who do not, however, similar benefit can be derived from understanding how the tools and traditions of the law are used and experienced by those who do.

B. The Model Juror's Traits

When we speak of the traits we hope to find in citizens as jurors, we usually speak in high-minded and obvious terms—what some might call platitudes. For example, according to the *Handbook for Trial Jurors Serving in the United States District Courts*, the optimal characteristics of jurors include integrity, intelligence, sound and good judgment, absolute honesty, a complete sense of fairness, an open mind, common sense, and "the general quality of citizenship."[16] Descriptions of ideal juror traits offered by various state courts include many of these same phrases,[17] as well as others such as "a readiness to work with the other jurors to make decisions."[18]

The trait most often stressed is impartiality. Indeed the only adjective in the United States Constitution regarding the character of a jury is "impartial." The Sixth Amendment states, "In all criminal prosecutions, the accused shall enjoy the right to a speedy and public trial, by an impartial jury." Though impartiality of jurors is lauded as fundamental,[19] its meaning is not always clear. As the Supreme Court observed years ago, "Impartiality is not a technical conception. It is a state of mind. For the ascertainment of this mental attitude of appropriate indifference, the Constitution lays down no particular tests."[20] Even earlier, Chief Justice John Marshall declared, in the trial of Aaron Burr:

> The great value of the trial by jury certainly consists in its fairness and impartiality. Those who most prize the institution, prize it because it

> furnishes a tribunal which may be expected to be uninfluenced by an undue bias of the mind. I have always conceived, and still conceive, an impartial jury as required by the common law, and as secured by the constitution, must be composed of men who will fairly hear the testimony which may be offered to them, and bring in their verdict according to that testimony, and according to the law arising on it . . . The jury should enter upon the trial with minds open to those impressions which the testimony and the law of the case ought to make, not with those preconceived opinions which will resist those impressions.[21]

Alongside customary recitations of model jurors' attributes, there are continuing debates about whether the reality matches the ideal. A considerable body of scholarship explores this question. It is not necessary to delve into it here, however, as the present inquiry seeks to draw guidance from the ideal, the model of the citizen as juror. Suffice it to note a few scholars' observations:

> The modern American jury has a bipolar presence in the popular consciousness. On the one hand, the jury is a cultural icon as revered in the United States as the flag, its contribution to democracy equated to voting. On the other hand, the jury is reviled as an agent of arbitrary injustice, its output considered evidence of the decline of moral consensus.[22]

> Trial by jury is about the best of democracy and about the worst of democracy.[23]

> Nowhere are the contrasting stereotypes of the legal process more seriously debated than over the American jury. Juries provide the most potent symbol of self-rule ever invented and represent the high-water mark of democratic understanding and republican principle. On the other hand, and at almost every stage of its existence, the institution has been found wanting or suspect in practical application. Disturbing examples of poor decisions made by juries can be found in every era, and systematic research into the workings of the modern jury system have exposed alarming instances of delay, inconsistency, misunderstanding, and outright nullification of the law.[24]

In sum, criticism of the jury has been asserted on at least three grounds: "it is incompetent, it is prejudiced, and it wages war with the law."[25] The validity of any of these assertions most likely will remain a matter of dispute for as long as America relies on juries.

C. TOOLS, TRADITIONS, AND THE JUROR

Service by the ideal juror fundamentally is engagement with the specific methods of the legal system explained in chapter 4. Adopting

Tocqueville's memorable phrase, we can say that this is how jury service "can communicate the spirit of the judges to the minds of all the citizens."

In some respects, the juror employs the law's tools and traditions himself, while in other respects the juror is largely an observer of their use by other participants in the justice process, mainly lawyers and judges. The distinction between what the juror *does* and what the juror *sees* is not precise, for in some aspects of his service he must do both. Similarly, the four broad goals earlier identified, for how legal work should be done, also apply to the juror but somewhat differently from the ways they apply to lawyers and judges. Specifically, jurors are certainly expected to stay focused on their duties and to appreciate the importance of an organized approach to them. However, they are not charged to find reliable information themselves, but they are counted on to grasp distinctions between reliable and unreliable information as it is presented to them. Probably most importantly, jurors must keep an open mind.

Because the tools that promote these goals apply differently to jurors than they do to others working in the law, it is not necessary to discuss all 12 tools in equal depth or in the order presented earlier. Instead, to best illuminate what is expected of the juror, the 12 tools can be divided into two rough categories: the methods the juror uses and those the juror observes. In the first category, the following six methods need to be both understood and acted on by the members of a jury:

- Separating facts from standards and evaluations
- Listening and learning
- Identifying bias
- Recognizing incomplete facts
- Making hard choices in gray areas
- Respecting procedure

For the other six features, the juror is largely an observer, though one who needs to absorb these aspects of what transpires before him. These elements are:

- Defining the issue
- Gathering the facts
- Dividing labor
- Using expertise
- Taking time
- Arguing and persuading

D. What the Juror Uses

Looking at the six factors the juror must both understand and use, *the separation of facts from legal standards and evaluations* is a good starting point, as it is critical for proper performance of the jury's function. It is commonly stated, particularly when judges instruct juries about their duties, that the jury's principal function is to determine what the true facts are, while the judge's duties include statement of the applicable law.[26] A standard jury instruction in Massachusetts courts, for example, declares:

> You must take the law as I give it to you. You should not be concerned about the wisdom of any rule of law that I give you. Whatever your private opinions about what the law is or ought to be, it is your duty to base your verdict on the law as I define it to you.[27]

The juror who does not grasp these distinctions and act accordingly is not doing the prescribed job. Delaware judges emphasize this with the following jury instruction:

> Nor are you to be concerned with the wisdom of any legal rule that I give you. Regardless of any opinion you may have about what the law ought to be, it would be a violation of your sworn duty to base a verdict on any view of the law other than what I give you in these instructions.[28]

It should be noted, however, that not all legal scholars or lawyers agree that juries have no power to depart from established law. Instead, there is a persistent line of thought urging the value and propriety of "jury nullification." "Jury nullification refers to the refusal of juries to apply the law when they believe that to follow the letter of the law would mean an unjust verdict."[29] Although many famous trials involved jury nullification, the practice is controversial:

> Those who oppose jury nullification in both principle and practice say that it is inconsistent with a society based on the rule of law. Allowing a jury to disregard the law and decide a case on the grounds of whatever it thinks is fair sets up a slippery slope.[30]

In a highly publicized example of jury nullification in 2012, a man who admitted before the jury to having beaten up an elderly priest was acquitted of criminal assault. Years earlier, as a young boy, the man had been sexually abused by the priest. A newspaper report on the verdict stated:

> Defense lawyers in California can't directly urge the jury to nullify, which is when a jury acquits a defendant despite evidence of guilt because it believes a conviction would be unjust. But during closing arguments [the defense lawyer] had managed to get his message across.[31]

Although the acquittal reflected widespread sympathy for the sexual abuse victim, not everyone agreed with the outcome. One newspaper columnist wrote that the defendant himself "said that he had expected to go to jail. If you believe—as I do—that we should not take the law into our own hands, he should have."[32]

In comparison to this controversy over the jury's power to depart from the law, there is little disagreement about the jury's primary responsibility, that is, to decide what the true facts are. Nevertheless, that is not a complete or precise description for all cases. As mentioned in earlier discussion of these distinctions,[33] the jury can be asked to determine the facts of what the automobile driver actually did, but also can be asked to apply the general legal standard of negligence. The jury must determine whether the driver's conduct meets that standard. The jury, in other words, is the fact-finder, not the lawmaker, but often is also responsible for evaluating how the facts fit the law. In performing these tasks, each juror needs to understand what she should and should not be doing. The evaluation function can involve the exercise of judgment, particularly in close cases, but that is judgment within the breadth of the law, rather than the creation of entirely new legal standards.

Looking at the *listening and negotiating* feature of the law, listening is certainly central to the juror's role. California jury instructions, for example, emphasize the "ability to listen carefully to all the testimony and to watch the witnesses as they testify."[34] To a greater degree than for any of the other participants in legal proceedings, the jury's dominant function is not to give but to receive, not to speak but to listen, not to convey evidence and argument but to absorb and evaluate them. This is obviously true during the course of a trial, in which the jury is a silent, listening presence.

Additionally, at the deliberation stage, when jurors are to interact with one another in exchanging views and seeking consensus, their listening skills are to be applied, though in a somewhat different way. Their interaction then requires them to listen to each other's reviews of evidence and expression of opinions in a manner similar to what lawyers so often must do, as earlier described.[35] That is, during deliberations the need to listen carefully to others' perspectives is heightened beyond simply listening to what the parties, lawyers, and judge have to say.

In the jury room, the juror should be an active participant in the collective deliberation process. Jury instructions in the federal courts and in California courts make this point well:

> Talk with each other, listen carefully and respectfully to each other's views, and keep an open mind as you listen to what your fellow jurors have to say.
>
> In the jury room it is your duty to discuss the case in order to reach an agreement if you can. Each of you must decide the case for yourself, but should do so only after considering the views of each juror.
>
> I am asking each of you to listen with deference to the views of other jurors who do not agree with you and to ask yourself if they may be right and you may be wrong in how you evaluate the evidence and apply it to the law. If you are convinced you are wrong, you must be willing to change your opinion and you should not hesitate to do so.[36]

The juror must hear well what is being said by others so that she can analyze the strengths and weaknesses of it all, formulate and express her own emerging views, and ultimately reach a reasoned conclusion to be expressed in her vote on a verdict.

It is tempting to characterize jury deliberations as something akin to a negotiation. There is a similarity in tone to the cooperative and open-minded search for agreement earlier described as a characteristic of negotiations.[37] However, because jurors have no personal stake in the outcome of the case, but instead are all seeking the same goal—a just verdict under the law—strictly speaking, they are not conducting a negotiation.

Turning to methods of *identifying bias*, we consider again the significance of impartiality, one of the key traits of a model juror. Its importance is invariably impressed on the juror in admonitions and instructions from the judge. New Jersey jurors are told:

> Your oath as jurors requires you to decide this case fairly and impartially, without sympathy, passion, bias or prejudice. You are to decide this case based solely upon the evidence that you find believable and in accordance with the rules of law that I give you.[38]

In Delaware, the admonition is:

> You have been chosen and sworn as jurors in this case to decide issues of fact. You must perform these duties without bias for or against any of the

> parties. The law does not allow you to be influenced by sympathy, prejudice, or public opinion. All the parties and the public expect that you will carefully and impartially consider all the evidence in the case, follow the law, and reach a just verdict, regardless of the consequences.[39]

More concretely, the questioning of prospective jurors by the parties' lawyers, the judge, or both, highlights for the jurors the importance of recognizing bias. The evident purpose of that questioning, commonly known as voir dire ("to speak the truth"), is to shine a spotlight on bias through inquiry into the individual's interests, associations, values, and knowledge that might influence his jury service in the specific case. The goal is to screen for preconceived notions or dispositions which would prevent the juror from being able to evaluate and resolve the parties' dispute with an open mind, without prejudgments, that is, without prejudice. As a Nevada court described it:

> The purpose of jury voir dire is to discover whether a juror will consider and decide the facts impartially and conscientiously apply the law as charged by the court.[40]

Conversely, when the juror listens to the parties, their lawyers, and the witnesses, the persuasive impact of their statements should be affected by any of their biases which seem to emerge. Again, the self-interest of parties should be no surprise, and their assertions can be evaluated in light of their fairly evident motivations. As to other witnesses, however, particularly those offered as objective, disinterested, or expert sources of information about the issues at hand, the jury faces a more difficult task. The biases underlying their testimony probably will not be as evident or predictable as the parties'.[41]

The juror then must be alert for indications that the witness's statements are motivated, or at least colored, by tangential considerations. The witness whose testimony is motivated by hope of financial reward resulting from the trial's outcome; the witness whose adverse testimony toward a party reflects personal hostility, jealousy, or racial antipathy; and the witness whose personal history predisposes him to always see certain types of events as having the same significance and to disregard even large differences among them—these are witnesses whose credibility must be carefully evaluated by the juror with an awareness of those ingrained inclinations and their potential for shading or distorting the truth.

When the juror arrives at the point of having to make a decision, to cast a vote on a verdict, one of the law's most challenging features may have to be confronted: *the recognition of incomplete facts.* The jury's function, of course, is not to gather facts, as that task is performed by the litigants and their lawyers. Jurors then observe the parties' presentation of that body of evidence for the jury's consideration. Unfortunately, but often inescapably, the evidence may be incomplete, because of unavailability of witnesses, faded memories, scientific uncertainty, or other obstacles, as earlier mentioned.[42]

Nevertheless, members of the jury are charged to reach a verdict if they possibly can agree. The need for a decision is thus impressed on each juror. It is not acceptable for jurors to decline to decide by retreating behind the incompleteness of the information before them. Jury instructions emphasize the duty to try to reach a conclusion, as in the following examples:

> Do your best to reach a verdict if you can reasonably do so. This case is important to the parties and has been expensive to try. If you fail to reach a verdict, the case will have to be tried by another jury selected in the same manner as you were. You are certainly as competent as any other jury.
>
> It is your duty as jurors to consult with one another and to deliberate with a view to reaching an agreement if you can do so without sacrificing individual judgment.
>
> You should consider also that this case must be decided at some time.[43]

Fortunately, the juror facing this challenge is entitled—indeed obligated—to formulate his decision by reference to the applicable standard of proof and the announced allocation of the burden of proof as between the parties.[44] In dealing with the information at hand and any troublesome gaps in it, the juror's quandary is somewhat eased by focusing on which party has the greater legal responsibility to provide the needed information—to carry the burden of proof on specific issues—and on the level of persuasive force, the standard of proof, that party's evidence must reach.

In the prototypical example, if a criminal prosecutor fails to produce enough evidence to show beyond a reasonable doubt that the defendant committed the alleged crime, the juror's uncertainty over what to decide in the face of inadequate information must be resolved against the prosecution. It has failed to prove what the law says it must. The juror still does not know everything he might wish to know about what happened, but he still can discharge his duty to decide. Of course, the juror's resolution of cases with information gaps is seldom as easy as this discussion might sound. In criminal cases and perhaps even more so in civil cases, where the preponderance of the evidence standard of proof contemplates a closer call, the juror may well find it difficult to conclude which way the evidence, incomplete as it is, actually points.

Not only in reviewing the evidence, but also in evaluating the parties' positions on how the law applies to the facts, the juror must often make difficult choices on questions that are factually uncertain and require *hard choices in gray areas.*[45] It was emphasized earlier that traditional wisdom says jurors are not supposed to make new law, nor are they to make the kinds of value judgments and policy choices expressed in the law as enunciated by judges. This delineation of jury tasks is imprecise, however, for often verdicts must embody the jurors' judgments on social policy.

Particularly when all that the law gives the jury to apply is a very general standard of conduct, the jury's application of it expresses a great deal of policy judgment. Was the truck driver's manner of navigating a turn careless or careful within the broad standard of "reasonable care" under negligence law? Did the corporate executive who sold stock in his public company at considerable personal profit "knowingly," and thus criminally, take advantage of inside information? Did the apartment building landlord comply with city ordinances requiring common areas to be "safe" for tenants and guests? Jurors must decide what these important, but very general, legal standards mean. In doing so, as it is often said, the jurors are bringing to bear on the case, and infusing into the law, the values of the community from which they come.[46] When jurors do this, they are performing neither a mechanical nor an easy task. Whether the facts are laid out before them completely or incompletely, jurors still may have to make hard choices about how the law applies.

The last of the law's traditions which directly affect the conduct of jurors is the need to *respect procedure.*[47] The trial process in which the juror participates is replete with formality and prescribed modes of conduct. An Ohio jury instruction summarizes the point:

> Jury service may be new to some of you, so a short explanation is in order. Those who participate in a law suit must do so in accordance with established rules. This applies to witnesses, lawyers, the judge, and jurors.[48]

Some of these rules directly regulate the conduct of jurors themselves, with respect to aspects of their role such as taking notes, shunning outside information related to the case, avoiding conversation about the case with other jurors until the designated time for deliberation, and requesting the rereading of portions of the transcript or of the judge's instructions.[49] California jury instructions, as an example, cover this ground emphatically:

> During the trial you must not listen to anyone else talk about the case or the people involved in the case. You must avoid any contact with the parties, the lawyers, the witnesses, and anyone else who may have a connection to the case...During the trial, do not read, listen to, or watch any news reports about this case...Do not do any research on your own or as a group...When you begin your deliberations, you may discuss the case only in the jury room and only when all the jurors are present.[50]

Illinois instructions also give extremely practical directives:

> During the course of the trial you may encounter some of the lawyers or parties, at one time or another, in public corridors or in public elevators, or perhaps during a noon recess in the restaurants that are in the area. If they don't engage in discussion or conversation with you, please don't be offended. They are simply following the rules.[51]

A juror, in short, is supposed to be in certain places at certain times to do certain things in certain ways, while avoiding certain others. This regimentation reflects long-standing traditions to promote the orderly, fair, and informed performance of jury functions. The juror who does not honor these procedures impedes that role for himself, other jurors, and the parties to the case.

The juror also has a front row seat from which to observe the vast array of procedural requirements applicable to other participants in the trial. Undoubtedly, some of these requirements at times may seem, especially to an impatient juror, to be merely time-consuming obstacles to the administration of justice. Overall, however, at least some of these procedures should be seen as serving important purposes of the sort earlier canvassed.[52]

For example, rules and procedures governing the admissibility of evidence are designed to weed out unreliable, speculative information in favor of more solid factual input. However, the operation of evidentiary restrictions can be perplexing. Head-scratching by jurors may well accompany rulings such as the sustaining of an objection to testimony even though the jurors have already heard it. Being then instructed to pretend they did not hear what they heard, and to not think about it again, poses an interesting challenge of a sort most people seldom encounter elsewhere in daily life.[53] Thus, in the jury nullification instance discussed above—the acquittal of the child sexual abuse victim in the criminal case for assaulting the priest who molested him—the jurors were instructed by the judge to "disregard" the testimony of the priest for various important legal reasons. Nevertheless, observers of the trial believed the jurors "could not forget the deceitful priest."[54] However, if jurors have some grasp of the importance of removing some types of statements from their consideration, the challenge of fictionally "unringing the bell" may be not quite so puzzling or daunting. Jury instructions purport to assist in this regard, as in the following Illinois statement:

> When you go back to the jury room, you are going to have to recall all of the evidence to assist you in arriving at your verdicts in this case. That is the reason that we do not let you consider inadmissible evidence; it just makes your job harder. Your job is going to be hard enough as it is.[55]

Another important example of purposeful procedure is alternation in the presentations of lawyers' arguments. The avoidance of shouting matches by requiring speakers to proceed one at a time—in part so the court reporter or electronic transcription device can accurately record what is said—can be appreciated for the added decorum, clarity, and civility this pattern promotes. Also, perhaps an implicit message of respect for the law and its processes is sent by the simple formality that everyone must stand when the jury enters and exits the courtroom and must rise for the judge's entrance and departure as well.

E. What the Juror Sees

Reference has already been made to the jury as a recipient of information provided by the parties through their lawyers. Much *gathering of the facts* is done well in advance of courtroom proceedings, and the trial process serves to publicly present and augment what the parties have already found out. The jurors can see for themselves what each of the parties thinks is the key evidence in the case. They also can see, through cross-examination of witnesses and the presentation of contrary testimony, the process of testing and challenging assertions in a battle for acceptance of one version or another of the facts. Jurors with open minds presumably can perceive that what one person persuasively asserts at one moment may later be cast into doubt by conflicting information from others. The jury thus observes the ultimate assembling of facts in all its complexity and ambiguity.

One of the most crucial tools of the legal system that jurors observe, as they listen to the evidence and the arguments of trial participants, is the *defining of the issues*.[56] Jurors do not define the issues in the case, of course. Rather, the issues emerge from written pleadings filed by the parties, their evidence and arguments at trial, and the judge's instructions to the jury as to what questions must ultimately be resolved to reach a verdict. During this process jurors are expected to consistently understand what those issues are.

Probably, the most frequent signal of that expectation centers on "relevance." Through parties' objections to each other's evidence and arguments, and through the judge's rulings on those objections, jurors repeatedly see attention given to a claim that some information is "irrelevant!" The juror cannot grasp the possible validity of that claim, and the judge's ruling on it, without having some sense of what is relevant, that is, what bears upon a real, disputed issue in the case. The responsible juror needs to understand that what matters are those issues and the evidence and argument pertinent to them, and not just anything and everything that a party might wish to say to sway the jury.

Closely linked to the primacy of issue definition, and the anchoring role of relevance, is understanding of the law's approach to *arguing and persuading*. The juror who realizes, as earlier discussed,[57] that legal issues are often susceptible to honest differences of interpretation and opinion, is much better prepared to complete his job well. He can grasp what most warrants his attention as he listens to each lawyer's attempts to persuade him of the rightness of his client's view of the facts and how the law applies to them. The responsible juror will understand that what matters are the identified issues, the proven facts, and the applicable rules, and not the drama or flamboyance of the style of argument. Subsequently, during his interaction with other jurors during deliberation, he should attempt to emulate this issue-based approach.

The remaining three tools and traditions play more of a backup role for jurors. The *division of labor*, which, as earlier discussed,[58] characterizes so much of the work of lawyers, and even judges, is not very apparent during courtroom proceedings. One aspect of the law's procedural traditions is that a party's case is ordinarily presented orally through a single lead lawyer, with occasional questioning of a witness or presentation of oral argument on a specific issue by an associate. The earlier, perhaps extensive, participation of additional lawyers, paralegals, investigators, consultants, and others in the collection and organization of evidence, writing of pleadings and briefs, and preparation of witnesses and oral arguments is for the most part hidden from what jurors see in the courtroom.

In performing her own role, each individual juror is expected to equally bear all the same responsibilities as the others as they hear the case and then deliberate and vote on the outcome. With the possible exception of some organizational and speaking duties assigned to the jury foreperson, there should not be any significant division of labor among the members themselves. As Ohio jurors are reminded, "Each of you must decide this case for yourself."[59]

Similarly, the *use of expertise* is something jurors may observe during a trial, but it is not part of their own work. Direct examination and cross-examination of expert witnesses sometimes constitute substantial portions of a trial. Jurors thus observe that many legal issues are complicated not only because of gaps in the facts or ambiguities in the law. Rather, jurors see that many legal disputes, at their core, raise difficult questions involving medicine, technology, finance, environmental protection, product design, building construction, accident or crime scene investigation, or a multitude of other fields.

Paradoxically, although they are exposed to the importance of expertise through courtroom battles of experts in sometimes arcane subjects, jurors often carry the daunting burden of resolving those disputes despite their own lack of expertise. Jury instructions in Ohio acknowledge this burden:

> On you alone rests the duty of deciding what weight to give to the testimony of the expert. In deciding its weight, consider the expert's skill, experience, knowledge, veracity, and familiarity with the facts of this case, and the usual rules for testing... believability and deciding the weight to give to the testimony.[60]

Indeed, individuals who have some relevant expertise or additional knowledge related to the subject of the controversy are commonly not selected as jurors. If they are selected to serve, they are instructed not to employ their expertise by bringing information into the jury's consideration beyond the evidence presented by the parties.[61] Expertise has its place in legal matters, but, as quoted earlier:

> We do not require any particular skills, expertise or education level of our jurors; in fact, just the opposite is true... Remember, the jury's task is to make a determination of the truth, and all of our citizens are equipped with the ability to undertake that responsibility.[62]

Finally, and perhaps most troublesome for jurors, is the law's approach to *taking time* to conduct and resolve legal proceedings. For the vast majority of people, jury service interrupts other commitments and pastimes the individual would prefer to attend to. When that interruption is coupled with a lot of waiting—to find out whether one needs to report to the courthouse on a particular day, to find out whether one will be called from the jury waiting room into a courtroom for *voir dire*, and on and on from there—it is difficult to expect a juror to draw positive meaning from the slowness of the legal system. An attempt to ward off juror frustration is reflected in the following Illinois instruction:

> At times, the jury will be excused from the courtroom, or the Judge and the attorneys will go into the Judge's chambers while the objections are being discussed or for other reasons. Under the law, various matters *must* be heard out of the presence of the jury. Also, when a case is recessed or adjourned and the trial does not commence promptly at the designated time, the delay may be caused by the Court's administrative duties or its transaction of emergency or other matters. When a trial is necessarily interrupted or delayed for any of these reasons, you should not feel that your time is being wasted.[63]

Courts across the country have tried various ways to minimize the inconvenience and waiting imposed on jurors. These methods include increased use of telephones, the Internet, and mobile phone texting to convey scheduling information. Nonetheless, the individual who is brought into jury duty still ordinarily faces the prospect that more of his time will be taken up than he would like.

Will he understand that the avoidance of error and the attainment of sound and fair results are hard to achieve quickly? Judges and lawyers usually try to promote such understanding by conveying sympathy for the disruption of jurors' lives, appreciation for their service, and good reasons why the wheels of the justice system often grind slowly. A statement for New Jersey judges to offer at the conclusion of cases is a good example:

> Let me take this opportunity to thank you for your service on this jury. We realize this case has interfered with your daily lives and probably caused you some inconvenience. However, our judicial system could not function without people like you willing to serve on juries. It is a job that has to be done in order that people can resolve their differences by jury trial. We are extremely grateful for the time you have spent here.[64]

Whether this type of effort succeeds is hard to gauge, especially since some proceedings move much more slowly than anyone can justify. In the end, jurors will come to understand that legal processes take time, yet it may be hard for them to accept that this is as it should be.

Hopefully, jurors also will come to understand the public importance and personal educational benefits of their service. If they do, they may be better prepared to meet their broader civic responsibilities when they conclude jury service, leave the courthouse, and return to daily life. Of course, what they cannot avoid noticing then is that the similarities between acting as a responsible citizen and acting as a responsible juror are limited because the everyday court of public opinion is vastly different from a court of law, as mentioned earlier. Chapter 6 illuminates some of the most important of those differences.

6

Inescapable Differences

The citizen forms her opinions each day in a world which is inescapably different from the narrower world of the legal system. There are aspects of public discussions and political decisions that inevitably diverge from the more systematic approach of legal decision making. Before concluding whether the law's tools can narrow that gap, we should understand some of the major ways in which the twain shall never meet.

A. The Fragility of Rationality

A plethora of researchers, scholars, and popular authors has asked whether people act rationally in conducting daily affairs and making many types of decisions, including voting. A common conclusion is that they do not. In the words of one scholar, "The Enlightenment view of reason and rationality has been shown to be completely inadequate to describe or explain contemporary human behavior. We are not all rational actors in our every action—not even close."[1] Many studies have shown that a host of psychological, sociological, cognitive, and emotional characteristics of the human species predispose us to make decisions that make little sense, that are, as one writer has said, "predictably irrational."[2]

The significance of these findings for fields such as economics and law has received considerable attention:

> While economists, lawmakers, and legal theorists were embracing the rational actor model (or the law's reasonable person norm) in the late 20th century, social psychology, social cognition, cognitive neuroscience, and other mind sciences were demonstrating its flaws... The mind sciences turned commonsense legal theory on its head by recognizing ideology—construed broadly to include numerous internal influences outside the norm of reasoning—as foundational to human behavior and "reasoning" as a potential façade behind which ideology operates.[3]

Another writer puts it this way:

> Ever since the ancient Greeks, these assumptions [about how humans make decisions] have revolved around a single theme: Humans are rational. When we make decisions, we are supposed to consciously analyze the alternatives and carefully weigh the pros and cons. In other words, we are deliberate and logical creatures... There's only one problem with this assumption of human rationality: it's wrong. It's not how the brain works... It turns out we weren't designed to be rational creatures. Instead, the mind is composed of a messy network of different areas, many of which are involved with the production of emotion.[4]

The extensive literature in this vein raises doubt about the utility of any plea for more systematic approaches to the formation of opinions by all of us. Therefore, unless we are writing fiction, we must assume that none of us is immune to the failings and foibles of our perception and understanding.

On the other hand, we must also assume that each of us has the ability to restrain those inclinations, at least to some degree, if we are aware of them and, even better, if we are aware of tools for more reasoned and informed development of our views.[5] This assumption is embedded in our expectations for jurors, as shown in chapter 5, and it is indulged here as well regarding individuals' discharge of broader civic responsibilities.[6]

Outside of legal forums, there obviously are far fewer prods toward rationality in the citizen's daily life than there are, for example, in jury duty. Indeed, many of the obstacles discussed in chapter 2 push us in quite the opposite direction: They are disincentives to careful, open-minded, internal deliberation. When complicated issues face us through a flood of information, and our opportunities to digest it all seem limited, our challenge is daunting.[7] Even just with regard to the environment, technologies, medicines, and foods we encounter daily, one author has observed that "the proportion of our surroundings that any ordinary person can explain today is minute—and it keeps getting smaller."[8] Add in a persistent dose of mistrust of many information sources to which we are exposed, and the temptation is great to ignore the issues, oversimplify them,[9] demonize people who disagree with us,[10] restrict conversations only to people with whom we agree,[11] or retreat to "any port in a storm" shortcuts as an alternative to careful thought.[12]

A related tendency, also standing in marked contrast to the legal system, reflects the citizen's ability to drop out of discussing public issues without any perceptible personal consequences. As noted in chapter 1, this can be a sensible option to exercise selectively, since none of us can be an expert or even solidly knowledgeable about all public issues. The citizen thus can be a nonparticipant on selected issues for that pragmatic reason, as well as for no reason at all, and, of course, anyone eligible to vote is free not to do so. In a legal dispute, however, it is impermissible for the judge or a juror to simply default on his responsibilities and blithely say with regard to the issues at hand, "I'm just not going to deal with them."[13]

The array of internal and external forces leading us away from thoughtful, reasoned formation of opinions constitutes the most important divergence from the way the law approaches its conclusions. In contrast, the tools and traditions of the law can be seen as a set of consciously designed responses to the fragility of rationality. The law's methods, and their ongoing message about the importance of systematic and open-minded decision making, aim to maximize the exercise of reason among participants in legal processes, while minimizing the influence of the contrary inclinations and pressures we all experience every day.

This is not to say that all lawyers always "think like lawyers" and act accordingly, or even that judges always conduct their work in full conformity with the law's tools and traditions. Being human, these professionals at times fail to honor the responsibility they have undertaken and the legal system's aspirations toward fair and rational action. Nevertheless, the aspirations remain prominent in the profession, and the vast majority of lawyers and judges consistently strive to honor them in both word and deed.

There are many, varying analyses of how and why we all shy away from rationality. It is often asserted that our national debates on important public issues have descended in recent years into "culture wars"[14] fueled by mistrust,[15] misinformation, polarization, political competition, indignation, blame, fear,[16] self-deception and wishful thinking,[17] and "a free-floating, self-perpetuating anger."[18] "Civic discourse is often driven more by emotion and dogma than by reasoned dialogue."[19]

Even in less contentious times, apart from the ebb and flow of political disputes and cultural divisions, people are predisposed to reach dubious opinions and conclusions, and even to engage in sustained disputation over demonstrable fact.[20] One author has catalogued "twenty-five fallacies of thinking that can lead anyone to believe weird things."[21] He also asserts:

> Thinking is skilled work. It is not true that we are naturally endowed with the ability to think clearly and logically—without learning how,

> or without practicing... We must always work to suppress our need to be absolutely certain and in total control and our tendency to seek the simple and effortless solution to a problem. Now and then the solutions may be simple, but usually they are not.[22]

Similarly, a prominent political commentator has written of our inclination to make life appear simpler and more understandable—the "timeless human craving... for banishing randomness and the inexplicable from human experience."[23] Succumbing to this inclination, and substituting "belief for thought," does seem to have a seductive, short-term benefit: "It protects you from self-doubt."[24] It results as well in a profound "incapacity for true dialogue."[25]

These tendencies toward irrationality, which are the subject of such an abundance of study and explanation, are operative in all of us. They cannot be banished from our daily lives, nor even entirely from our legal forums. Indeed, the emphasis on rationality here is not intended to suggest that emotion, intuition, sympathy, and feeling must always be shunned in addressing public issues or even legal matters. Instead, the intention is to emphasize the primary importance of reasoned consideration of issues but coupled with awareness of the influence of other predispositions and responses. Emotional reactions undoubtedly are inevitable, and may at times even help us to reach sound conclusions, especially if we try to understand how we get to them.[26]

In the legal system, the attempt to constrain the impact of these other influences is persistent, is embodied in many of the law's tools and traditions, and achieves a good measure of success. No comparable structure or methodology exists in the court of public opinion. Nevertheless, despite the differences between these contexts, some borrowing and adaptation of the law's methods may still be beneficial to the individual citizen and thus to society generally.

B. Importance of the Personal

We are often told that ours is a government of laws, not of men. "Equal justice under law" is proclaimed above the entrance to the Supreme Court. Who you are—your wealth, religion, race, age, friendships, or eye color—is not supposed to matter in the ordinary legal dispute. A strength of the American legal system is its ability to view disputes with a focus on the issues the parties raise, rather than who the parties are. Sometimes, this tendency to look away from the persons involved and toward the more abstract issues at stake is taken to an uncaring extreme, leading to unnecessarily harsh results for people affected by the law.[27] Nevertheless, and while recognizing that it is difficult to define the best balance in this regard, occasional insensitivity may be an acceptable price to pay for our commitment to "blind justice," to impersonality in the law.

An alternative approach, giving great weight to individual, personal characteristics, would profoundly impede fair treatment under the law. However, some legal scholars, advancing what is called "critical race theory," "argue that the legal system cannot ignore the racial dynamics underlying many cases." They emphasize that, "even though national ideals aspire to equality, not all Americans receive equal treatment and opportunities. Furthermore, treating those situated differently in merely an equal manner can produce systematic injustice."[28] Critical race theory, and related perspectives, focus on "the systems of privilege that exist in our society," affording preferred treatment in many ways to certain groups over others, based on considerations of race, gender, sexual orientation, and economic class.[29] To the extent that the impersonality of the legal system perpetuates unjustifiable privileges and discrimination against persons as members of certain groups, the system's supposed objectivity is to be condemned. To the extent that impersonality ensures that one individual ordinarily is treated the same as another, the system is to be appreciated.

Outside of legal processes, in everyday discussions and decisions about issues and candidates for elective office, things are very different. Public views of politicians and other celebrities are inevitably influenced by individual and group characteristics such as wealth, religion, race, appearance, and age. Voters frequently factor into their decisions the gender or ethnicity of candidates. In contrast, jurors—who are usually voters, of course, but performing a different civic duty—are supposed to disregard such information, unless it is specifically relevant to the issues in the case at hand.

The law, in other words, is fundamentally and purposely impersonal, while politics and many other realms of public discourse are decidedly and inevitably very personal. As an illustration of the latter, a newspaper commentary at the start of the 2012 presidential primary elections season observed:

> Issues have declined in importance as a factor in the campaign... Instead, the [Republican Party] contest reflects an intensifying search by voters for the candidate they believe has the strongest chance of unseating President Barack Obama next November...The salience of issues as a way of sorting through the crowded GOP field has declined sharply during the preprimary campaign...More than emphasizing issues, the

> leading contenders have often framed their candidacies as a cultural contrast with Obama, in what Democrats say are unsubtle attempts to distance the president from ordinary Americans.[30]

Not infrequently such discourse descends into extremely negative criticisms and verbal attacks on individuals. In this highly personal arena,"while often petty or just plain rude, impoliteness may, however, be a necessary evil in political discourse."[31]

C. Follow the Leader

A reflection of the personal nature of much opinion formation is the tendency to let other people decide for you. It is not unusual for an individual to take a particular position in public discussion, or to cast a particular vote in an election, largely because someone else has reached that conclusion. The person whose lead we follow may be a relative, friend, minister, celebrity, politician, or just about anything else. At times, it seems both easier and sensible to do what others are doing, and say what others are saying, rather than develop one's own analysis of the issues.[32]

In the legal realm, with jury service as the prime example, this approach is presumed to be unacceptable, or at least undesirable. Standard practice in jury trials, after a verdict has been announced, is for the judge to poll the jurors individually to make sure that each one who has voted in favor of the verdict does indeed subscribe to that outcome. This polling does not absolutely guarantee that some jurors have not just "gone along" with the views of others, or been persuaded by a particularly persuasive or engaging fellow juror, but it presumably encourages jurors to resist those tendencies and instead think for themselves.

At its worst, to follow the lead of others is to forfeit the individual's responsibility to reach his own conclusions. This is especially true if it is done for reasons that have nothing to do with the merits of the issues. If I learn that a popular music star whose music I like is against gun control or opposed to abortion, and that alone is enough to solidify my position, I am basing my conclusion on inclinations that are irrelevant to the issues.

At its best, however, taking cues from others for the development of my views on a particular issue can be based on my determination that a certain individual or organization is knowledgeable and thoughtful, does its homework, and shares important values with me. On these bases, "we tend to rely on opinion leaders, who are more or less like ourselves but who know more about the subject than we do."[33] This is quite different from blind, unthinking allegiance. It also can be an important, perhaps dominant, basis for an individual's ongoing affiliation with a particular political party. Over time the voter has discerned that one party rather than another tends to take positions and put forward candidates that correspond with his own inclinations.

D. EVERYBODY HAS OPINIONS

In legal proceedings, only a limited number of voices are heard. The prototypical lawsuit involves just two contending parties. Often there are more, even many, but at a certain stage the door to further participants is closed. Even when a lawsuit is brought on behalf of a multitude of individuals, as in a class action, procedures are in place to make sure that just a few people are identified as representatives of the various categories of class members.

In the public arena, there are no such limits. Everybody who has an opinion, or a question, can try to be heard in one forum or another. Anyone who wishes to do so can be part of the flood of information discussed in chapter 2. In a free society, discussion of public issues should be open to everyone, and increasingly it is.

The definition of issues is also quite a different matter in a legal forum as compared to daily conversations, media presentations, and Internet blogs and such. Legal proceedings provide substantial clarity about the specific content of the matters to be resolved, the "issues." In open public debates, in contrast, often the ongoing opinions are about competing characterizations of what is at stake and what is to be decided. For example, in a controversy over an Illinois requirement that foster care and adoption organizations receiving state funds must consider same-sex couples, Catholic bishops saw the requirement as infringing religious freedom while supporters of the requirement saw it as promoting equality and preventing unlawful discrimination.[34]

There is an important concomitant of this openness to many voices and many viewpoints. By a specified point in a legal proceeding, each party's position on the issues has become fixed. The decision maker has received the parties' statements of their views, and those views are no longer subject to restatement or amendment, because it is time for a decision. In public debates, however, views are constantly changing and there is no authoritative voice to declare that you have stated your position unalterably.

E. WHO'S TALKING?

In public debates, especially as elections approach and political advertising increases, it is at times hard to know who is speaking. In a newspaper, on television, or in a website, a group may forcefully assert its position, but it may be difficult for the reader or viewer to know who that speaker is. The "Citizens for [insert principle, value, or noble sentiment]" group may perhaps present a thoughtful, articulate perspective, but its name and other minimal identifying information still may not be enough to disclose what individuals or other organizations comprise and fund the group. Thus, "of $266.4 million spent by outside groups to influence the 2010 elections, $135.6 million was spent by groups that did not reveal any details about their funders."[35]

In an election in 2012 in California, "the largest anonymous political donation in state history"—$11 million—was made by a group based in Arizona and known only as Americans for Responsible Leadership. Because the real identity of this group and its members was secret, California officials filed a lawsuit shortly before the election. The lawsuit sought a court order permitting the officials to conduct an audit that could disclose more information about the organization.[36]

This lack of identifying information in and of itself may not be problematic, for the ideas and information presented presumably can be evaluated on their own merits. What is missing, however, is collateral information that could help us to assess the credibility, possible biases, and hidden agendas of the speaker, as well as the extent to which the group has significant membership or other support from very many people.[37] Some observers even have suggested we should "assume that contributors are withholding their identity because they think their identity might undermine their message."[38]

In stark contrast, hidden identities are anathema in most legal proceedings. At times, vaguely named groups whose backers are hard to identify are heard from in proceedings such as government agencies' consideration of proposed new regulations. In the prototypical lawsuit, however, the decision maker and parties know the identities of all the participants. Furthermore, the tools of adversary contests, such as discovery of documentary evidence and cross-examination of witnesses, are available to bring to light hidden affiliations and biases. Outside of courtrooms, however, the mystery of who is speaking is often much harder to solve.

F. Minimum Skills

It was pointed out in chapter 1 that not all citizens are equally well-equipped to grapple with public issues. It also should be just about as self-evident that not all of us are equally able to be heard, to have access to forums and tools for expressing our views. The range of capabilities and resources in the citizenry in general is vast. Similarly, within members of the legal profession, there are analogous differences in levels of intelligence, experience, and powers of expression, but there the range of such differences is much, much narrower.

As a function of required educational training—generally four years of college and three years of law school—and other hurdles such as bar examinations and continuing legal education requirements, we presume that lawyers and judges possess at least a substantial minimum of skills, knowledge, intellectual capability, and comfort with the language, content, and methods of the law. It is difficult to gauge a comparable minimum set of abilities for the ordinary citizen. Nevertheless, as discussed in chapter 5, when individuals are called for jury service, our society makes just such an assumption of adequate and equal capability to think and act responsibly in that role. In citizens' unstructured daily conversation about public issues, however, and even in voting behavior, it is much harder to make such an assumption.

Perhaps the most significant respect in which the lawyer's minimum skills stand in marked contrast with the ordinary citizen's is in the ability to be heard. By virtue of their training and their credentials to practice law, including the privilege of initiating and advancing legal proceedings in courts and other forums, lawyers know how to make themselves heard on behalf of their clients. They are, as is often said—albeit usually pejoratively—"mouthpieces." They know how and where to express interests, rights, and grievances. Among other capabilities lawyers offer, this ability to be the client's voice is one of the main reasons that any of us, when facing a difficult situation, often want the help of a lawyer.

Commentators on modern American politics and culture have observed that many Americans feel that their views and concerns are not being heard and that they do not have the ability or power to make them heard. This perspective breeds frustration, injecting additional elements of anger and resentment into understanding of social policy and cultural developments. Whether this perspective is or is not always justified, it is fundamentally understandable. It is not always easy in a large and complex society such as ours to know how and where to try to express your views and have some impact by doing so, as the following observation emphasizes:

> Modern communication media and devices have multiplied the outlets for active voter participation in conversational interactions. But given the size of the American population and the role of mass media, most popular participation in primary and secondary conversation about public affairs must be as readers and listeners rather than as writers and speakers. Indeed, greatly unequal citizen contributions to any ongoing dialogue about public matters seems an irreducible fact of our public life.[39]

In contrast, lawyers virtually always can find a way to be heard and in a forum that matters.

G. Debate Never Ends

In public discussions, there are seldom, if ever, deadlines or time limits. In legal proceedings, timelines are set for when written briefs must be submitted, testimony presented, and oral arguments heard, and even for how long written and oral submissions can be. After a time limit is first fixed by the law, of course, often there are extensions or continuances. Even legally mandated election dates seem to not always have as firm significance as is usually thought. The 2000 presidential election was not decided for over a month after election day,[40] and the November 2008 election of a United States senator in Minnesota remained undecided until mid-2009.[41] These are unusual episodes, and yet even within them there is no doubt that eventually the disputes—like other processes structured by law—will be settled once and for all through prescribed procedural routes.

In public discussions, there need never be an end. The Warren Commission's 1964 report on the assassination of President Kennedy seemed to mark the official end of investigations of the event. Nevertheless, other inquiries followed, books are still written,[42] films are made,[43] and decades later the issue is still with us. As other examples, Newsweek magazine observed in the summer of 2009, "The war over Watergate never ends,"[44] and even though the legal fight over the 2000 election is over, as is the presidency of George W. Bush, more debate over that tumultuous contest may still lie ahead.[45]

The processes of the law, in other words, produce a decision sooner or later. It may be followed by reversal or modification through legislation or judicial decree, but those later responses also embody specific decisions and concrete milestones. There are important reasons why legal decisions are sometimes replaced by subsequent rulings. There may have been mistakes in the original proceeding, new information may have come to light, and, perhaps most importantly, complex and ambiguous issues—and related legal precedents or statutory and constitutional language—may deserve to be reconsidered in light of changing social trends or community values.

As earlier discussed in chapter 4, lawyers and judges know that many issues are not black or white, and that, therefore, it is not surprising when they are revisited. The difficulty, of course, is that society expects the legal system to produce decisions—to say "yes" or "no" or to require action in one direction and not another, despite the complexity of the issues. In daily discourse, there is no such endpoint.

Plainly in this respect, as well as in the others discussed above, there are marked differences between the context of public discussions and the context of legal proceedings. Nevertheless, as will be explored in chapter 7, the differences are not so great as to make it unworkable or foolhardy to seek guidance from the legal system for citizens participating in the court of public opinion.

7

Guidance from the Law

The previous chapters described the individual's civic responsibility, identified the major obstacles she faces, and surveyed conventional sources of guidance to aid her in grappling with public issues. A dozen of the law's principal tools and traditions for sound decision making were explained, followed by the expectations placed on jurors for engagement with this web of methods. A summary of inescapable differences between legal forums and everyday life was then offered.

This chapter distills the preceding material into the guidance aimed at from the beginning: how the law's methods can help us form our opinions and conclusions on public issues. Before doing so, we may ask again whether, realistically, the law's tools and traditions can be useful to the ordinary citizen for this purpose. If we assume that he is unable or unwilling to understand issues and reach his own thoughtful conclusions, then the answer must be "no." If a more optimistic—though some might say "naïve"—assumption is made, a different answer emerges.

As suggested earlier, we ought to assume that we each can restrain our tendencies to shun careful, rational attention to public issues. "We can actively improve on our irrational behaviors. We can start by becoming aware of our vulnerabilities."[1] If this hopeful assumption is correct, then the law's methods can assist us, just as they assist lawyers, judges, and jurors. The citizen who understands what these tools are, and who is discerning about which ones he can employ and when, will be better able to make up his mind about public issues and express his conclusions. His engagement with the issues will reflect the four broad goals promoted by the law's methods, as explained in chapter 4. He will be more capable of focusing on his task, taking an organized approach to it, finding reliable information, and keeping an open mind.

This chapter will examine what each of the law's methods offers as a way to reduce both the obstacles considered in chapter 2 and the inescapable differences in context explored in chapter 6. The methods will be discussed in the same order presented earlier, that is, the 12 tools and traditions will be grouped within the same four general goals they promote. Echoing that order, the Appendix will offer a brief review of this chapter's guidance.

Many of the tools will be seen as overlapping or intertwined with others, enhancing their potential benefit. Similarities between the law and conventional guidance will be recognized as well. A variety of examples of possible application of the law's tools to specific public issues will be offered, with frequent emphasis on two difficult, current issues—global climate change and gun control. With the aid of these examples, we will focus on what the citizen can do with each particular legal method, when faced with a specific issue, to diminish the obstacles and grapple more effectively with the issue.

When looking at the juror's role, we saw that some of the law's methods could be actively used by jurors while others were only to be observed. Similarly, for the citizen's broader role, some methods can be actively used while others can be helpful largely through changes in the individual's thinking about issues and about her own capabilities to understand them. At times, probably the most the citizen can gain by thinking like a lawyer is a better ability to decide what makes sense and what does not. Though that may not sound very concrete, or like much of an achievement for the individual, it could be a major step toward more informed and effective civic engagement.

A. FOCUSING ON THE TASK

Just as individuals working in the law need to understand each problem or question on which they work, so too should the ordinary citizen try to develop and maintain clear focus as she addresses public issues. It is undoubtedly more difficult for the citizen to do this in the course of her daily life than it is for the lawyer, judge, or juror. People working in the law are trying to stay focused within structured decision-making processes, and at least for lawyers and judges this is an integral aspect of their jobs. The citizen, in contrast, is functioning in the much more chaotic context of everyday life, trying to meet a dynamic array of work, family, and community responsibilities. Nevertheless, two of the law's methods—defining the issue and separating facts from standards and evaluations—can be helpful as the citizen strives to maintain a clear orientation toward his civic duty.

1. Defining the Issue

All participants in legal work have to be able to clearly identify the specific questions their work is addressing.[2] Law students, for example, must develop the habit of identifying the issues raised by the cases they are studying. Lawyers' arguments and judges' decisions must home in on the precise matters at stake in a case, making clear which issues are the most critical for its resolution. Once they have done this, the relevance of evidence and the persuasiveness of arguments become more evident.

Discussion of public issues does not ordinarily demand, much less invite, this type of clarity. The tumult of information in public forums can make it difficult, if not impossible, to get a good sense of what is at stake, what really matters, in debates on just about any matter of broad interest. Interest groups, politicians, or others may even purposely or carelessly create confusion about the issues, and in any event they may be habitually inclined to emphasize one way of framing the matter rather than another.

A good example is the debate over the question of whether same-sex couples should be legally entitled to marry. That question states the "case" or problem in a simple, straightforward way, but as anyone who has paid even minimal attention to this issue knows, it raises serious contending considerations. In order to sensibly debate the question, those underlying concerns must be addressed, for they are what is fundamentally in dispute.

From one perspective, the main underlying concern is equality. Advocates of gay marriage assert that all couples committed to a long-term relationship should be equally entitled to enjoy the benefits of the legally recognized status of marriage. Such advocates state, "Principles of equality require that we do not impose a higher standard for judging the desirability of same-sex marriage than we do for opposite-sex marriage."[3]

From a slightly different perspective, the key concern is personal privacy. "It may also be argued that the right to gay marriage falls under the general 'right to privacy' as explicated in the [Supreme] Court's prior jurisprudence."[4] It is claimed that an individual's sexual and relationship preferences are no one's business but his or her own, and therefore the right to marry should not depend at all on such preferences.

In marked contrast, people opposed to same-sex marriages see matrimony as fundamentally defined and governed by historic traditions, moral values, and procreation objectives, which have long cast it as a heterosexual union. Their views rest on propositions such as these:

1. Gay marriage threatens the institutions of marriage and the family.
2. Same-sex relationships are not the equivalent of traditional marriage.
3. Gay marriage is not a civil rights issue.
4. Americans overwhelmingly reject gay marriage.
5. Gay marriage is not a moral alternative to traditional marriage.
6. Homosexuality is rightly viewed as unnatural.[5]

Amidst these divergent, forcefully expressed views on what is at stake, it is not easy to know just what the issue is. Obviously, there is no taskmaster demanding that citizens must answer the "What is the issue in this case?" question, which professors pose to students and judges pose to lawyers. But that does not mean citizens are excused from asking it of themselves, and each other, as they discuss contemporary problems. Quite to the contrary, posing this question at least to oneself is pivotal if one is to participate sensibly in discussion of public matters.

A good starting point for the citizen on the contentious public question of same-sex marriages is simply to grasp these various definitions of what is at stake. As some commentators have suggested for better understanding of what an issue is, "like a 'fork' you encounter in a real road, an issue presents you with a choice between two (and sometimes more) paths leading in different directions."[6] In the present example, should resolution of the same-sex-marriage debate turn on equality and privacy considerations or on traditional moral values and practices? This choice is the fork in the road. It is the issue that needs to be resolved before the question of the legality of same-sex marriages can be answered.

As a citizen, if you clearly focus on what the issue is with respect to a problem such as same-sex marriage, you are accomplishing a few things. First, you are enabling yourself to determine much more readily which information and assertions are relevant and which are not. Facts may be offered in support of one side's claim or to undercut a contrary position. As long as those facts, and arguments based on them, help to illuminate considerations germane to the issue, they are worthy of attention. Other information is not, and the citizen who sees what the issue is, what the fork in the road is, can assess this other information as superfluous or, at best, just providing background or context.

This type of understanding can diminish the obstacles posed by the complexity of the issue and the flood of information surrounding it. The citizen can develop a clearer sense of what is under discussion and more readily discern what portions of the flood deserve his attention. The complexity obstacle will not be entirely eliminated, but at least issues will not be seen as more complex and confusing than necessary.

Having reached your conclusion as to what the issue is, you also should be positioned to realize that other people may continue to define it differently, emphasizing other considerations—taking other forks in the road—which you may have rejected, overlooked, or found less compelling. With this realization, you are better able to hear what they have to say and evaluate its worth. What may seem irrelevant to you may be central to the issue as they see it, the choices they believe are worthy of consideration. Once you realize that different people are using different issue definitions, your openness to listening and learning enables you to respect their expression of their views and even perhaps change your mind and redefine the issue in your own thinking. Perhaps most importantly, as you proceed with a clear definition of the issue, you are better oriented toward developing a reasoned opinion and reaching a sensible conclusion.

Another example of multiple issue definitions was presented in the Supreme Court's consideration of the constitutionality of the historic health care reform law—the Patient Protection and Affordable Care Act—championed by President Obama and enacted by Congress. Before the Court decided the case, commentators realized that issue definition was going to be critical:

> How [the Supreme Court] answers the question depends in large part on how the justices decide to frame the core issue. The law's challengers...present the central question as one of individual liberty. May the federal government, they ask, compel individuals not engaged in commerce to buy a product, here health insurance, from private companies? The Obama administration, by contrast, urges the court to answer a different question. May Congress decide, in fashioning a comprehensive response to a national crisis in the health care market, to regulate how people pay for the health care they will almost inevitably need?[7]

When the Court rendered its decision in June 2012, the justices continued to reflect different views on how to frame the constitutional issue raised by the statute's requirement that individuals purchase health insurance. Most of them saw the issue as a question of Congress's power to regulate commerce, and a majority opined that this specific requirement was beyond that power.

However, the Chief Justice and four others formed a majority to uphold the law on the basis of an alternative definition of the legal question before the Court. They rested their votes on Congress's power to impose taxes. The Chief Justice stated that the law's "requirement that certain individuals pay a financial penalty for not obtaining health insurance may reasonably be characterized as a tax."[8] The justices concluded that this "tax" was within Congress's authority under the Constitution. The majority thus provided another definition of the determinative issue, and a different legal outcome as well: Viewing the statute's requirement as an attempt to regulate commerce, it would be unconstitutional. Viewing the requirement as imposing a tax, it passed constitutional muster.

The problem of global climate change is another instructive example. Some people believe that there is no problem and that climate fluctuations are no worse now than they have been historically.[9] Others perceive that there is destabilization of climatic conditions but claim there are no significant human contributions to these changes.[10] A third position is that there is scientific uncertainty as to whether climate change is happening and whether human activities are making a significant contribution to it, but that in the face of this uncertainty, wise policy calls for precautionary measures to be implemented.[11] An additional definition of the issue is that serious climate destabilization is underway, humans are causing it to a great degree, and there is no time to waste in taking measures to combat it. Lastly, although this list is not exhaustive, there are those who accept that adverse climate phenomena are occurring and that human activities are part of the problem, but who also assert that current needs for economic growth and improvement in global living conditions should take precedence over mitigation measures that might impede the satisfaction of those needs.

On this problem, as with many others, numerous alternative or overlapping definitions of the issue are offered. Indeed, for complex problems such as this, more than one issue may need resolution before a conclusion can be reached as to whether anything needs to be done. That is, there can be a batch of interrelated issues: Is global warming happening? If so, are human activities causing it? If we are not causing it, does that mean society need not try to do anything about it? If we are causing it, does that mean measures to combat it should be taken or do competing economic and current welfare needs militate against such measures?

These are serious forks in the road, all being raised at the same time in public discourse, even if some of them logically depend on the prior resolution of others. The citizen who tries to understand and participate in the debate about this type of multilayered public question will be better prepared to do so if he understands this array of underlying disagreements. Similarly, whenever he is exposed to information about the problem, he should be better able to assess whether it has relevance to one or more of these underlying issues and, if so, which ones.

In other words, even though legal disputes tend to crystallize into resolution of a more or less mutually agreed upon definition of what is at stake, in the public arena, competing definitions of the core issue or issues often persist. This does not mean that the citizen should not try to reach a definition for herself. Quite to the contrary, in order for the individual to ask probing questions, assert informed and relevant opinions, and cast votes or take other actions to promote her conclusions, she needs to develop her own individual perspective on what is at stake. With this perspective in mind, and recognizing that she may later find good reason to modify it, she is better prepared to proceed on the collective path toward resolution of the problem.

Lawyers often revise their approaches to arguing a case, and judges also frequently do so as they deliberate on cases they must resolve. They realize that the way an issue is first framed—what they first thought was at stake—is not correct, or at least not the most accurate way or the only way to understand the matter. This is what transpired in the Supreme Court's decision on the health care reform law, as explained above. If citizens are similarly prepared to engage in this process, and to realize that it is a strength rather than a weakness to be open to evolving understanding of an issue, they will be better positioned to speak and act on it intelligently and effectively. As we have seen, not everyone will always agree on what the issue or group of related issues is, for the choice to emphasize some values or concerns over others is likely to be reflected in issue definition. Nonetheless, for the individual to have carefully sorted out what he thinks the issue is remains a crucial first step toward meeting his civic duties.

2. Separating Facts from Standards and Evaluations

Public issues, like legal disputes, usually comprise facts, standards, and evaluations of the facts according to the standards. Some set of real circumstances—facts—is at the issue's core. Various values, criteria, and policies—standards—have bearing on the problem. The debate over gun control provides a useful example, particularly since "few issues generate more disagreement between ordinary citizens, or peril for elected officials, than gun control."[12] Frequently, the debate focuses on factual questions such as the extent of gun violence, the ease of access to firearms by different sectors of society, and the likelihood that various behaviors will change in response to various regulatory measures.

It may well be, however, that conflicting cultural values held by different groups are what fundamentally stokes the continuing controversy. As one scholar asserts:

> Positions on gun control vary across social groups, the members of which attach competing social meanings to guns.
>
> What makes the gun control debate so intense is not a disagreement about the facts—does private ownership of guns promote or deter violent crime?—but a disagreement about "alternative views of what America is and ought to be."[13]

The citizen who tries to make sense of divergent positions in the debate is well advised to try to ascertain whether specific statements reflect divergent assertions of facts, cultural standards, or policy implications of applying selected standards to selected facts.

Teenage pregnancy, another serious social concern, provides another example.[14] Understanding of the problem begins with some grasp of the facts, the actual demographic data. Values brought to the fore include the morality of young people's behavior, the optimal allocation of health care and child care responsibilities and costs, the importance of uninterrupted education for young people, and the desirability of intact nuclear families. Discussion of teen pregnancy thus links the facts to these types of values, and ultimately attempts to apply the standards to the facts in order to develop policies.

Similarly, with respect to the wisdom of imposing the death penalty for certain crimes, the discussion should be based on facts—for example, the frequency of death sentences, the frequency of actual executions nationally and in different regions, data on whether the possibility of a death sentence deters crime, the financial costs associated with appeals and incarceration pending appeals, and proven instances of death sentences being imposed on people who are later proven innocent. Again, various standards are expressed by various groups.[15] They include divergent views on the propriety of this extreme punishment for severe crimes, the morality of the taking of life by the state, and the fairness of the distribution of death sentences among different racial groups and geographic regions. The citizen who seeks to form an opinion about the death penalty ought to have some understanding of the facts and a grasp of the contending values being asserted. He then can decide for himself which of those standards he believes are most important and then apply them to the facts to reach his conclusion.

An unusually clear example of distinguishing standards from facts regarding the death penalty was recently presented by a California politician. His father, who also had been a politician, was a principal sponsor of the successful 1978 ballot measure expanding use of the death penalty in that state. The son wrote a newspaper article in 2012 in which he described the objective of his father's measure "as a warning to evildoers that the state would deliver swift and final justice." The article then explained his and his family's more recent conclusion "that the death penalty isn't working for California." He wrote of "the fiscally ruinous effect of our death penalty initiative," quoted his late father's reminder that "facts are stubborn things," and indicated that "three decades of obstinate data" convinced his "family that we created a fiscal monster that's taking a human toll on the very people we wanted to protect." He recognized that the accumulated facts had made clear that the original "warning" objective or standard was not being achieved and that other values were being impaired.[16]

The distinction among facts, standards, and their application is deeply engrained in legal work. The challenge for the citizen is to keep the distinction in mind whenever public issues are under discussion: What facts are being asserted? What standards—whether legal rules, cultural preferences, or moral values—are being promoted? What outcomes are being urged through suggested application of standards to the facts? Too often public debates are clouded by speakers' failure, inadvertent or intentional, to keep this three-part distinction clear. Even when it is clear, however, the citizen who fails to be aware of it, and who does not try to identify which component is being emphasized at a given time, will be hampered in his attempt to understand the issue and develop his own sound opinion.

Instead, he will probably be more confounded than necessary by the complexity of the issue and the barrage of information of varying types to which he is exposed. Recognizing that public debate has these three fundamental aspects can help reduce the individual's confusion and combat the tendency to conclude that public issues are just too complicated to deal with at all.

B. Taking an Organized Approach

For most people, engagement with public issues is a sideline. It is neither their regular job nor even a major part of their activities and conversations with families, friends, coworkers, and neighbors. Amid the press of other commitments, finding time and energy to learn about and understand the issues is challenging, so the individual's attention to the issues can easily be random and rushed.

In stark contrast, the legal system is based on orderly, deliberate decision making. Despite this great difference, at least two of the law's traditions may help bridge the gap and enable the citizen to be at least somewhat more organized in addressing the issues. These two methods are respecting procedure and taking time.

1. Respecting Procedure

The legal system emphasizes adherence to prescribed processes in order to promote a number of important values.[17] From the practice of only one party speaking at a time, to the acquittal of a criminal defendant because damning evidence was inadmissible, to methodical phases in gathering evidence and providing testimony in trials, to the rules for step-by-step information gathering and evaluation in the making of government regulations, the legal system recognizes the benefits of orderly procedure. Of course, as most everyone knows, the law's processes sometimes seem frustratingly slow, inefficient, or even pointless. That perception is undoubtedly accurate at times, but sometimes it simply reflects limited understanding of the importance of procedure.

There is no comparable array of procedures to lend structure to the way in which the citizen arrives at his conclusions on issues. The procedures observed in legal forums do not lend themselves to easy adaptation to daily life outside of those forums. Nonetheless, the law can offer some instructive examples. One example is suggested by the Supreme Court's decision in 2007 on the question of whether the federal air pollution law, the Clean Air Act, applies to greenhouse gases and requires the Environmental Protection Agency (EPA) to enact regulations to restrict emissions of those gases from cars and trucks.[18] Before that case came to the Court, a group of states and other organizations had availed themselves of a statutory procedure allowing anyone to petition the EPA to enact new regulations.

In response to the petition, the EPA invited public comment on the issues raised in the petition, "adding a 'particular' request for comments on 'any scientific, technical, legal, economic or other aspect of these issues that may be relevant to EPA's consideration of this petition.'"[19] The EPA was following an open process for obtaining a broad range of factual material and diverse arguments on whether it should take the important regulatory step urged in the petition. During the five months following EPA's invitation, the Agency received more than 50,000 comments.

After receiving all those comments and reviewing them—obviously a time-consuming task—the EPA denied the petition. It explained the reasons for the denial, as applicable legal procedures required. The petitioning groups, however, appealed to the Supreme Court. The Court found that the EPA's denial was legally incorrect, and the justices ordered the Agency to reconsider the petition in accordance with the criteria and procedural steps set forth in detail in the Clean Air Act.[20]

The Court, in other words, insisted that the government's environmental officials follow the legally prescribed procedures for obtaining and evaluating a tremendous and complex batch of information on this major public policy issue. That information falls within the category of "legislative facts" earlier discussed, that is, information that can help in the resolution of questions of law, policy, and discretion. Those were the kinds of questions the EPA would have to resolve in deciding what, if anything, to do about climate change.[21] After taking the required procedural steps, the EPA enacted a variety of regulations to begin to control greenhouse gases not only from vehicles, but also from other major emitters such as electrical power plants.[22]

Obviously, a massive, multiyear process such as this is something probably only the government can undertake. Nevertheless, this example of step by step development of information, evaluations, and conclusions through required legal processes emphasizes the importance of trying to methodically gather the facts, argue the issues, consider opposing views, and otherwise emulate the legal system's approach to decision making. Even very small steps the citizen can take along these lines can help him to better understand the issues and arrive at his own conclusions.

Additionally, appreciation of the importance of procedural requirements can guide the citizen to better understanding of the substance of some specific public controversies. Again, it is worth recalling the O. J. Simpson cases—the judgment of acquittal in the criminal trial for murder and the judgment of liability for millions of dollars in the civil case for wrongful death brought by the families of the two victims.[23] Many people were puzzled by these apparently inconsistent results: The acquittal suggests he did not commit the homicides, but the liability says he did.

However, even assuming that the evidence in the two proceedings was exactly the same, the criminal jury's finding that the prosecution failed to carry its burden of proving guilt at the "beyond a reasonable doubt" standard of proof does not necessarily mean that the civil jury erred in finding that the plaintiffs had met their burden of proving liability "by a preponderance of the evidence."[24] Instead of quickly concluding that one jury or the other must have gotten it wrong, the citizen who understands these procedural differences is better able to understand the outcomes. Of course, she still may conclude that one or the other jury was wrong. That conclusion, however, will simply express the more thoughtful view that the jury was incorrect in its application of the pertinent standard of proof to the evidence.

Another example of how appreciation of the importance of procedural requirements can foster better understanding of controversial topics is the Supreme Court's decision in 2003 in Stogner v. California.[25] There was considerable public outcry over this ruling, for the Court prohibited the prosecution of a man charged with sex-related child abuse committed at least 22 years in the past.[26] Part of this outcry derived from growing public understanding that before child victims of sexual abuse can come forward and report the crimes, they usually must "overcome shame and the desire to repress these painful memories."[27] Many years may pass before the victim is able to do so.

Recognizing this, the California legislature had enacted a new statute of limitations governing this type of crime, and the statute would have allowed this particular prosecution to be brought despite the expiration—many years earlier—of the three-year limitations period in force when the alleged crime was committed. In other words, three years after the crime, it became too late for any prosecution of it. The new statute, however, tried to revive the possibility of prosecution for this crime allegedly committed many years in the past.

The Supreme Court ruled that the new statute of limitations violated the Constitution's prohibition on enacting a retroactive criminal law, that is, an ex post facto law. The new law was trying to make past conduct criminal even though that conduct was not criminal when the new law was passed. The new statute of limitations "authorized criminal prosecutions that the passage of time had previously barred."[28] The Court reviewed the important purposes behind the constitutional ban on ex post facto laws and concluded that this case required the ban to be applied in order to serve those policies.

With this ruling, the Court in the *Stogner* case made a hard choice between the objectives of the new statute of limitations (to allow child abuse cases to be brought in later years when the victims are able to come forward) and the objectives of the ex post facto law prohibition (to avoid the unfairness of penalizing someone for conduct that was not considered criminal when it was committed or that was not subject to criminal prosecution by the time the later law was enacted). In a sense, the Court had to sacrifice the former objectives in order to serve the latter ones. Citizens who were outraged by the Court's squelching of the prosecution probably focused only on the former, and probably also felt some lack of trust in the justices' judgment. That reaction, however, ignores the complexity of the case, especially the important values embedded in the procedural requirements of statutes of limitations and the ex post facto law prohibition.

In contrast, the Court understood that, despite strong public sentiment about the need for punishing this type of crime even long after its commission, the procedural mandate of the Constitution and the important policies behind it had to be respected. By the same token, citizens could more accurately understand the outcome if they too were prepared to understand and respect the purposeful procedural requirements of the law.

2. Taking Time

One of the citizen's obstacles already discussed is that most people are so busy with a variety of concerns and obligations that they do not have time to study public issues. In contrast, when discussing the law's traditions, we noted that legal processes often, and for good reasons, take a great deal of time. If the citizen does not have much time for complex issues, but the law recognizes the need to take lots of time for them, it is hard to see that the legal system can offer the citizen much guidance to overcome this obstacle. Nevertheless, the legal system does suggest some helpful practices.

First, the deluge of information and opinion at hand need not swallow us up if we can efficiently manage our time for engaging with the issues. For example, we each do not have to have opinions on everything, and for the issues we do choose to concentrate on, we can be selective in the information sources we rely on. We can distinguish information sources that provide serious, useful information on the issues from those which provide content of a more simply entertaining nature. We may find a particular newspaper, magazine, website, or blog that presents concise summaries of information and analysis of issues that concern us. Observation of televised or online speeches, debates, or panel discussions can also be effective and fairly quick sources of information. They are particularly valuable when they present nonhearsay evidence, such as when elected officials or candidates for office are speaking for themselves, rather than being paraphrased or selectively quoted by others.

Second, the demands on the citizen's time will be diminished to the extent that she divides the labor and uses expertise. Ways of applying those methods will be discussed below.[29] Those traditions, used in the law as well as in many other aspects of our lives and work, help the citizen with the complexity and flood of information problems. By enabling her to rely on others for assistance, they also take some time-consuming burdens from her shoulders.

A few minutes or an hour of concentrated attention with thoughtfully selected sources often can be helpful as we explore information and ideas and "build" the foundations for our conclusions. To speak of the citizen's task as "building" echoes what lawyers do, for we often speak of lawyers "building a case." That phrase connotes a step by step and inherently time-consuming process of evidence collection, analysis, and reasoning. No lawyer worthy of her license to practice can take on a case and instantly know all that she needs to know about it and how to handle it. Similarly, to gather information and collect her thoughts, the citizen needs to take her time, too.

Although there is reason to believe that most of us do not have much time for this type of effort, there also is reason to think we can readily make—or take—the necessary time. Particularly through the extraordinary accessibility of information on the Internet, the vast majority of Americans can learn a lot fairly quickly about most anything if they wish to do so. Even for persons who live alone, "New communications technologies make living alone a social experience...The person alone at home can digitally navigate through a world of people, information and ideas."[30]

To analogize once again to jury service, when the legal system interrupts our daily lives to call us for jury duty, we must make the time to respond to the call. If then selected as a juror, we are forced to take the necessary time—even at the sacrifice of some of our leisure time—to hear the case and deliberate on a verdict. Similarly, we can put ourselves on "civic duty" and choose to take the time we each need to engage with the issues.

For the citizen to take his time does not mean he can take forever. In the most obvious example, if an election is coming up and the citizen needs to decide what his votes will be, he faces a time limit. Similarly, lawyers and other participants in legal proceedings often may take a long time in their work, but they cannot take forever, although it sometimes seems that way to anxious clients.[31] Lawsuits and other disputes in legal forums always embody deadlines and schedules.[32] What "taking your time" then means, both for lawyers and ordinary citizens, is trying to make the best use of the time available to you amidst your other activities and as allowed by deadlines imposed by others.[33]

When a particularly dramatic or catastrophic event brings sudden, massive attention to an issue, it is particularly difficult to respect the need for deliberate consideration rather than quick action. In the aftermath of the tragic December 2012 shooting of children at a Connecticut public school, opinions quickly hardened for many people on different sides of the gun control debate. It is often the case, however, even with incidents of gun violence, that within a matter of weeks most people's attention shifts to other news events and the urgency of the issue fades. In a sense, this tendency is both bad news and good news.

It is bad because an important social concern ceases to receive as much attention as it deserves. The good news is that the citizen who is suddenly sensitized or reenergized to think about the issue probably now has valuable time in which to learn more and formulate her opinion more thoughtfully. This is particularly important because, as with many of the recurring mass shooting incidents, the initial definition of the issue as simply and overwhelmingly a gun control issue may, with time, come to be reconsidered. A more multifaceted and precise redefinition may emerge, highlighting other important concerns such as mental illness, the availability of psychological treatment, and security measures in schools and other public facilities.

The point is that we should neither rush to hasty conclusions nor dawdle and passively wait for information to come our way randomly to gradually nudge us in one direction or another. Instead, we can do as lawyers do and actively investigate selected issues to consciously build our positions. Particularly with nettlesome, lingering issues such as gun control and climate change, their importance and difficulty are so great that the likelihood of quick resolution is slim—arguably too slim—and yet the slowness of our society's democratic processes for resolving them does give each of us time to clarify our views.

Once we each grasp the importance of managing our civic duty time wisely and giving ourselves opportunities to think things over, we may be a bit better able to evaluate whether others also are doing so and whether the information and opinions they are presenting to us are sound. For example, it is not unusual in media-intensive political campaigning for a candidate to garner strong, immediate popular support, only to quickly fall out of favor when additional information about him or her comes to light.[34] Early supporters of such candidates, as well as supporters who have donated money to them, may wish they had taken more time before declaring their allegiances.

A particularly disturbing rush to public judgment occurred in 2010 when the US Secretary of Agriculture forced the sudden resignation of an African American midlevel official in his department. The secretary's actions occurred within hours after a videotape came to light showing portions of a speech in which the official made statements suggestive of racial bias.[35] The remarks had been widely publicized, in a torrent of coverage, by some websites, the Fox News Channel, other news outlets, and the NAACP.

Shortly after the resignation, however, examination of the full speech demonstrated that the publicized portion had been taken out of context and highly edited by a blogger, creating a seriously misleading message. There had been no real basis for the firing of the employee or for her reputation to be besmirched in the eyes of millions of people. Unfortunately, probably very few of those people had reserved judgment on the initial reports until more time had passed. In this instance, as in many others, a habit of taking time before reaching a conclusion would have served all the participants in the matter, and the public, much better.

C. Finding Reliable Information

In our earlier exploration of obstacles the citizen faces, and of inescapable differences between the court of public opinion and courts of law, the difficulty of knowing what and whom to believe was emphasized. It capsulizes many aspects of the challenges the responsible citizen faces. Fortunately, many of the law's tools and traditions are designed to help us overcome that difficulty and instead find reliable information. These methods can be adapted to assist the citizen in gathering the facts, recognizing incomplete facts, dividing labor, using expertise, and identifying bias.

1. Gathering the Facts

In legal proceedings such as courtroom trials or legislative hearings, there comes a point at which no more information is allowed to come in. In legal parlance, "the record is closed." The debate has reached its end, and no more evidence will be allowed for consideration by the decision maker.[36] The information in the record has been received in accordance with the rules of evidence. Depending on the type of proceeding, oral evidence may have been received under oath, and much or all of the evidence will have been subject to limitations based on relevance, the hearsay rule, rights of cross-examination, and other procedural safeguards.[37]

In the public arena, the flow of information could not be more different. The "record" is never closed, and the volume of available information—facts, standards, and evaluations—on any major issue is so vast that no one individual could ever be exposed to it all, much less digest it. Similarly, we all face the difficulty of knowing what information and sources to trust. Unlike a court of law in which witnesses testify under oath, with the threat of prosecution for perjury hovering in the background, the public arena does not require that the truth, the whole truth, and nothing but the truth be spoken. The rules of evidence, and procedural rights to cross-examination and to confront one's accuser, do not apply. Nevertheless, the legal system's approach to fact-gathering offers clues on how to deal with the flood of information and assess its trustworthiness. Some of the law's tools for this purpose can be approximated in daily life.

The best starting point is for the citizen to see that he can actively gather information, rather than just passively receive it. An experienced judge, as quoted earlier, succinctly described this task:

> In the law, as well as in life itself, judging is the act of selecting and weighing facts and suggestions as they present themselves, as well as deciding whether the alleged facts are really facts.[38]

The citizen presumably has the capability to seek out helpful information, as well as to sift carefully through uninvited information that happens to come his way. In doing so, he can more effectively select and weigh facts, and distinguish proven information from unsupported allegations, if he keeps in mind certain of the law's tools. He may be aided, for example, by the law's approach to direct versus circumstantial evidence, hearsay, cross-examination, the standard of proof, and the burden of proof. None of these tools is fundamentally difficult to understand, and indeed in many respects they are just refinements of common sense. Nonetheless, reminders of how they can help us may be worthwhile.

Also fundamental to the gathering of facts is relevance, which can only be gauged in relation to a defined issue or set of issues, as already discussed. If the citizen has an understanding of the issue, and of other people's varying definitions of it as well, he will be able to ascertain whether information and arguments are rationally connected to the discussion. Similarly, if he keeps in mind the differences among facts, standards, and evaluations of facts under standards, he can try to discern which category fits the information he is receiving. If it is factual, he can ask, does it really bear on the problem at hand, or is it tangential or superfluous? Returning to the death penalty example, the height of defendants sentenced to death may be of some peripheral interest to someone, but it would seem to be of no utility in discussions of the wisdom of executions.

If the information is an asserted policy value or standard, does it have anything to do with the problem? Someone might argue that executions should always take place at a particular time of day, whether to reduce crowds of protesters, deter inmate outbursts, avoid electricity disruptions, or for other practical reasons. However, the relevance of this assertion to the core issue is hard to see.

When the application of a standard to the facts is asserted, would it resolve the problem or even touch on important aspects of it? An argument, for example, that the death penalty should not be applied to a person convicted of parking violations might make sense if the possibility of such a sentence even arose, but it would have hardly any relevance to the fundamental issue.

With these three components of the information flow in mind, the citizen ought to be better able to determine what is relevant and what is not, and thus to lower the chances of being confused or overwhelmed by all the available information.

Direct versus Circumstantial Evidence

The distinction between direct and circumstantial evidence also can be useful. Is the speaker or writer who appears to be delivering facts actually providing direct evidence, that is, telling of something she herself fully experienced, observed, or investigated? Alternatively, is she offering circumstantial evidence, painting an incomplete picture from her limited contact with the subject and then suggesting we draw certain inferences to fill in the factual gaps? There is nothing sinister or inherently untrustworthy about it, but circumstantial evidence is generally not as conclusive and persuasive as direct evidence, for, by definition, it does not tell us as much.[39]

If circumstantial evidence is offered, it should be viewed cautiously. It is especially wise to be on the lookout for other evidence that may corroborate it, or undermine it. All parties in a trial are entitled to provide evidence, and the result is usually a batch of conflicting descriptions of key factual information. Out of these disagreements, the decision maker presumably is able to determine what has been successfully proven as true. This process includes in-depth inquiry to see whether additional evidence confirms earlier testimony or contradicts it.

Similarly, the citizen who makes sure that his fact-gathering efforts explore multiple, diverse sources of information, and who pays close attention to whether information already received is corroborated or contradicted by other evidence, is likewise preparing himself to reach a more informed, solid conclusion. Conversely, the individual who always looks to only one source, or to a few that always take the same viewpoint, is closing himself off to deeper understanding of the issues.

Hearsay

We also should ask if the speaker is expressing her own views or others'. Others' alleged statements fall into the hearsay category, and the listener usually has only limited ability to get the full version of what the original source had to say and to evaluate her demeanor in saying it. In the climate change debate, for example, where statements about conflicting scientific findings are frequently offered, it is wise for the listener to try to assess whether the speaker is the original source of the findings in question or is instead repeating or paraphrasing what someone else supposedly has concluded. This distinction was dramatically illustrated when 16 scientists published a newspaper article, based explicitly in part on an economist's work, in which they disputed the incontrovertability and urgency of global warming.[40] The economist soon replied:

> My response is primarily designed to correct their misleading description of my own research ... I did the research and wrote the book on which they base their statement ... The authors summarize my research incorrectly.[41]

On a technical subject like climate change, of course, it is seldom this easy to ascertain speakers' relationship to the information they are putting forward. This is particularly true because scientists' findings often are embodied in dense, technical reports and the scientists themselves are not usually the main speakers in public arenas. The citizen has no choice, in a sense, but to rely to a large extent on hearsay, what others—often politicians—say the scientists have said. As will be discussed below, one aspect of the law's possible assistance with this difficulty will be addressed through the use of expertise.

Cross-Examination

We are bombarded daily with hearsay. The information we receive through media sources such as television and the Internet is often in that category, and opportunities for questioning akin to cross-examination obviously are absent. Occasionally, however, online exchanges between those who post their views in articles, blogs, and similar formats on the Internet, and those who comment on them in response, partake of some of the probing, testing, and challenging aspects of courtroom cross-examination. Additionally, of course, in that vast electronic forum, the search for confirming or contradictory evidence always can continue, and it can be especially helpful in the assessment of whether hearsay statements are reliable or not.

Apart from reading online sources of information and disputation, we also may find a partial substitute for cross-examination through viewing, reading, and listening to live, printed, televised, or Internet-streamed debates and interviews in which the source of the information is questioned and challenged by others, whether they be opponents on the issue or more or less unbiased journalists. Exposure to dialogue of this sort offers a more in-depth basis for evaluating the credibility of the speaker and her information, as compared to simply listening to her speech.

Standard of Proof and Burden of Proof

Lastly, the significance of the facts we gather, and the persuasiveness of opinions and arguments we hear, can be evaluated more soundly if we understand the standard of proof we bring to the issue in question. Do we each demand to be persuaded beyond a reasonable doubt of the correctness of what we are being told? Alternatively, it is enough that, instead of applying that criminal law standard, something like the civil standard of proof is satisfied, that is, that it is more likely than not that the position being asserted is true and sensible?

Do we even go to an extreme and believe that the correctness of an assertion must be shown to a virtual certainty? At the other extreme, is it enough that the position seems merely to make some minimal sense or that we feel personal comfort or affinity with the speaker regardless of whether he or she is making much sense? There is no requirement anywhere that we all apply the same standard of proof to any specific issue or all issues. Nevertheless, it would be helpful for us each to examine just what level of persuasiveness we are looking for on each issue we are concerned about.

The burden of proof concept also can be challenging to apply. With multiple views expressed on any major public issue, rather than the customary two as in courtroom matters, it is difficult to say that one public participant rather than another bears the burden of proof. Sometimes, however, we can identify a sensible reason for allocating the burden of proof to one participant rather than another. Thus, if the status quo is considered desirable or at least satisfactory, the person arguing that it should be changed probably should have the burden of proving and persuading that change is needed.

With respect to disputes over environmental quality, for example, it makes sense that "in both pollution cases and conservation cases [we] should place the burden of proof upon the party which already has created or wishes to create some damaging disruption of the environment."[42] Similarly, when fundamental rights are in question, arguably the burden of proof should be on those in favor of abridging those rights. Some advocates of same-sex marriage have taken this view, as in the following statement:

> Principles of equality require that we do not impose a higher standard for judging the desirability of same-sex marriage than we do for opposite-sex marriage... Legally, the burden of proof is on those who want to treat people unequally; the burden is especially high with respect to those rights deemed fundamental, like the right to marry.[43]

If, on the other hand, a social problem is widely acknowledged to need correction, then the many contending parties and their viewpoints do not seem to require that one, rather than another, should bear the burden of being the most persuasive, that is, of satisfying the applicable standard of proof. Consider the question of the individual's right to own firearms. This right arguably is based on the Second Amendment of the Constitution, as the Supreme Court has concluded, even though the Amendment's language is far from crystal clear.[44] As a question of social policy, there is a wide range of viewpoints on whether individuals should be able to own firearms, and, if so, whether some weapons should be allowed and others disallowed. Related points of contention include background check and licensing requirements, permissible types of ammunition, and restrictions on carrying weapons in vehicles or in personal concealment.

Each of these issues presents a policy choice. If your view is that no individual should be allowed to own an assault rifle, and that it is better to preserve present circumstances in which fewer people have that weapon, you may believe that others who see the question differently, and would allow for expansion in possession of such rifles, have the burden of proving that their position embodies a better policy. The standard of proof you apply might be that they must prove beyond a reasonable doubt that possession of such weapons is a good idea.

Conversely, if you believe that the right to own a firearm is an important personal interest, you would expect others to try to persuade you differently, that is, to carry the burden of proving that no such right is warranted or that it should be severely circumscribed. If you feel strongly about your starting position, you similarly may be applying a stringent standard of proof. You will not change your mind unless it is shown beyond a reasonable doubt that gun ownership is a bad idea. If you start out with a less firm view, however, you may be open to the burden of proof being carried—and to being persuaded to change your mind—by a lesser showing, such as that gun ownership more probably than not is unwise policy. What matters, for the clarity of your thought and the rational development of your views, is that you have some sense of how open you are to being persuaded to agree with a particular position and whom you expect to bear the burden of proof and persuasion.

2. Recognizing Incomplete Facts

Even if jurors do not have all the evidence they would like to have in order to reach a well-informed conclusion in a case, that frustration does not allow them to shirk their responsibility to make a decision.[45] The same is true for judges when they must render decisions, and for government officials when the law requires them to make regulatory rulings.[46] Similarly, the ordinary citizen often faces a complex public issue but only has incomplete information about it, even despite his conscientious efforts to gather the facts.

In contrast with decision makers in the legal system, the citizen is not subject to any requirement that he must reach a conclusion despite this quandary. He is free to drop out of discussion of most any issue for this reason, any reason, or even no reason at all, without suffering any significant consequences. As earlier discussed, sometimes that is the sensible thing to do.[47]

At other times, the absence of complete information ought not to dissuade the citizen from reaching a conclusion. At those times, she can choose to do what legal decision makers must do, which is to exercise her judgment to make the most sensible decision she can on the basis of the limited information at hand. She need not pretend that her conclusion is based on all the necessary information. Instead, she should acknowledge, at least to herself, that more facts might later become known and that additional information might later lead her to a different conclusion. In the meantime, she can recognize that she is making her best guess, in a sense, as to what outcome seems most sound.

Many citizens have taken this approach to the debates in recent years about whether global warming is occurring, whether humans are contributing to it, what its impacts may be on climatic events, ocean temperatures, and other phenomena, and whether various possible measures to combat it are needed, affordable, and likely to be effective. The challenge has been well described as follows:

> Predictions of the future climate are surrounded with considerable uncertainty which arises from our imperfect knowledge both of the science of climate change and of the future scale of the human activities that are its cause. Politicians and others making decisions are therefore faced with the need to weigh all aspects of uncertainty against the desirability and the cost of the actions that can be taken in response to the threat of climate change.[48]

On the subject of gun control, despite the growing volume of information in the public arena, there still are serious gaps in our knowledge, as the following statements emphasize:

> Without question, guns are inextricably linked to violence in America. The available evidence does not, however, answer the causal question of whether guns cause violence or whether the violence-prone simply turn to guns. The most likely answer to this riddle is probably a combination of both conclusions. If guns disappeared tomorrow, violence would surely continue. But it would probably be less devastating.[49]
>
> Crime and mortality statistics are often used in the gun control debate. According to a recent study, however, none of the existing sources of statistics provide either comprehensive, timely, or accurate data with which to definitively assess whether there is a causal connection between firearms and violence.[50]

Even beyond such gaps in our understanding of the problem, there are substantial gaps in our knowledge of the likely efficacy of proposed solutions. How much added safety would America actually receive from increased criminal background checks, bans on specific weapons, limits on ammunition magazine capacities, prohibitions of certain types of bullets, or other measures? We do not have all the information we wished we had, and even important information we do have is subject to dispute. Nevertheless, the need for decision and action may be inescapable, or at least the expressed preference emerging from our democracy.

In recognizing that incomplete facts are at times the only facts available on climate change, gun control, and many other issues, the citizen may be helped by applying some pertinent legal tools. For example, jurors evaluate incomplete or ambiguous information according to the standard of proof and the burden of proof applicable in the case. They must determine whether the evidence presented satisfies the required level of persuasiveness for the party who bears the burden of proof. Similarly, the individual who feels stymied by a lack of complete information will be better able to reach a rational conclusion if he stops to assess what standard of proof he is applying and whom he expects to carry the burden of proving the standard is met.

Consider, for example, a proposal for a "three strikes law." These are laws passed by legislatures, or by voters through ballot propositions, requiring that lengthy prison sentences must be imposed on anyone convicted of a serious crime and who has previously been convicted of two such crimes. Even assuming that the law was written so clearly that there would be no significant ambiguities in how it would be applied, the range of factual information a voter might wish to have before voting on such a proposal is great: How many mandatory third strike sentences would be imposed under a new law like this? Do the state's prisons have room for all the persons who would be sentenced under the law? What would be the financial cost of these incarcerations? Would this law cause greater, more dangerous resistance to arrest by persons subject to mandatory third strike punishment? Would third strike defendants be less likely to enter guilty pleas and, if so, what added burden and cost would that development place on criminal prosecutors and the courts? The answers to these and many other questions would help to educate the voter as to the wisdom of the proposed law, but it is unlikely that all such answers would be available.

Faced with information gaps such as these, the voter must form his opinion on the basis of whatever he can learn now, while realizing that later on, as the gaps are filled, he may see things differently.[51] As for the burden of proof, he may consider that the proponents of the new law—changing the way judges impose sentences and increasing the likelihood of long incarceration for convicted individuals—have the burden of demonstrating that it is a good idea and deserves his vote. Conversely, if his main concern is getting criminals off the street, he may view the burden of proof as more sensibly resting on those who oppose the three strikes law.

What standard of proof he will apply is also likely to vary, depending on his personal assumptions about crime, punishment, and the judicial system. If he believes crime is rampant, long prison sentences are effective deterrents or appropriate punishment for many crimes, and judges have too much discretion and impose lenient sentences, then he can be easily persuaded that this law should be enacted. In other words, he will apply a low standard of proof. If, however, he has doubts about the effectiveness and fairness of long prison sentences and trusts judges generally to impose appropriate sentences, his standard of proof will be more demanding. He will not be swayed to vote for the law unless its proponents make a strong case for it, persuading him that it is more probable than not, or even persuading him beyond a reasonable doubt, that this law should gain his vote.

In sum, the citizen should recognize that often her views on issues can only be based on incomplete information. She should also try to discern how readily she can be persuaded despite the incompleteness of information. The citizen who absorbs this guidance will be able to approach an issue with greater clarity at the outset and with a more realistic, open-minded perspective on it in the future.

3. Dividing Labor

Our focus here on guidance for the individual should not blind us to the possible benefits she might gain from teamwork, from dividing her labor in some fashion. It is quite common for legal work to be done by a team, with different members assigned different tasks.[52] Is there some way in which each of us can approximate this in daily life? If there is, then we can reduce the obstacles posed by the complexity of issues, the flood of information, the trust challenge, and the limits of our available time and space for grappling with the issues.

At the simplest level, we know that our friends, relatives, and co-workers have varying levels of interest in different public issues, just as we do. Some of us pay more attention to the quality of public education, others to economic concerns such as government spending and deficits, others to foreign policy in particular regions of the world, and so on. Their knowledge may be easily accessible to us, and we can gain from simply questioning them and listening, trying to discern as we do so, of course, whether they really know what they are talking about.

To the extent that our close associates seem to be well-informed, open-minded, and trustworthy, there is a lot we can learn from them with minimal effort. In relying on our circle of acquaintances in this way, we are in effect making them part of our own personal "staff," analogous to the types of assistants relied on by lawyers, judges, and legislators. They can help us by gathering information, analyzing it, and sharing it with us. Tocqueville recognized the necessity and desirability of reliance on others for assistance in developing our opinions, although he described this benefit oddly:

> A man who should undertake to inquire into everything for himself, could devote to each thing but little time and attention... He must therefore make his choice from amongst the various objects of human belief, and adopt many opinions without discussion, in order to search the better into that smaller number which he sets apart for investigation. It is true, that whoever receives an opinion on the word of another, does so far enslave his mind; but it is a salutary servitude which allows him to make a good use of freedom.[53]

Beyond nearby sources of help, we can also each create a more extended, "virtual" staff by choosing other sources of information and opinion we find worthy of ongoing reliance. In seeking such sources, we are looking for someone to do some of our homework for us, though not so much as to displace our ultimate responsibility to form our own opinions. This strategy is by no means unique to the legal system, of course. When we earlier examined sources of conventional guidance, we found this same approach suggested in some types of citizens group guides and even in the comments of assorted celebrities about the value of learning the opinions of other respected persons.[54]

We may find that a particular newspaper or magazine's editorial board, a radio or television commentator, an Internet blogger, a politician or political party, or a particular civic organization consistently appears to provide solid, well-researched information. Again, as emphasized with regard to gathering facts, we can actively choose sources of help, rather than passively accept sources of information with which we just happen to have contact. As with any team effort or division of labor, reliability becomes a key criterion. Is this person or organization one which applies energy and intelligence to identifying issues clearly, gathering information carefully, formulating positions thoughtfully, and communicating its views understandably? If so, it is worthy of our reliance.

Remembering the importance of the personal, and the tendency to follow the leader, it may be tempting to choose our virtual staff on the basis of inclinations and habits such as those. If we do so, we may be letting someone else do all our homework and form opinions for us on dubious bases. However, if the opinion leaders or groups we choose are knowledgeable and thoughtful, share important values with us, and make explanations of their views available to us, and if we pay enough sustained attention to be sure they continue to deserve our reliance, the benefits can be considerable. Others will not be making decisions for us, but helping us by sharing some of the labor as we do so ourselves.

4. Using Expertise

The complexity of many public issues implies that expert knowledge is valuable, and often essential, for understanding them. This need is also compelled in many legal proceedings.[55] In lawsuits, legislative hearings, and other forums, expertise is brought to bear through the input of technically specialized staff employees of government agencies, companies, and other interested parties, as well as the input of paid consultants. High-stakes battles of highly paid experts are thus quite common in the legal system.

How can the ordinary citizen approximate expert assistance for his own opinion formation? There is no easy answer. Perhaps in no other aspect of the citizen's task do the obstacles of complexity and the flood of information present more of a problem. Issues such as climate change, government budgets and spending, stem cell medical research, health care reform, and many others raise difficult questions in science, technology, economics, and many other fields. The vast amount of information and debate on such questions includes technical data and expert opinions, making complex issues appear impenetrable for the vast majority of us.

Perhaps the most that can be drawn from the legal system's use of experts is a reiteration of the value of careful selection of one's own virtual staff. With the plethora of written and electronic sources of information, it is not difficult to find expert sources of information on any subject, including controversial topics. Since we obviously cannot hire our own experts, we have to pick and choose from among the sources presented to us in various media. Again, criteria of ability, thoroughness, open-mindedness, and shared values properly come into play.

Often we are exposed to information or opinions from someone who claims to be an expert, and yet we may not be sure just how justified the claim actually is. The legal system itself faces this same difficulty. It is not unusual in a court proceeding, or in administrative or legislative forums considering the enactment of new regulations or statutes, for a purported expert's credentials or experience to be closely scrutinized or challenged. In courtroom trials, experts are allowed to state their opinions and conclusions on scientific, technical, and other specialized questions while ordinary witnesses may not do so. Because of this added force of expert testimony, it is important, and frequently a subject of dispute and intensive cross-examination, to determine whether a particular individual legally qualifies as an expert witness in a particular case.

In the federal courts, the rule governing expert witnesses reads as follows:

> A witness who is qualified as an expert by knowledge, skill, experience, training, or education may testify in the form of an opinion or otherwise if:
>
> (a) the expert's scientific, technical, or other specialized knowledge will help the trier of fact to understand the evidence or to determine a fact in issue;
> (b) the testimony is based on sufficient facts or data;
> (c) the testimony is the product of reliable principles and methods; and
> (d) the expert has reliably applied the principles and methods to the facts of the case.[56]

When the ordinary citizen encounters a purported expert on an issue of public concern, some of the considerations emphasized in this rule may be helpful. Has it been shown that the so-called expert has pertinent scientific, technical, or other specialized knowledge? Is her information or opinion based on identified facts or data? Has she given any indication of the principles or methods she applied in reaching her conclusions?

As difficult as it may be to come to firm answers to these three questions, the last consideration is probably the most challenging: Has the expert "reliably applied" those principles or methods to the issue at hand? This last question would seem to require our evaluation of whether, after we have reflected on the expert's statements, they seem well supported and fundamentally sensible. Answering this question is not something that can be done by applying any clear, bright line test. Even when the Supreme Court issued its leading decision on expert scientific testimony, it said, "We do not presume to set out a definitive checklist or test."[57] Instead the Court offered "general observations" and a flexible set of factors for trial judges to consider in deciding what scientific testimony to admit into evidence.

The Court also said, "The trial judge must ensure that any and all scientific testimony or evidence admitted is not only relevant, but reliable."[58] Perhaps the Court's emphasis on relevance and reliability provides the best, shorthand guidance for the citizen's effort to evaluate claims of expertise he encounters on public issues. As to relevance, do the expert's statements shed light on the issue as we are coming to understand it, or are they unrelated or tangential? As to reliability, if the statements are relevant, do they appear to be based on solid knowledge and evidence? In other words, has the expert approached the issue with an open mind, applied specialized knowledge to it, and reached informed conclusions that make sense?

As we go about recognizing sources of expertise to assist us in developing our views, another important attribute to assess is the ability of our "staff" to communicate sophisticated subjects clearly. Without presuming to understand all the ins and outs of a difficult, specialized topic, we should seek sources that can translate experts' information and views into digestible terms. Even fairly short summaries of technical material can be extremely helpful, whether found in newspapers, magazines, newsletters, television, the Internet, or elsewhere. In any of these places, we should not ask for material to be "dumbed down" into overly simplistic, and thus potentially misleading or biased, presentations. Instead, we should seek aids to our understanding that respectfully recognize that although we are not experts, we want to understand the fundamentals of the issues at hand and the divergent views on them. Again, we need some help with our homework, especially in highly complex subjects, but ultimately it is our job to form our own opinions and reach our own conclusions.

5. Identifying Bias

The legal system recognizes that self-interest normally and properly motivates most transactions and litigation. The law also strives to identify, publicize, and neutralize self-interest, prejudice, favoritism, dogmatism, and other forms of bias, which are improper when they interfere with the law's search for accurate information and fair decision making.[59] In the daily life of the citizen, there are no such traditions and tools for identifying bias and taking it into account as we express our own views and are exposed to others'. If we did notice bias more readily, however, we would be better positioned to grapple with the issues.

First, and probably most difficult, is the challenge of becoming aware of our own predispositions which color our responses to public concerns. Just as jurors are closely questioned by the lawyers or judge in a case to ascertain their ability to evaluate disputes with an open mind, self-questioning about our own preconceptions and self-interests ideally would be useful. But the ancient challenge to "know thyself" has never been easy to meet. Accordingly, it would be unrealistic simply to suggest we can extrapolate from the legal system so as to more readily identify our own biases and set them aside when public issues come to our attention. The structured processes of the law aim at fostering objectivity, but outside of those processes it is difficult to expect major changes in the individual's awareness of his own blinders.

What is easier for us to achieve is enhanced awareness of biases that others bring to public debates. Just as the juror has to be alert to indications that a witness's testimony is shaded by tangential considerations, so too should we be on the lookout for signs that people urging information or opinions on us may be influenced by dubious motives. The state legislator who argues that a proposed redrawing of voting district lines is right and just may really believe that, but he also may be motivated by the benefits those lines will create for his own political longevity or the power of his party. In a Supreme Court decision in 2012, the Court "instructed a lower court in Texas to take a fresh look at election maps it had drawn in place of a competing set of maps from the Texas Legislature. One set of maps was drawn by the Legislature, which is controlled by Republicans. Those maps seem[ed] to favor Republican candidates."[60]

In another example, an historic public vote in California in 1986 removed from office the chief justice and two other justices of the state supreme court. Much of the expensive publicity targeting the three justices concentrated on their resistance to imposing the death penalty.[61] Undoubtedly, many of the individuals and groups sponsoring that publicity honestly disagreed with the justices' approach to that question. However, close examination of the organizations providing the major funding for that publicity identified business and insurance interests that were adversely affected economically by the justices' decisions in certain regulatory and tort liability cases, but not in the death penalty cases. Those economic grievances were largely eclipsed from public view by the loud drumbeat about the death penalty. Would it have been helpful to the ordinary voter to understand that the issue being pressed by these opponents was not the issue of real concern to them? At a minimum, the diversion of attention from the opponents' main, economic motivation to the hot button death penalty question made it harder for voters to understand the true nature and extent of the justices' alleged failings in their judicial role.

At times during the controversies in recent years over global warming, it has been charged that research findings of some scientists are open to question because the sources of monetary support for their work lead them to biased results. For example, the environmental organization Greenpeace USA maintains an online database, called "ExxonSecrets," which states that it "compiles Exxon Foundation and corporate funding to a series of institutions that have worked to undermine solutions to global warming and climate change." Greenpeace charges that the Exxon Mobil Corporation and other companies provide funding for scientists who challenge the growing consensus of many climate scientists regarding the nature and urgency of the problem.[62]

Serious charges of this sort, particularly when tarnishing the work of particular scientists, should not be uncritically accepted, but they do deserve careful attention. If they are valid, they raise serious doubts about whether information presented to the public as technically sound instead reflects a built-in bias. In an unusual variation on the theme of corporate-funded climate research, a scientist whose work on global warming had earlier identified problems in some others' prominent climate findings publicly declared himself "a converted skeptic." He explained:

> Last year, following an intensive research effort involving a dozen scientists, I concluded that global warming was real and that the prior estimates of the rate of warming were correct. I'm now going a step further: Humans are almost entirely the cause.[63]

What was surprising about this scientist's change of views was that his research had been funded by a foundation that "has a considerable history of backing groups that deny climate change."[64] Either the assumption that the funder's desire was to skew the scientific findings was unfounded, or the scientist was principled enough to flout such a desire. Either way, this episode appeared to provide evidence for the public that the scientist's new position was his honest, unbiased, scientific conclusion.

In addition to being on the lookout for biases arising from economic or political self-interest, there are benefits in simply identifying purveyors of dogma. As noted in the discussion of jurors' obligations, the witness who is consistently predisposed to view events as having the same significance despite substantial differences among them is not a witness whose testimony is altogether reliable. Similarly, a judge whose decisions are highly predictable because of his or her rigid application of certain fixed preconceptions, while disregarding differences among the facts and policy impacts of different cases, is not approaching the judging function with the open-mindedness and breadth of reasoning that the legal system fundamentally expects. In other words, the credibility of a witness's testimony or the quality of a judge's decisions is undermined when excessive consistency characterizes his or her work.

The same kinds of doubts should arise when any speaker on public issues is identified as virtually always adopting the same viewpoint. There is, of course, much to be admired in a person who has thoughtfully developed a perspective on many public issues and who brings a coherent set of values or personal philosophy to bear. To the extent that the individual's perspective is so rigid, however, as to blind him to competing views and information and the possibility of changes in his viewpoint, that individual becomes far less constructive as a contributor to public debates and as someone others should listen to and learn from.

The earlier-quoted conventional guidance of Walter Cronkite expresses essentially this same point. When asked whom the public can trust, he said,

> I think they're most likely to trust that source which they have learned is fair and impartial in gathering the facts and presenting the facts... That opinion which I think is fair and worth listening to is that which you can't predict is going to take a stand one way or the other on any particular issue, but bases the position upon the facts of that alone.[65]

Cronkite thus describes the open-minded citizen whose opinions are unbiased, solid enough to be acted upon, and worthy of trust and reliance by others.

D. Keeping an Open Mind

An eminent judge once described open-mindedness as fundamental in a free society. He wrote, "The spirit of liberty is the spirit which is not too sure that it is right."[66] In the same vein, of the four broad objectives promoted by the law's methods, perhaps the most important one for improving citizen engagement with public issues is keeping an open mind. Just as the legal system operates at its best when the people working within it are receptive to new and differing aspects of the problems before them, so too is the ordinary individual best prepared to be a responsible contributor to public discourse when she embraces that approach. The law's tools most directly designed to assist in this way focus on arguing and persuading, listening and negotiating, and making hard choices in gray areas.

1. Arguing and Persuading

We all should argue more, and welcome other people's arguments, about public issues. Of course, the type of "argument" to be encouraged is not heated, angry discourse, but rather argument in the legal system's sense, as discussed earlier.[67] Arguments by lawyers are statements of position on particular legal issues. Because legal issues are often complicated, and seldom invite an indisputably "right" answer, the expression of multiple conflicting perspectives on them is a good thing.

In this vein, a popular study of the human brain's decision-making processes focused on the common inclination to assume a firm position while ignoring contrary perceptions that challenge our "bias for certainty":

> We must force ourselves to think about the information we don't want to think about, to pay attention to the data that disturbs our entrenched beliefs. When we start censoring our minds, turning off those brain areas that contradict our assumptions, we end up ignoring relevant evidence... But the certainty trap is not inevitable. We can take steps to prevent ourselves from shutting down our minds' arguments too soon. We can consciously correct for this innate tendency. And if those steps fail, we can create decision-making environments that help us better entertain competing hypotheses.[68]

Legal argumentation provides just such a decision-making environment, forcing the participants to "entertain competing hypotheses." Airing of different arguments and viewpoints helps to illuminate disagreements, and in the legal system it frames the issues more fully for the decision maker.

In contrast, much of the flood of information on public issues is presented as argument in the ordinary sense of angry disagreement, often impugning the character and motivations of those with whom one disagrees. This is not surprising in a climate in which strong feelings abound on hot button issues and in which personal factors play an important role, especially in political allegiances. In response to these tendencies, it would be foolish to suggest that everyone should just calm down, set aside emotion and personality, and just "play nice" in all settings. What hopefully is not folly is to suggest that citizens' participation in public discourse, and their observation of others' participation, could be enhanced by awareness of the important difference between ordinary arguments and legal arguments.

Lawyers' arguments emphasize the relevant facts, interpretations of applicable legal standards, and competing views of good policy outcomes. In these substantive respects, lawyers are expected to disagree in order to advance their clients' interests and lend clarity to differences of view on the issues. What they are not supposed to do, and usually do not do, is to become disagreeable as they disagree. The civility of legal argument helps to ensure that issues are not obscured, and decisions skewed, by anger and excessive emotion.

Much public debate involves angry voices speaking loudly at the same time, fighting to be heard. All too often, televised panels or debates, even television courtroom shows, descend into shouting matches.[69] The conventional courtroom pattern of one speaker at a time is decimated in "a political discourse that increasingly resembles professional wrestling."[70] Although this kind of lively, even clever, verbal jousting may make for good entertainment, it also should be understood as often not much more than that.

Angry, turbulent disagreement and appeals to emotion and fear increase the risk of distorting the issues, distracting from the difficult decisions being pursued, and destroying opportunities for constructive dialogue and reasoned persuasion. Although the connection is hard to verify, vitriolic speech may even increase the risk that disagreements on social issues will precipitate violence, as evidenced in incidents of physical, even fatal attacks on abortion providers by anti-abortion advocates and on scientific researchers by animal rights activists.[71]

In the aftermath of the school shooting in Connecticut in December 2012, one byproduct of the heated public arguments about gun control was a reaction to the position in favor of gun control strongly expressed by a British broadcaster on his American cable interview show. Also, during one of his shows, the broadcaster had called one of his guests, the leader of a gun owners group, "an unbelievably stupid man." The reaction to the broadcaster's position and intemperate comment was a petition, signed by over 100,000 people, demanding that the Obama Administration deport him back to Britain.[72] Considerable attention was thus diverted from the gun issue itself to the status and free speech rights of a British citizen in America who favors greater control of firearms. Similarly, President Obama's prominent presentation of children and their letters calling for gun control, as part of his effort to build support for new gun regulations, was criticized by some as an emotionally exploitive diversion from the real and difficult policy issue at hand.[73]

Public issues are already complex enough in their substance and policy implications. Obfuscation through uncivil disputation is of no benefit to anyone, except a speaker or media outlet that seeks to draw more attention to itself. Citizens who hear such speakers should be prepared to distinguish argument addressed to the merits from argument addressed to peripheral considerations such as publicity for its own sake or the venting of personal hostility. The former type of argument can help us learn more about what is really at stake, while the latter does not. If we become aware of this difference in what we hear from others, hopefully we will also be better equipped to focus our own speech to make our arguments more constructive and persuasive, just as a good lawyer tries to do.

2. Listening and Negotiating

One clear benefit of the law's tradition of people speaking in turn, rather than fighting simultaneously to make their points, is that it facilitates listening. Obviously, if you are speaking, you cannot listen very well. If more than one person is speaking at a time, it is hard for anyone to hear anything clearly. This is true, of course, in every aspect of our lives, and not just in legal forums.

As earlier emphasized, even though we habitually think of lawyers as speakers—as "mouthpieces" for their clients—lawyers must be good listeners in order to understand others' views and formulate their own views in response. Advocates, in other words, must listen to those with whom they disagree, and judges and jurors must listen to all parties and their differing evidence and arguments. Although good listening is by no means a unique aspect of legal work, it is of fundamental importance there.

Understanding of the content of legal issues, and of what is relevant to them, is vastly improved by careful attention to what is being said and even how it is said. These same benefits can accrue to the citizen who is a good and patient listener to facts and arguments on public issues. Early in his presidency, President Obama expressed confidence that people are inclined to listen well. He opined that, by doing so, people both understand others' viewpoints better and gain the reassurance that they too are being heard. He said:

> I've always been struck by the fact that, if you can get me in a room with a group of people, even who disagree with me violently on an issue, they'll still take the time to listen. They might not, at the end of it, agree with me, but having seen how I'm thinking about a problem, having a sense of how I'm making decisions, that I understand their point of view, that I can actually make their argument for them, and that that's part of the decision-making process, it gives them a sense, at least, that they've been heard, and I think...it pushes us away from the

> dogmas and caricatures that I think get in the way of good policymaking and [fosters] a more civil tone in our politics.[74]

In these statements, the President embraced a rosier view of common behavior than many others would, and perhaps even a rosier view than he held later in his presidency. Nevertheless, just as we assume that citizens have the capacity to listen, learn, and work through disagreements when they serve as jurors,[75] we also should assume they can exercise this capability in other parts of their lives. If they do so, the complexity of public issues may be less daunting and confusing, and the ability to discern which voices to trust will be enhanced.

3. Making Hard Choices in Gray Areas

Many legal questions are complicated because they require hard choices among respectable but competing policies or concerns. As Justice David Souter put it, often a court is faced with "a conflict of approved values," and the court then "has to decide which of our approved desires has the better claim, right here, right now."[76] The citizen has an analogous challenge in trying to reach conclusions on complex public issues, for in this broad realm as well, hard choices in gray areas are needed.

Perhaps the most important guidance the law can offer the citizen with regard to these choices is its express recognition that the answers to complex questions *do* require choices and that seldom is there an indisputably right answer. Lawyers' arguments in legal disputes highlight the different choices available, depending on what facts and standards are considered most important by one party or another. The decisions by judges similarly embody choices among the available answers to the hard questions the cases raise. The Alabama Supreme Court explicitly acknowledged this challenging task, as it reviewed the parties' opposing views and stated in a difficult case:

> We have given serious consideration to these concerns and, as meritorious as they are, their counter-arguments must also be given due legal consideration...We believe that Alabama law...must be applied to balance the delicate and competing policy considerations presented here.[77]

If citizens similarly could remind themselves that their positions on public issues involve choices, and that other positions usually express different but not necessarily irrational or irresponsible choices, the quality and civility of public dialogue could be substantially enhanced. Disagreement on issues could be more readily accepted as normal and productive, just as it is in the law.

It is easy to identify public issues that call for hard choices among competing approved values, for there are always many of them at hand. Consider, for example, the imposition of term limits on members of a state legislature. Proponents of term limits emphasize the lengthy tenure of some legislators, especially those whose talents seem to wane over time. These proponents argue that more frequent turnover in the membership of lawmaking bodies would promote fresh ideas and skills, as well as greater representation of younger, more diverse constituencies. Conversely, those who oppose term limits point to the sacrifice of accumulated wisdom and expertise that would follow from limiting the length of an individual's legislative service. These opponents highlight the sagacity of experienced legislators who continue to make wise, skillful contributions to the legislative process.[78] In this debate, neither side is necessarily wrong, in either the facts it emphasizes or the policy arguments it advances. The disagreement is real, and ultimately the democratic process will result in a policy choice being made.

The issue of global climate change poses a host of such difficult choices, most of which are by now extremely well-known: Should drastic changes in our consumption and fuel use options be made even if immediate economic hardship, or substantial changes in our patterns of living, may result? Should richer, industrialized nations make sacrifices through such changes while poorer, less developed nations continue unabated and even increased emission of greenhouse gases as a concomitant of their efforts to grow their economies and improve their standards of living? Should long-term benefits to future generations and environmental quality be given greater or lesser weight than the needs and preferences of the current residents of the planet? Again, the array of policy choices ultimately to be made is daunting, but the citizen who acknowledges these choices and their difficulty at least is in better touch with the realities of what must somehow be resolved.

Gun control, too, is a powerful example of a conflict of approved values and the need for hard choices among them. At one level of discourse, the question is simply framed by competing perspectives on the principal use of guns as a tool:

> They can be a tool for recreation, for personal or family protection, or for crime, unwarranted and unjustified, or death. Like any tool, a firearm's use is largely determined by its owner.[79]

At a deeper level, there are broader concerns at work. Gun control advocates focus on public safety and the ability of the government to contribute to it, while contrary voices emphasize individual autonomy and concern about both the effectiveness of government regulation and its potential infringement of personal liberty.

> To gun control advocates, the opposition is out of touch with the times, misinterprets the Second Amendment, and is lacking in concern for the problems of crime and violence. To gun control opponents, advocates are naïve in their faith in the power of regulation to solve social problems, bent on disarming the American citizen for ideological or social reasons, and moved by irrational hostility to firearms and gun enthusiasts.[80]

In light of the importance of the values being advanced by each side, and the depth of feeling those values arouse, it is obvious that gun control poses one of the most contentious and difficult of the hard choices modern America faces.

Occasionally a court will decide a case by making a hard choice that ignites great public controversy. One such decision was Kelo v. City of New London, decided by the Supreme Court in 2005.[81] With four justices dissenting, the Court upheld the city's exercise of its eminent domain power to buy a number of privately owned properties from unwilling sellers. The Court found the city's action constitutional because the property was to be taken for "public use." That use was the implementation of a development plan to revitalize blighted sections of the economically distressed city. What made the taking of property so controversial was the city's plan to transfer some of the acquired properties to other private owners for projects in keeping with the city's development plan.

In a narrow sense, the Court's job was to interpret the meaning of the constitutional phrase "public use." Within that limited chore, however, the Court was called upon to make a hard choice: On the one hand, the city's interest in shoring up its economic viability and municipal vitality was being promoted. On the other hand, private property was being taken by the government for ultimate transfer to other private owners. The majority opinion explicitly recognized the conflicting policies:

> Two polar propositions are perfectly clear. On the one hand, it has long been accepted that the sovereign may not take the property of *A* for the sole purpose of transferring it to another private party *B*, even though *A* is paid just compensation. On the other hand, it is equally clear that

> a State may transfer property from one private party to another if future "use by the public" is the purpose of the taking.[82]

A majority of the justices resolved the case in favor of the city's interest, while the dissenters railed against that interpretation. They asserted that "under the banner of economic development, all private property is now vulnerable to being taken and transferred to another private owner, so long as it might be upgraded."[83]

Once again, a conflict of approved values was presented, and the judges had to make the choice. In this instance, however, the Court's choice rested in large part on the type of reasoning from precedents discussed in chapter 4.[84] The decision analyzed a number of analogous, though not precisely the same, prior cases involving interpretation of "public use." The justices concluded that "over a century of our case law dictates" the answer in this case. Examination of what "a court *has* held" was found to be instructive on "how future courts *ought* to hold,"[85] and the benefits of reasoning from precedential analogies presumably were realized.

What was particularly noteworthy about the *Kelo* decision's reliance on precedent was a subsequent speech by the author of the majority opinion, Justice John Paul Stevens. Stevens asserted that "if I were a legislator," with the freedom to make a fresh policy choice, instead of being a judge obligated to promote consistency in the law through adherence to precedents, he would have chosen a different result. Principled constraints on judges' choices are reflected in Stevens's statement that "my opinion of what the law authorized is entirely divorced from my judgment concerning the wisdom of the program."[86]

The tools of the law make it relatively easy for lawyers and judges to research past decisions to see if there are pertinent precedents to help in the resolution of present disputes. Ordinary citizens do not have comparable tools or skills, but they may find helpful wisdom by examining new disputes with some recollection of how analogous disputes in the past were resolved. The reasoning, policy arguments, and actual experiences related to prior disputes may help illuminate choices to be made in the present.

When President Clinton was impeached by the House of Representatives in 1998, the analogous proceedings against President Andrew Johnson in 1868 were recalled. Similarly, the contested 2000 presidential election invited reexamination of some aspects of the disputed 1876 election.[87] Controversy over US military actions in Iraq was often linked to recollections of the Vietnam War's policies and impacts, and, more recently, the Vietnam and Iraq experiences have been cited in discussions of US policy in Afghanistan.[88] To suggest that there are benefits to this kind of examination of precedent is not to say that the individual citizen is expected to become a skilled researcher of history. Rather, the previously mentioned tools for gathering facts, dividing labor, and using expertise should enable the citizen to acquire more of this type of information and analysis from readily available sources of reliable information.

If citizens develop a stronger grasp of the hard choices public issues present, the issues will not magically become less complex and the flood of information will not be reduced. Nonetheless, the individual's competency in understanding the issues may be improved. Furthermore, her level of trust and respect for those with whom she disagrees may be raised. She may be more inclined to listen to them, learn from them, and develop her own views in a more informed manner. This is what lawyers must do relative to their adversaries all the time, and what judges and jurors must do as they listen to the evidence and arguments presented to them. The result in the legal system is more thoughtful and informed decisions. The result of an analogous approach for the citizen would be more thoughtful and informed opinions on difficult questions of the day.

8

Conclusion: About Responsibility

The preceding chapters explored whether the legal system can provide useful guidance to anyone who wishes to be a responsible citizen in dealing with public issues. The key word is "responsible," and perhaps the best way to sum up the guidance offered in this book is to say that ultimately it is all about the exercise of responsibility. As was stated at the beginning, if democracy is to be more than a hollow word, we each have a civic responsibility to make up our mind about public issues and to express our conclusions. The point was well stated in a 2012 national report on civic learning: "To be an American means to take responsibility for democratic purposes, practices, vitality, and viability."[1]

Again, a comparison to the ways lawyers do their work is instructive. When a lawyer begins working on a case, the lawyer commits to focusing his attention and talents on the client's concerns. Courts have described this obligation in terms of professional responsibility:

> Lawyers in the practice of law have a formidable responsibility to protect their clients' "property, their freedom, and at times their very lives."[2]
>
> Professional ethics requires of a lawyer a decent sense of responsibility to all those he serves.[3]
>
> An attorney has certain obligations and duties to a client once representation is undertaken, and his obligations in that respect do not evaporate because the case becomes more complicated or the work more arduous or the retainer not as profitable as first contemplated or imagined.[4]
>
> Unquestionably, "an attorney has the responsibility to investigate and prepare every phase of his or her client's case."[5]

In the same vein, the American Bar Association's Model Rules of Professional Conduct declare:

> A lawyer must also act with commitment and dedication to the interests of the client.[6]

Similarly, with respect to jury service, we often speak of the responsibilities the citizen assumes in that role:

> [Jury duty] is an awesome responsibility...Remember, the jury's task is to make a determination of the truth, and all of our citizens are equipped with the ability to undertake that responsibility.
>
> We regard the activity of dispensing justice in the courts as a responsibility all citizens should share.
>
> To meet their responsibility, jurors must decide the facts and apply the law impartially.[7]

This book's attempt to translate the law's tools and traditions into ways in which the citizen can more effectively engage with public issues might be seen as simply a general plea for people to be more responsible about their civic duty. Hopefully, however, it is more than that. By gaining a better grasp of how people in the legal system go about their work in understanding and resolving difficult questions, each of us can become better equipped to perform our task as citizens. Just as a lawyer commits to serious, focused actions when taking on a case, so can each of us, when trying to understand and form an opinion on a public issue, be more focused on the task, take an organized approach, find reliable information, and keep an open mind.

Another way to look at this responsibility is to imagine that we each could afford to hire a lawyer who would know us and our interests and values well, and who would do the work for us in investigating and analyzing public issues and recommending conclusions to us. We would want that lawyer to be committed to serving us, and to be well-versed in the law's methods so that he or she could apply all of the tools and traditions discussed here. The advice we would receive from that competent, diligent, and responsible lawyer would be extremely helpful in our preparation to participate in discussion of issues and to act on our opinions through voting and other involvement in public affairs.

We would want our lawyer to know how to define the issues, separate facts from standards and evaluations, gather the facts, and employ any or all of the other tools and traditions of the law as needed. Her exercise of her professional responsibility through application of those methods would help us to understand public issues, just as the application of those methods by lawyers, judges, and jurors helps them to understand legal issues.

Obviously, very few of us could afford to hire lawyers for that kind of ongoing advice. Also, by doing so, we would be distancing ourselves from public discourse on the issues and, in a sense, delegating a big part of our civic duty to others. As earlier mentioned, there is a big difference between, on the one hand, dividing labor and getting some expert assistance with our civic homework and, on the other hand, delegating the whole task to someone else.

If we cannot and should not have a lawyer do this work for us, but the tools lawyers use can be helpful as suggested here, the message is clear: We each must act essentially as our own lawyer for this purpose. If we develop and express our opinions by applying the tools and traditions the legal system uses to reach conclusions—if we think more like lawyers—we can better fulfill the civic responsibility that modern democracy requires.

Appendix: Reviewing the Guidance

As an aid to reviewing the guidance presented in chapter 7, each section of that chapter is listed below. Key statements are excerpted (with page number references) to summarize and highlight some of the main points of each section.

A. Focusing on the Task

"Just as individuals working in the law need to understand each problem or question on which they work, so too should the ordinary citizen try to develop and maintain clear focus as she addresses public issues" (104).

1. Defining the Issue

"The citizen can develop a clearer sense of what is under discussion and more readily discern what portions of the flood [of information] are worth his attention" (107).

"Having reached your conclusion as to what the issue is, you also should be positioned to realize that other people may continue to define it differently, emphasizing other considerations" (107).

2. Separating Facts from Standards and Evaluations

"The challenge for the citizen is to keep the distinction in mind whenever public issues are under discussion: What facts are being asserted? What standards—whether legal rules, cultural preferences, or moral values—are being asserted? What outcomes are being urged through suggested application of standards to the facts?" (111).

"Recognizing that public debate has these three fundamental aspects can help reduce the individual's confusion and combat the tendency to conclude that public issues are just too complicated to deal with at all" (111).

B. Taking an Organized Approach

"Amid the press of other commitments, finding time and energy to learn about and understand the issues is challenging... At least two of the law's traditions may help bridge the gap and enable the citizen to be at least somewhat more organized in addressing the issues" (112).

1. Respecting Procedure

"Step-by-step development of information, evaluations, and conclusions through required legal processes emphasizes the importance of trying to methodically gather the facts, argue the issues, consider opposing views, and otherwise emulate the legal system's approach to decisionmaking. Even very small steps the citizen can take along these lines can help him to better understand the issues and arrive at his own conclusions" (113).

"Additionally, appreciation of the importance of procedural requirements can guide the citizen to better understanding of the substance of some specific public controversies" (113).

2. Taking Time

"We each do not have to have opinions on everything, and for the issues we do choose to concentrate on, we can be selective in the information sources we rely on. We can distinguish information sources which provide serious, useful information on the issues from those which provide content of a more simply entertaining nature" (115).

"We should neither rush to hasty conclusions nor should we dawdle and passively wait for information to come our way randomly to gradually nudge us in one direction or another. Instead, we can do as lawyers do and actively investigate selected issues to consciously build our positions" (117).

C. Finding Reliable Information

"The difficulty of knowing what and whom to believe... capsulizes many aspects of the challenges the responsible citizen faces. Fortunately, many of the law's tools and traditions are designed to help us overcome that difficulty and instead find reliable information. These methods can be adapted to assist the citizen in gathering the facts, recognizing incomplete facts, dividing labor, using expertise, and identifying bias" (118).

1. Gathering the Facts

"The citizen presumably has the capability to seek out helpful information, as well as to sift carefully through uninvited information that happens to come his way. In doing so, he can more effectively select and weigh facts, and distinguish proven information from unsupported allegations, if he keeps in mind certain of the law's tools. He may be aided, for example, by the law's approach to direct versus circumstantial evidence, hearsay, cross-examination, the standard of proof, and the burden of proof" (119).

2. Recognizing Incomplete Facts

"The absence of complete information ought not to dissuade the citizen from reaching a conclusion. At those times, she can choose to do what legal decisionmakers must do, which is to exercise her judgment to make the most sensible decision she can on the basis of the limited information at hand. She need not pretend that her conclusion is based on all the necessary information. Instead she should acknowledge, at least to herself, that more facts might later become known and that additional information might later lead her to a different conclusion. In the meantime, she can recognize that she is making her best guess, in a sense, as to what outcome seems most sound" (124).

3. Dividing Labor

"To the extent that our close associates seem to be well-informed, open-minded, and trustworthy, there is a lot we can learn from them with minimal effort. In relying on our circle of acquaintances in this way, we are in effect making them part of our own personal 'staff,' analogous to the types of assistants relied on by lawyers, judges, and legislators" (127).

"Beyond nearby sources of help, we can also each create a more extended, 'virtual' staff by choosing other sources of information and opinion we find worthy of ongoing reliance. In seeking such sources, we are looking for someone to do some of our homework for us, though not so much as to displace our ultimate responsibility to form our own opinions" (128).

4. Using Expertise

"How can the ordinary citizen approximate expert assistance for his own opinion formation? There is no easy answer. Perhaps in no other aspect of the citizen's task do the obstacles of complexity and the flood of information present more of a problem" (129).

"When the ordinary citizen encounters a purported expert on an issue of public concern...has it been shown that the so-called expert has pertinent scientific, technical, or other specialized knowledge? Is her information or opinion based on identified facts or data? Has she given any indication of the principles or methods she applied in reaching her conclusions?...Has the expert 'reliably applied' those principles or methods to the issue at hand? This last question would seem to require our evaluation of whether, after we have reflected on the expert's statements, they seem well-supported and fundamentally sensible. Answering this question is not something that can be done by applying any clear, bright line test" (130).

5. Identifying Bias

"The structured processes of the law aim at fostering objectivity, but outside of those processes it is difficult to expect major changes in the individual's awareness of his own blinders. What is easier for us to achieve is enhanced awareness of biases that others bring to public debates. Just as the juror has to be alert to indications that a witness's testimony is shaded by tangential considerations, so too should we be on the lookout for signs that people urging information or opinions on us may be influenced by dubious motives" (132).

D. Keeping an Open Mind

"Just as the legal system operates at its best when the people working within it are receptive to new and differing aspects of the problems before them, so too is the ordinary individual best prepared to be a responsible contributor to public discourse when she embraces that approach. The law's tools most directly designed to assist in this way focus on arguing and persuading, listening and negotiating, and making hard choices in gray areas" (134).

1. Arguing and Persuading

"Obfuscation through uncivil disputation is of no benefit to anyone, except a speaker or media outlet which seeks to draw more attention to itself. Citizens who hear such speakers should be prepared to distinguish argument addressed to the merits from argument addressed to peripheral considerations such as publicity for its own sake or the venting of personal hostility. The former type of argument can help us learn more about what is really at stake, while the latter does not" (136–137).

2. Listening and Negotiating

"Understanding of the content of legal issues, and of what is relevant to them, is vastly improved by careful attention to what is being said and even how it is said. These same benefits can accrue to the citizen who is a good and patient listener to facts and arguments on public issues" (137).

"Just as we assume that citizens have the capacity to listen, learn, and work through disagreements when they serve as jurors, we also should assume they can exercise this capability in other parts of their lives" (138).

3. Making Hard Choices in Gray Areas

"Perhaps the most important guidance the law can offer the citizen with regard to these choices is its express recognition that the answers to complex questions *do* require choices and that seldom is there an indisputably right answer" (138).

"If citizens similarly could remind themselves that their positions on public issues involve choices, and that other positions usually express different but not necessarily irrational or irresponsible choices, the quality and civility of public dialogue could be substantially enhanced. Disagreement on issues could be more readily accepted as normal and productive, just as it is in the law" (138–139).

"If citizens develop a stronger grasp of the hard choices public issues present, the issues will not magically become less complex and the flood of information will not be reduced. Nonetheless, the individual's competency in understanding the issues may be improved. Furthermore, her level of trust and respect for those with whom she disagrees may be raised. She may be more inclined to listen to them, learn from them, and develop her own views in a more informed manner" (142).

Notes

1 The Citizen's Task

1. Sean Wilentz, "History and Democracy," *Harvard Magazine*, September–October 2006, 37.
2. Robert W. Bennett, *Talking It Through: Puzzles of American Democracy* (Ithaca, NY: Cornell University Press, 2003), 34.
3. John Locke, *The Second Treatise of Government*, ed. Thomas Reardon (Indianapolis: Hackett, 1985), 56.
4. Alexander Hamilton, *The Federalist No. 71*, ed. E. H. Scott (Buffalo: William S. Hein & Co., 2002), 393.
5. Michael Schudson, *The Good Citizen: A History of American Civic Life* (Cambridge: Harvard University Press, 1998), 9. As used in this book, the word "citizen" refers generally to an inhabitant of the United States. This usage encompasses not only people who have the status of legal citizenship by virtue of birth or naturalization, but also others residing here legally or even otherwise.
6. California Secretary of State, *Voter Information Guide, California General Election*, November 4, 2008.
7. Whitney v. California, 274 U.S. 357, 375 (1927) (Brandeis, J., concurring).
8. Dr. Michael Hartoonian, Panel Discussion on Civics Education at the American Bar Association Symposium II: "Public Understanding of Perceptions of the American Justice System," *Albany Law Review* 62 (1999): 1451, 1456; see Jamin B. Raskin, "No Enclaves of Totalitarianism: The Triumph and Unrealized Promise of the Tinker Decision," *American University Law Review* 58 (2009): 1193, 1198, which states, "The citizen occupies the highest office in the land…"
9. Letter from Thomas Jefferson to Colonel Yancey (January 6, 1816), quoted in Martin H. Redish and Abbie Marie Mollen, "Understanding Post's and Meiklejohn's Mistakes: The Central Role of Adversary Democracy in the Theory of Free Expression," *Northwestern University Law Review* 103 (2009): 1303, 1305.
10. Harry G. Frankfurt, *On Bullshit* (Princeton: Princeton University Press, 2005), 63–64.
11. Kazuo Ishiguro, *The Remains of the Day* (New York: Random House, 1988), 194.

12. Yves R. Simon, *Philosophy of Democratic Government* (Chicago: University of Chicago Press, 1951), 78.
13. Algernon D. Black, *The Young Citizens: The Story of the Encampment for Citizenship* (New York: Ungar Publishing Company, 1962), 5–6.
14. Ted Gup, "So Much for the Information Age," *Chronicle of Higher Education*, April 11, 2008, A37.
15. Judith Barad, "Stewart and Socrates: Speaking Truth to Power," in *The Daily Show and Philosophy*, ed. Jason Holt (Hoboken: Wiley-Blackwell, 2007), 76.
16. Allan Bloom, *The Closing of the American Mind* (New York: Simon & Schuster, 1987), 246.
17. Black, *The Young Citizens*, 9.
18. San Antonio Independent School District v. Rodriguez, 411 U.S. 1, 113–15 (1973) (Marshall, J., dissenting).
19. Alex S. Jones, *Losing the News: The Future of the News That Feeds Democracy* (New York: Oxford University Press, 2009), 1.
20. A similar distinction has been suggested in an analysis of the Supreme Court's approach to the First Amendment protection of speech on "matters of public concern." The distinction first identifies a "normative conception of public concern," which is about "matters that are substantively relevant to the processes of democratic self-governance." This is contrasted with a "descriptive conception of public concern," which simply addresses "issues that happen actually to interest the 'public,'" even though the matters may "seem trivial and irrelevant to democratic self-governance." Robert C. Post, "The Constitutional Concept of Public Discourse: Outrageous Opinion, Democratic Deliberation, and *Hustler Magazine v. Falwell*," *Harvard Law Review* 103 (1990): 667–674.
21. Morris P. Fiorina et al., *The New American Democracy*, 6th ed. (Upper Saddle River: Pearson, 2009), 9–11. See Andrew Rehfeld, "Representation Rethought: On Trustees, Delegates, and Gyroscopes in the Study of Political Representation and Democracy," *American Political Science Review* 103 (2) (2009): 214–215, observing that the relation between citizens and their representatives in a democracy is commonly "framed by the terms 'trustees' and 'delegates,' denoting whether political representatives—in their capacities as lawmakers—act as they believe is best for the nation versus acting as their electoral constituents desire."
22. For example, see Rehfeld, "Representation Rethought," 221–223, arguing that "the terms 'trustee' and 'delegate' were labels imposed on top of a more complicated set of distinctions," resulting in "eight possible permutations" rather than just two ideal types of representatives.
23. Bennett, *Talking It Through*, 38–40.
24. Kay Lehman Schlozman, Sidney Verba, and Henry E. Brady, *The Unheavenly Chorus: Unequal Political Voice and the Broken Promise of American Democracy* (Princeton: Princeton University Press, 2012), 5–6.
25. Ibid., 7.

26. Andrea Louise Campbell, "America the *Politically* Unequal," *Harvard Magazine*, September–October 2012, 22–24.

2 The Citizen's Obstacles

1. Leo Tolstoy, *War and Peace*, trans. Ann Dunnigan (New York: Penguin, 2007), 1126.
2. Alexis de Tocqueville, *Democracy in America*, trans. Henry Reeve (London: Oxford University Press, 1961), 124, quoted in Robert D. Putnam, *Bowling Alone: The Collapse and Revival of American Community* (New York: Simon & Schuster, 2000), 337.
3. Mike Cassidy, "Democracy 2.0," *San Jose Mercury News*, May 19, 2009, 1C.
4. An optimistic view is presented in Caroline J. Tolbert and R. McNeal, "Unraveling the Effects of the Internet on Political Participation," *Political Research Quarterly* 56 (2003): 175. A more skeptical perspective can be found in David H. Weaver, "What Voters Learn from Media," *Annals of the American Academy of Political and Social Science* 546 (1996): 44, which states, "Because political interest, voting, and learning from the media reinforce each other over time, it is difficult to tell whether additional exposure to media results in increased interest and intention to vote, or whether the opposite is true."
5. Jason Gainous and Kevin M. Wagner, *Rebooting American Politics: The Internet Revolution* (Lanham, MD: Rowman & Littlefield, 2011), 6.
6. Ted Gup, "So Much for the Information Age," *Chronicle of Higher Education*, April 11, 2008, A37.
7. Gainous and Wagner, *Rebooting American Politics*, 27.
8. Jack Citrin, "Political Culture," in *Understanding America: The Anatomy of an Exceptional Nation*, ed. Peter H. Schuck and James Q. Wilson (New York: PublicAffairs, 2008), 177.
9. Michael Schudson, *The Good Citizen: A History of American Civic Life* (Cambridge, MA: Harvard University Press, 1998), 189.
10. Varieties of difficult public issues are often listed by journalists, scholars, and political observers, as in the following statement: "Our challenges aren't becoming any easier. The state budget, global warming, health care reform, wars in Iraq and Afghanistan, an economy in tatters, a national reputation tarnished. It's natural to wonder who's going to grapple with this stuff": Mike Cassidy, "Democracy 2.0," *San Jose Mercury News*, May 19, 2009, 1C. See Jason Zinser, "The Good, the Bad, and the Daily Show," in *The Daily Show and Philosophy*, ed. Jason Holt (Hoboken, NJ: Wiley-Blackwell, 2007), 52, referring to "the great debates of our time (for example, abortion, euthanasia, the war in Iraq, and stem cell research, to name a few)"; David S. Broder, *Democracy Derailed: Initiative Campaigns and the Power of Money* (New York: Mariner Books, 2000), 3–11, discussing ballot initiatives on controversial issues, including affirmative action, decriminalization of hard drugs,

medical marijuana, campaign spending, casino gambling, abortion, animal rights, and property taxes; Patrick J. Buchanan, op-ed., "Is America Coming Apart?" *San Jose Mercury News*, September 13, 2009, A19, which observes, "Consider but a few issues on which Americans have lately been bitterly divided: school prayer, the Ten Commandments, evolution, the death penalty, abortion, homosexuality, assisted suicide, affirmative action, busing, the Confederate battle flag, the Duke rape case, Terri Schiavo, Iraq, amnesty, torture."; and Nathaniel Persily, Jack Citrin, and Patrick J. Egan, eds., *Public Opinion and Constitutional Controversy* (New York: Oxford University Press, 2008), 3, noting "constitutional controversies" in the Supreme Court raising "highly emotional issues," such as "racial integration [,] abortion, school prayer [,] gay rights, flag burning or the right to die."

11. "The public's general awareness [of climate change] does not, however, reflect widespread accurate knowledge of particular controversies related to global warming...Americans are also uninformed about the specific dynamics of climate change...Despite considerable recent media coverage of the relationship between global warming and natural disasters, the public's beliefs are not in accord with those of the scientific community." Deborah L. Rhode and Lee D. Ross, "Environmental Values and Behaviors: Strategies to Encourage Public Support for Initiatives to Combat Global Warming," *Virginia Environmental Law Journal* 27 (2008): 163.
12. Mike Antonucci, "Our Fractured Discourse," *San Jose Mercury News*, July 11, 2004, 1P. For a study of the impact of major Supreme Court decisions on public opinion concerning controversial and complex public issues, see Persily et al., eds., *Public Opinion and Constitutional Controversy.*
13. Robert B. Cialdini, *Influence: Science and Practice*, 3rd ed. (Mundelein, IL: Writers of the Roundtable Press, 1993), 6. See George Lakoff, *Don't Think of an Elephant: Know Your Values and Frame the Debate* (White River Junction, VT: Chelsea Green, 2005), arguing that cognitive science and linguistics explain the influential, divergent metaphors, or "frames," underlying competing views on many issues as between US conservatives and progressives.
14. Jesse Kornbluth, "Whole Earth Discipline: An Ecopragmatist Manifesto," October 22, 2009, quoting Stewart Brand, http://www.headbutler.com/print/books/non-fiction/whole-earth-discipline-ecopragmatist (site discontinued).
15. Gainous and Wagner, *Rebooting American Politics*, 104.
16. Citrin, "Political Culture," 176.
17. Cialdini, *Influence: Science and Practice*, 240.
18. Christine Barbour and Gerald C. Wright, *Keeping the Republic: Power and Citizenship in American Politics*, 4th ed. (Washington, DC: CQ Press, 2009), 519.
19. A less sanguine perspective is possible because, although polls indicate that as many as 40 percent of American voters identify themselves as

independent, research suggests that for some people this status may reflect apathy, procrastination, or ambivalence more than open-mindedness and self-determination. Lauren F. Friedman, "Swing: Think Independent Voters Are Honorable Upholders of Democracy? Not So Fast," *Psychology Today*, September–October 2012, 9.

20. Zinser, "The Good, the Bad, and the Daily Show," 52.
21. Jacob Weisberg, *The Bush Tragedy* (New York: Random House, 2008), 106.
22. Lauryn Axelrod, *TV-Proof Your Kids* (New York: Birch Lane Press, 1997), 172. See Howard Kurtz, *Reality Show* (New York: Free Press, 2007), 36, which states, "The debate...was between 'back fence' stories—the kind that the neighbors would gossip about—and 'civics lesson' stories, which tended to involve government and diplomacy. Sometimes civics just lost out."); and Putnam, *Bowling Alone*, 217, which observes, "Although modern media offer both information and entertainment—indeed, they increasingly blur the line between the two—it is important from the point of view of civic engagement to treat the two somewhat separately."
23. Al Gore, *The Assault on Reason* (New York: Penguin, 2007), 17. Some observers assert that the television medium is inherently biased toward entertainment, rather than informative rational discourse, even in the presentation of news and discussion of important social and political issues. See Neil Postman, *Amusing Ourselves to Death: Public Discourse in the Age of Show Business* (New York: Penguin, 1985), 80, suggesting that "television speaks in only one persistent voice—the voice of entertainment."
24. Keith Melville, John Dedrick, and Taylor Willingham, "National Issues Forums: A Network of Communities Promoting Public Deliberation," in *The Deliberative Democracy Handbook: Strategies for Effective Civic Engagement in the 21st Century*, John Gastil and Peter Levine, eds. (Hoboken, NJ: Jossey-Bass, 2005), 37–42.
25. Axelrod, *TV-Proof Your Kids*, 169.
26. Gore, *Assault on Reason*, 6. There is disagreement, however, about the continuing prominence of television. Cf. Robert L. Lineberry, George C. Edwards, and Martin P. Wattenberg, *Government in America: People, Politics, and Policy*, 6th ed. (Upper Saddle River, NJ: Pearson, 1994), 206, which declares, "Unfortunately, today's generation of young adults is significantly less likely to watch television news than their elders."; and Alex S. Jones, *Losing the News: The Future of the News That Feeds Democracy* (New York: Oxford University Press, 2009), 3–4, which contends, "It is the nation's newspapers that provide the vast majority of iron core news...While people may *think* they get their news from television or the Web, when it comes to this kind of news, it is almost always newspapers that have done the actual reporting."
27. Axelrod, *TV-Proof Your Kids*, 191. "During the 1990s,...the media landscape suddenly included such alternatives as political talk radio,

competitive cable news networks, and numerous applications of the Internet, along with the convergence of multiple media via the personal computer. This fragmentation of the media, and the twenty-four -hour news cycle that accompanied it, have brought about the most massive change in journalism since the arrival of television." S. Robert Lichter, "The Media," in *Understanding America: The Anatomy of an Exceptional Nation*, ed. Peter H. Schuck and James Q. Wilson (New York: Public Affairs, 2008), 213.

28. Jeff Brazil, "Can Newspapers and Journalism Survive the Digital Age?" *Santa Clara Magazine*, Spring 2011, 20, 25.
29. Anne Colby, Elizabeth Beaumont, Thomas Ehrlich, and Josh Corngold, *Educating for Democracy: Preparing Undergraduates for Responsible Political Engagement* (Hoboken, NJ: Jossey-Bass, 2007), 48.
30. Antonucci, "Our Fractured Discourse," 1P. For a perspective on the sources of these changes in the media, see Lichter, "The Media," in *Understanding America*, 196, which states: "Beginning in the late 1960s and 1970s, many reporters seized the opportunity to act as the nation's teacher as well as its conscience. Professionally, this development dealt a heavy blow to the old ideals of detachment and neutrality. News analysis, context, and interpretation gained a new cachet. The new breed viewed 'objectivity' as problematic at best, and a dangerous illusion at worst. It was gradually superseded by the ideal of 'fairness,' an inherently more subjective standard."
31. Jim Rutenberg, "State of Campaign Changes If You Flip Cable Channels," *San Jose Mercury News*, November 2, 2008, 20A.
32. Kurtz, *Reality Show*, 361.
33. Gainous and Wagner, *Rebooting American Politics*, 104.
34. Elizabeth Gehrman, "'Likemindedness' Can Be Stulfifying," *Harvard Gazette Online*, September 25, 2008, http://news.harvard.edu/gazette/story/2008/09%e2%80%98likemindedness%e2%80%99-can-be-stultifying (site discontinued), describing Professor Cass Sunstein's presentation of Harvard Law School's Fourth Annual Constitution Day Lecture, September 7, 2008.
35. Gainous and Wagner, *Rebooting American Politics*, 105.
36. Antonucci, "Our Fractured Discourse," 1P.
37. Samantha Young, "Prop. 87 Campaign is Notable for Expense, Fact-Twisting," *San Jose Mercury News*, October 26, 2006, 5B, which further elaborates, "'What is a voter to believe?' said Brooks Jackson, director of the Annenberg Political Fact Check, a non-partisan, non-profit group...that studied the advertising related to [a major ballot proposition]. 'Both sides are saying contradictory things. Both sides are being misleading and overselling.'" See Rhode and Ross, "Environmental Values and Behaviors," 164, which notes, "In a 2005 Yale University School of Forestry and Environmental Studies poll, a majority of respondents (53%) agreed with the statement that 'there is so much information and disagreement in the media that I don't know who to

believe about what is best for the environment.'" In the unusual situations in which it is found that the facts underlying a journalist's work are clearly false, public confidence is further damaged. In the wake of one such scandal, a newspaper editorial observed: "People are struggling in this Internet age to find reliable sources of information. Many turn to mainstream media; others seek out activists who base their opinion on facts rather than shaping facts to match preconceived opinion. When those who claim to be truth-tellers lie, trust in the entire journalistic fabric crumbles." Editorial, "Daisey Damage was Done Long before Apology," *San Jose Mercury News*, March 28, 2012, A10, concerning a false report presented on National Public Radio by performer Mike Daisey regarding working conditions in an Apple supplier's manufacturing plant in China.

38. This statement has been attributed to James R. Schlesinger, US Secretary of Defense from 1973 to 1975. Reportedly the American financier Bernard M. Baruch earlier said, "Every man has a right to his own opinion, but no man has a right to be wrong in his facts," and US Senator Daniel Patrick Moynihan also later is quoted with a similar statement. See www.barrypopik.com, accessed February 15, 2013.

39. Buchanan, "Is America Coming Apart?" A19. See Al Franken, *Lies and the Lying Liars Who Tell Them* (New York: Plume, 2003), 9, quoting Ann Coulter, *Slander: Liberal Lies about the American Right* (New York: Three Rivers Press, 2002), 10. Coulter also said, "Instead of actual debate about ideas and issues with real consequences, the country is trapped in a political discourse that increasingly resembles professional wrestling." A similar observation appears in W. Lance Bennett, "Changing Citizenship in the Digital Age," in *Civic Life Online: Learning How Digital Media Can Engage Youth* (Cambridge, MA: MIT Press, 2008), 1, which asserts, "Young people see the media filled with inauthentic performances from officials who are staged by professional communication managers."

40. Eric Burns, "Media Lend Credence to Patently False Information," *San Jose Mercury News*, August 13, 2009, A10. See James Stewart, *Tangled Webs: How False Statements are Undermining America from Martha Stewart to Bernie Madoff* (New York: Penguin, 2011), 441, discussing false statements by celebrities and public officials, and stating, "We appear to be on the brink of becoming a society where perjury is the norm."

41. Harry Frankfurt, *On Bullshit* (Princeton: Princeton University Press, 2005), 63. See David Britt, "Internet Introspection," *Harvard Magazine*, May–June 2009, 5 (commenting on media trends "away from emphasis on consensus facts [remember them?]" and asserting that "Internet technology...abandons altogether the pretense of facts."); and Jones, *Losing the News*, 55, which comments, "The culture of Web journalism, which is rapidly becoming the delivery system of choice for younger audiences, generally does not support news in depth or investigative journalism."

42. Leonard Pitts Jr., "'Birthers' Movement: How Far Removed from the Real World?" *San Jose Mercury News*, August 2, 2009, A13. "Two years into the Obama administration, so-called birthers continue to argue that Obama isn't a natural-born citizen...Birth records in Hawaii haven't dissuaded them." "House Leader Cantor believes Obama is a U.S. Citizen," http://news.yahoo.com/s/ap/20110123/ap_on_re_us/us_cantor_birthers (site discontinued).
43. "For example, a kind of 'science by press release' has repeatedly produced public panics and inflated reports of health risks...Many people still accept such spurious statistics as valid, even though they have been repeatedly refuted. Of course, accusations are big news; refutations aren't. But they also stay in circulation because they are put forward by groups that aim to promote the public interest by making all Americans aware of the problems that they perceive. For 'public interest groups' on the left and (less frequently) the right, making news is the first step toward creating conventional wisdom." Lichter, "The Media," 201.
44. Paul Krugman, "Health Reform Opponents Tap into Deep Well of Anger," *San Jose Mercury News*, August 9, 2009, A13. Cf. Broder, *Democracy Derailed*, 230, stating: "And the breach of trust cuts both ways: people in government are as skeptical of the citizenry as the citizens are of government. [A 1998] Pew Research Center Study...concluded that 'public distrust of government is paralleled by a belief among members of Congress, presidential appointees, and senior civil servants that the American public is too ill-informed to make wise decisions about important issues.'"
45. Putnam, *Bowling Alone*, 27. Commenting on *Bowling Alone*, one scholar summarized as follows: "What sustains viable democratic politics is the underlying strength of social bonds that people can draw on to propel them into and sustain them in civic affairs. Voluntary organizational involvement, from bowling leagues to the PTA, are the signs of community health. They provide the social resources and the civic training that citizens need to make democracy tick"; Schudson, *The Good Citizen*, 296. Cf. Bob Herbert, op-ed, "The Public Thinker," *New York Times*, February 14, 2005, A21, which opines, "Americans not only seem to be doing less serious thinking lately, they seem to have less and less tolerance for those who spend their time wrestling with important and complex matters."
46. Citrin, "Political Culture," 178, which observes, "The empirical status of Putnam's claims about the United States remains unsettled."
47. Putnam, *Bowling Alone*, 189.
48. Allan Bloom, *The Closing of the American Mind* (New York: Simon & Schuster, 1987), 77.
49. Putnam, *Bowling Alone*, 190.
50. Gainous and Wagner, *Rebooting American Politics*, 41.
51. John Gastil et al., "A Nation that (Sometimes) Likes to Talk: A Brief History of Public Deliberation in the United States," in *The Deliberative*

Democracy Handbook, 3, 9. See Bennett, "Changing Citizenship in the Digital Age," 1, 9, exploring "how to use the media that are now so richly developed for social and entertainment purposes to build civic and political communities" and "to encourage the creative involvement of young people in politics"; and Eric Klinenberg, "One's A Crowd," *New York Times*, February 4, 2012, discussing increased numbers of persons living alone in many countries and noting, "New communications technologies make living alone a social experience...The person alone at home can digitally navigate through a world of people, information, and ideas."

52. Jon Meacham, "A New Magazine for a Changing World," May 25, 2009, 9 (quoting President Barack Obama). Some scholars have offered a similarly positive perspective, as in the following statement: "The public has the capacity to deal with complex public issues; the difficulty is that it normally lacks an institutional context that will effectively motivate it to do so...Opinion change does not seem to correlate with any of the standard sociodemographic factors, including education. Deliberation is not just for the more educated or more privileged; it is democratic in its potential for everybody"; Bruce Ackerman and James S. Fishkin, *Deliberation Day* (New Haven, CT: Yale University Press, 2004), 4, 59.

3 Conventional Guidance

1. Anne Colby, Elizabeth Beaumont, Thomas Ehrlich, and Josh Corngold, *Educating for Democracy: Preparing Undergraduates for Responsible Political Engagement* (Hoboken, NJ: Jossey-Bass, 2007), 45, 49. The Political Engagement Project is more fully explained at "www.aascu.org /programs/adp/engagement.htm".
2. Colby et al., *Educating for Democracy*, 295, 297.
3. See Arthur Bestor, "The Role of the Common Schools," in *Crucial Issues in Education*, ed. Henry Ehlers and Gordon C. Lee (New York: Holt, 1959), 267, describing the "five great areas" of twentieth-century schooling, including the study of history and its "political and constitutional aspects sometimes called, in public school jargon, 'civics.'"
4. Benjamin R. Barber, *Strong Democracy: Participatory Politics for a New Age* (Berkeley: University of California Press, 1984), 234.
5. W. Lance Bennett, "Changing Citizenship in the Digital Age," in *Civic Life Online: Learning How Digital Media Can Engage Youth*, ed. W. Lance Bennett (Cambridge, MA: MIT Press, 2008), 16–17.
6. Charles N. Quigley, "Civics Education: Recent History, Current Status, and the Future," *Albany Law Review* 62 (1999): 1426–1427.
7. Colby et al., *Educating for Democracy*, 5.
8. Bennett, "Changing Citizenship in the Digital Age," 7. See www .ourcourts.org, noting that "civics education is being marginalized in our country."; and www.rockthevote.com/about/democracy-class .html, observing that "over the past 30 years, civics education has been

systematically cut from public schools. Opportunities to learn about politics and government are rare, and programs to register [as voters] newly eligible high school students are not widespread."

9. Anne Colby, Thomas Ehrlich, Elizabeth Beaumont, and Jason Stephens, *Educating Citizens: Preparing America's Undergraduates for Lives of Moral and Civic Responsibility* (Hoboken, NJ: Jossey-Bass, 2003), 32.
10. Kevin F. Ryan, "Lost in the Cave: Citizenship and the Decline of Public Education," *Vermont Bar Journal* 29 (2004): 9–10. Ryan also states that recent emphasis on standardized testing in English and mathematics contributes to neglect of civics education.
11. Robert L. Lineberry, George C. Edwards, and Martin P. Wattenberg, *Government in America: People, Politics and Policy*, 6th ed. (Upper Saddle River, NJ: Pearson, 1994): 204–206. The Political Engagement Project also recognizes that there are conflicting research conclusions as to whether civics courses contribute significantly to political knowledge and sufficient understanding for responsible political participation. Colby et al., *Educating for Democracy*, 45.
12. Mitch Smith, "Massachusetts System to Track Civic Engagement," accessed March 7, 2012, http://www.insidehighered.com/news/2012/03/07/massachusetts-system-track-civic-engagement, quoting Carol Geary Schneider, president of the Association of American Colleges and Universities.
13. Bennett, "Changing Citizenship in the Digital Age," 17.
14. "We the People…The Citizen and the Constitution," Center for Civic Education, accessed October 25, 2009, http://www.civiced.org/index.php?page=we_the_people_the_citizen_and_the_constitution.
15. Quigley, "Civics Education," 1441. See "About the Foundation," Close Up Foundation Online, accessed October 25, 2009, http://www.closeup.org/aboutcuf.
16. David H. Souter, "Remarks on Civic Education at the American Bar Association Opening Assembly," August 1, 2009, speech transcript, http://www.americanbar.org/content/dam/aba/images/public_education/justicesouterremarksoncviceducationatabaannualmeetingaugust_2009.pdf-8k-2011–06–29. The Obama Administration program is described in Sonal Shah and Robynn Sturm, "Strengthening Civic Participation," White House's Open Government Initiative, accessed June 11, 2009, www.whitehouse.gov/blog/Strengthening-Civic-Participation. The initiative's website explains, "Now we address what government can and should be doing to support civil society…in helping to educate and prepare the public to engage with critical public issues and play a more effective role in new, open public policymaking processes." Information about programs of the Office of Social Innovation and Civic Participation, part of the White House Domestic Policy Council, can be found at www.whitehouse.gov/administration/eop/sicp/.
17. The National Task Force on Civic Learning and Democratic Engagement, *A Crucible Moment: College Learning & Democracy's*

Future, (Washington, DC: Association of American Colleges and Universities, 2012), 31–33. Similar reports and recommendations of other organizations to address "the critical need to incorporate civic education in university-wide curricula" are discussed in Angelique Davis and Brian Mello, "Preaching to the Apathetic and Uninterested: Teaching Civic Engagement to Freshmen and Non-Majors," *Journal for Civic Commitment* 18 (2012): 3.

18. *A Crucible Moment*, 69.
19. Davis and Mello, "Preaching to the Apathetic and Uninterested," 2. Another recent report and set of policy recommendations entitled "Guardian of Democracy: The Civic Mission of Schools" was issued in 2012 by the Campaign for the Civic Mission of Schools in partnership with the Annenberg Institute for Civics at the University of Pennsylvania and other organizations. The report can be found at www.civicmissionofschools.org.
20. See Quigley, "Civics Education," 1429–1430.
21. See "Our Mission," Pennsylvania Coalition for Representative Democracy, accessed October 24, 2009, http://www.penncord.org/mission; New Hampshire Supreme Court Society, accessed October 25, 2009, http://www.nhsupremecourtsociety.org, which emphasizes the importance of an independent judiciary; Constitutional Rights Foundation, accessed February 18, 2013, www.crf-usa.org; Center for Civic Education, accessed February 18, 2013, www.civiced.org; and American Bar Association, Division for Public Education, "Who We Are, What We Do," accessed February 18, 2013, http://www.abanet.org/publiced/PED_Brochure(Final).pdf, promoting "active participation in civic life" and advocating "for effective public legal education and civic learning in our schools." Evaluations of various alternative approaches to civic education can be found at the website of Tufts University's Center for Information and Research on Civic Learning and Engagement, accessed February 18, 2013, http://www.civicyouth.org.
22. "What is iCivics," iCivics, accessed February 18, 2013, www.icivics.org. See Mark Hansen, "Flunking Civics: Why America's Kids Know So Little," *American Bar Association Journal* (May 2011): 32; Fred Hiatt, Editorial, "Justice Souter's 'Safe Place,'" *Washington Post*, May 25, 2009, A21, discussing Justice David Souter's participation in Our Courts events and his lamenting "how many Americans today do not grow up understanding even the most basic truths about U.S. democracy."); and AnnMarie Timmins, "Civics Instruction Souter's Priority," *Concord Monitor* (Concord, NH), August 3, 2009, www.concordmonitor.com, which reports, "New Hampshire is one of a few states at work on reintroducing civics education to the curriculum from kindergarten to grade 12."
23. See Jon M. Ericson, James J. Murphy, and Raymond Bud Zeuschner, *The Debater's Guide* (Carbondale: Southern Illinois University Press, 1987), 3, noting that debate education strengthens abilities "to

collect and organize ideas," "to evaluate evidence," and "to see logical connections."

24. Chad R. Derum, "Practicing to Practice: Scholastic Debate as Law-Related Education," *Utah Bar Journal* 20 (2007): 34–35.
25. Ibid., 32.
26. Ibid., 35.
27. The National Forensics League, a large debate society, boasts over 1 million members. "About the NFL," National Forensics League, accessed February 18, 2013, http://www.nationalforensicleague.org/aspx/nav.aspx?navid=37&pnavid=0. The National Association of Urban Debate Leagues is a "nonprofit network of policy debate teams made up mainly of minority students from urban high schools in 24 large cities." Yvonne Villarreal, "No Argument: High School Debate Is Popular Once Again," *Los Angeles Times*, January 20, 2009. Cf. Derum, "Practicing to Practice," 32. Regarding high school programs in Utah, Derum states, "Programs that once flourished are now struggling to survive—the victims of evolving standards for academic achievement and slim budgets that strain resources for extracurricular activities like debate."
28. Michael Shermer, *Why People Believe Weird Things: Pseudoscience, Superstition, and Other Confusions of Our Time* (New York: Holt, 1997), 19. "The scientific method involves making qualitative observations, forming hypotheses and performing experiments to test the hypothesis." Lisa M. Agrimonti, "The Limitations of Daubert and Its Misapplication to Quasi-Scientific Experts," *Washburn Law Journal* 35 (1995): 143.
29. Timothy Ferris, *The Science of Liberty: Democracy, Reason, and the Laws of Nature* (New York: Harper, 2010), 13.
30. As discussed earlier in chapter 2, note 26, there is disagreement about which medium actually is the dominant source of news.
31. "National USC Annenberg-Los Angeles Times Poll Shows Local Television News Rules with Voters," USC Annenberg School for Communication and Journalism, accessed August 24, 2012, http://annenberg.usc.edu/News%20and%20Events/News/120824LATimesPoll.aspx.
32. Cox Broadcasting Corp. v. Cohn, 420 U.S. 469, 492 (1974).
33. David H. Weaver, "What Voters Learn from Media," *Annals of the American Academy of Political and Social Science* 546 (1996): 37.
34. "Think Like a Journalist," News Trust, accessed February 18, 2013, http://newstrust.net/guides.
35. Christine Barbour and Gerald C. Wright, *Keeping the Republic: Power and Citizenship in American Politics*, 4th ed. (Washington, DC: CQ Press, 2009), 24–25. The text also offers suggestions on "How to Be a Savvy Web Surfer." Ibid., 196–197.
36. A description of the processes of direct lawmaking, and criticisms of how they have evolved, are presented in David S. Broder, *Democracy*

Derailed: Initiative Campaigns and the Power of Money (New York: Mariner Books, 2000). See Juliet Williams, "State's Initiative System Hits 100-Year Milestone: Experiment in Direct Democracy Has Been Hijacked, Critics Say," *San Jose Mercury News*, October 10, 2011, B4, which claims, "A process that was intended to curb the influence of special interests has evolved into a tool for corporations and wealthy individuals to enact changes they desire... As ubiquitous as ballot measure campaigns seem to be, of the 1,657 initiatives titled and summarized for circulation from 1911 to 2010, just 348—or 21 percent—made the ballot. Of those, voters approved 116, or one-third."

37. "Easy Voter Guide," League of Women Voters of California, http://lwvc.convio.net/site/PageServer?pagename=easyvoter_guide_propositions (site discontinued). Examples of other branches' offerings can be found at League of Women Voters of Michigan, http://www.lwvmi.org/voterinfo.html; League of Women Voters of Texas, "Voters Guide: 2010 Primary Election Edition," http://www.lwvtexas.org.; and League of Women Voters of Wisconsin, http://lwvwi.org.
38. "Pros and Cons: State Ballot Measures for California Election," League of Women Voters, accessed October 24, 2009, http://ca.lwv.org/lwvc/edfund/elections/2006nov/index.html.
39. "Easy Voter Guide for California Election", League of Women Voters, November 7, 2006, accessed October 24, 2009, http://ca.lwv.org/lwvc/edfund/elections/2006nov/index.html.
40. "How to Judge a Candidate," League of Women Voters, accessed February 18, 2013, www.smartvoter.org/voter/judgecan.html.
41. "Ballot Initiatives: May 2009 Special Election," Institute for Governmental Studies Library, accessed October 25, 2009, http://igs.berkeley.edu/library/hot_topics/2009/endorseMay2009.html.
42. TransparentDemocracy, accessed October 24, 2009, http://transparentdemocracy.org/, encouraging visitors to "see how people and organizations you trust recommend you vote."
43. Pros and Cons of Controversial Issues, accessed February 18, 2013, www.procon.org.
44. University of California, Berkeley School of Law, *Newsletter* (October 2008).
45. Official Massachusetts Information for Voters: The 2008 Ballot Questions 2, 6.
46. Bruce Ackerman and James S. Fishkin, *Deliberation Day* (New Haven, CT: Yale University Press, 2004), 162.
47. California Presidential Primary Election: February 5, 2008, Official Voter Information Guide, accessed October 26, 2009, http://february2008.sos.ca.gov/voterguide/.
48. 2008 Florida Voter Registration and Voting Guide, Florida Department of State, accessed February 18, 2013, http://election.dos.state.fl.us/publications/pdf/2007–2008/2008VoterRegisVoteGuide.pdf.
49. City of Los Altos, California, *Communique,* Fall 2007.

50. John Gastil et al., "A Nation that (Sometimes) Likes to Talk: A Brief History of Public Deliberation in the United States," in *The Deliberative Democracy Handbook: Strategies for Effective Civic Engagement in the 21st Century*, ed. John Gastil and Peter Levine (Hoboken, NJ: Jossey-Bass, 2005), 3, 9. See Amartya Sen, *The Idea of Justice* (Cambridge, MA: Harvard University Press, 2009), 324. He writes: "In contemporary political philosophy the view that democracy is best seen as 'government by discussion' has gained widespread support... The understanding of democracy has broadened vastly, so that democracy is no longer seen just in terms of the demands for *public balloting*, but much more capaciously, in terms of what John Rawls calls 'the exercise of public reason.'"
51. Chad Flanders, "Deliberative Dilemmas: A Critique of Deliberation Day from the Perspective of Election Law," *Journal of Law and Policy* 23 (2007): 147. See James S. Fishkin, *The Voice of the People: Public Opinion and Democracy* (New Haven, CT: Yale University Press, 1997), 4. Fishkin observes, "The public can best speak for itself when it can *gather together* in some way to hear the arguments on the various sides of an issue and then, after face-to-face discussion, come to a collective decision."
52. Colby et al., *Educating for Democracy*, 173. "The framers of the American Constitution attempted to create a deliberative democracy, that is, a system that combines accountability with a measure of reflection and reason-giving." Cass R. Sunstein, "On a Danger of Deliberative Democracy," *Daedalus* 120 (2002): 123.
53. Amy Gutmann and Dennis Thompson, *Democracy and Disagreement* (Cambridge, MA: Harvard University Press, 1996), 347–348.
54. Cass R. Sunstein, "Group Judgments: Statistical Means, Deliberation, and Information Markets," *New York University Law Review* 80 (2007): 963.
55. Sunstein, "On a Danger of Deliberative Democracy," 123–124.
56. Ackerman and Fishkin, *Deliberation Day*.
57. Fishkin, *The Voice of the People*, 40. Discussing "decision costs: the time and effort required to reach an agreement," Fishkin says, "In the real world, people cannot ignore decision costs. Indeed, calculations about the decision costs for voters, given the paltry benefits and voters' lack of influence on the process, provide the basis for... 'rational ignorance.'" See "Deliberation Day: A Two-Day Presidents' Holiday Every Second October," CitizenSovereignty.org, www.CitSov.org., stating: "Six decades of modern public opinion research has [*sic*] established the general public's ignorance of important factual background to major civic and political debates. This is perfectly understandable. Time spent on public affairs competes with the need for information on more personal matters, such as price and quality of a home or car, in which ignorance can have a direct cost. In contrast, no voter perceives a consequential price for voting ignorantly, since the outcome of a major election never hinges on a single ballot."

58. Ackerman and Fishkin, *Deliberation Day*, 175. These scholars' approach relies heavily on the "social capital" analysis advanced by Robert Putnam, as discussed earlier in chapter 2. They state, "The new holiday is precisely the sort of new initiative that promises to reverse the current decline in social capital accumulation" (p. 177). Fishkin, in *The Voice of the People*, also has explained: "Tocqueville's observations on civic life have stimulated a fertile new branch of modern social science, the study of 'social capital.' The dense network of civic associations Tocqueville discovered created patterns of behavior, norms for how people join together—how they can trust or rely on each other—that can, in themselves, be considered a resource or a form of 'capital.' Social capital... seems to facilitate the public connectedness of ordinary citizens" (p. 146).
59. Ackerman and Fishkin, *Deliberation Day*, 3. Two consecutive days would be designated, but an individual could only participate on one.
60. Ibid., 164.
61. Ibid.,150. Not all public deliberation exercises have this emphasis, as other scholars have noted: "To date, most public deliberation has had low stakes, especially in the United States. In some cases, there is no serious effort to change public policy to match the results of the public conversation. The goal of a meeting may be to build networks of citizens, to develop new ideas, to teach people skills and knowledge, to change attitudes, but not to influence government. In other cases, deliberation does have direct consequences for policy." Peter Levine, Archon Fung, and John Gastil, "Future Directions for Public Deliberation," in *The Deliberative Democracy Handbook*, 278.
62. Ackerman and Fishkin, *Deliberation Day*, 172.
63. Fishkin, *The Voice of the People.*
64. See CitizenSovereignty.org, accessed February 18, 2013, http://citsov.org/, advocating deliberative polling, and tracking recent uses of deliberative polls in various nations; "Reports," National Issues Forums, accessed February 18, 2013, http://www.nifi.org/reports/index.aspx, compiling reports on "forums held across the nation about a particular issue"; The Center for Deliberative Democracy, accessed February 18, 2013, http://cdd.stanford.edu/, creating and compiling reports on deliberative polls, and noting usage in various nations, including China; Will Oremus, "Dense Housing Can Win Support," *San Jose Mercury News*, March 30, 2008, discussing use of deliberative polling in San Mateo, California, to assist in development of local plan to address housing shortage; "Deliberative Poll about Unemployment and Job Creation in the Area of Kaposvar," Center for Deliberative Democracy, accessed February 18, 2013, http://cdd.stanford.edu/polls/hungary/2008/kaposvar-results-summary.pdf; Susan Jakes, "Dabbling in Democracy," *Time Magazine*, April 16, 2005, which reported, "[The Chinese poll's] format, from the way its participants are selected to the way questionnaires are worded, adheres closely to the rules of the 'Deliberative Poll,' an approach to public consultation

devised by James Fishkin, a professor at Stanford University"; and "Poll Results: Deliberative Poll," What's Next California, August 20, 2011, stating that "on June 24, 2011, a scientifically selected random sample of 412 registered voters from throughout the state participated in California's first ever statewide Deliberative Poll on governance reform, in Torrance, CA," accessed February 18, 2013, http://www.nextca.org.

65. Fishkin, *The Voice of the People*, 43.
66. "This new form of opinion polling first became a reality on national television in Britain on 8 May 1994." James S. Fishkin, "The Televised Deliberative Poll: An Experiment in Democracy," *Annals of the American Academy of Politics & Social Science* 132 (1996): 136.
67. Ibid., 162–164.
68. Fishkin, *The Voice of the People*, 205–209, 214–221. "We have conducted more than twenty Deliberative Polls—half in the United States and half abroad, in countries ranging from Britain and Denmark to Australia and Bulgaria." Ackerman and Fishkin, *Deliberation Day*, 45. See "Deliberation Day: A Two-Day Presidents' Holiday Every Second October," CitizenSovereignty.org, accessed February 18, 2013, www.CitSov.org. This website declares, "Over thirty-five deliberative poll experiments demonstrate that when ordinary people have the chance seriously to consider competing sides of an issue, they take the opportunity to become far more informed, to hear out spokespersons for different sides, and to change their minds on the basis of greater familiarity with arguments and evidence."
69. A critique of deliberation day can be found in Flanders "Deliberative Dilemmas," 154, suggesting that the advocates of deliberation day "miss the ways in which deliberation might be biased, unproductive, or incomplete," especially by structuring deliberation day in a way which "maintains the two-party system, and prevents serious challenges to it." For a rebuttal to such critiques, see Ackerman and Fishkin, *Deliberation Day*, 61–65. For brief discussion of the structure and effectiveness of other deliberative democracy methods, see ibid., 202–204, 233. More extensive discussion of alternative methods—including the National Issues Forum, consensus conferences, planning cells, citizens juries, online dialogues, town meetings, and study circles—can be found in *The Deliberative Democracy Handbook*. Similar information appears at "What We're All About," National Coalition for Dialogue and Deliberation, accessed February 18, 2013, http://ncdd.org/; "Our Vision," Everyday Democracy, accessed February 18, 2013, http://www.everyday-democracy.org/; and Public Agenda, accessed February 18, 2013, http://www.publicagenda.org/.
70. Keith Melville, John Dedrick, and Taylor Willingham, "National Issues Forums: A Network of Communities Promoting Public Deliberation," in *The Deliberative Democracy Handbook*, 37, 41.
71. *Merriam-Webster's Collegiate Dictionary*, 11th ed., 329, defines deliberation as "a discussion and consideration by a group of persons (as a jury

or legislature) of the reasons for and against a measure." and *Black's Law Dictionary*, 7th ed., 428, presents a broad definition not limited to communication within a group.

72. Robert E. Goodin, "Democratic Deliberation Within," in *Debating Deliberative Democracy*, ed. James S. Fishkin and Peter Laslett (Hoboken, NJ: Wiley-Blackwell, 2003), 54, 55, 71.
73. Fishkin, *The Voice of the People*, 20–21.
74. Ackerman and Fishkin, *Deliberation Day*, 173.
75. "One of the most appropriate and most practical defenses of deliberative democracy is one that views it as part of a wider and longer-term effort to enliven active democratic citizenship and to bolster a democratic culture that will sustain such citizenship." Mark Button et al., "What Can We Learn from the Practice of Deliberative Democracy," in *The Deliberative Democracy Handbook*, 31.
76. The History Channel, *Events That Shaped Our Lives*, Audio CD (Cedar Knolls, NJ: Radio Spirits, 2004), Disk 1, Track 8.
77. Natalie Portman, "10 Questions for Natalie Portman," *Time Magazine*, March 10, 2008, 4.
78. Tim Russert, "10 Questions for Tim Russert," *Time Magazine*, February 25, 2008, 4.
79. While discussing her involvement in an effort to encourage young people to vote, one young television actress acknowledged that it is easier for a celebrity to just encourage voting than it is to support a specific candidate and risk alienating fans. She said, "Why wouldn't you want to get involved? I'm not saying 'Hey, go vote for this person.' I'm just saying 'Hey, go vote.'" Cindy Clark, "Voter Registration Gets Celebrities' Endorsement," *USA Today*, August 5, 2008, 13B. See William J. Watkins, Jr., "Don't Rock the Vote," *Washington Times*, November 3, 2008, A16, criticizing organizations aimed at encouraging young people to register to vote and stating, "But for elections to serve [their] lofty purpose, the people must be informed... Today's mass voter drives stand this notion on its head. Because it is already so easy to register without the aid of Rock the Vote or bothervoting.org, one must wonder what sort of person the mass voter drives are reaching."
80. A study of the influence of celebrity endorsements of candidates can be found in David Jackson and Jesse Neal, "Celebrity Politics and Young Adults' Political Beliefs in the United Kingdom," paper presentation, Midwest Political Science Association, Chicago, IL, April 3, 2008, http://www.allacademic.com/meta/p266657_index.html. See Dan DeLuca, "Celebrities Step Up to Try to Swing Votes," *Philadelphia Inquirer*, October 4, 2008, A01, which reports, "Jersey rockers [Bruce Springsteen] aren't the only marquee musicmakers lining up to support presidential candidates. Everyone from the Puerto Rican reggaeton star Daddy Yankee... to the bluegrass legend Ralph Stanley... has spoken out."

4 THE LAW'S TOOLS AND TRADITIONS

1. Peter T. Wendel, *Deconstructing Legal Analysis: A 1L Primer* (Minneapolis: Wolters Kluwer, 2009), 29. Notwithstanding his own caveat, Wendel ventures to describe "thinking like a lawyer" in terms of the interaction of three conceptual levels, or "planes," of legal analysis of a case. Ibid., 29–33 (factual plane, rule plane, and public policy plane).
2. Anne-Marie Slaughter, "Thinking Like a Lawyer," speech transcript, University of Miami School of Law Class of 2006, May 14, 2006, http://www.law.miami.edu/graduation/AMslaughter_may2006.html.
3. In an analysis of whether judges' written opinions actually demonstrate the reasoning that has led to the decisions, a prominent legal scholar was quoted as "viewing [opinions] no longer as mirroring the process of deciding cases, but rather as trained lawyers' arguments made by the judges (after the decision has been reached), intended to make the decision seem plausible, legally decent, regally right, to make it seem, indeed, legally inevitable." Brian Z. Tamanaha, *Beyond the Formalist-Realist Divide: The Role of Politics in Judging* (Princeton: Princeton University Press, 2010), 234, quoting Karl Llewellyn, "Some Realism about Realism: Responding to Dean Pound," *Harvard Law Review* 44 (1931): 1238–1239.
4. "The [legal] profession honors, in tradition at least, the connection between the discipline of law and other sciences which relate to human nature...The discussion of cases themselves [in law schools] is in the liberal arts tradition of the examination of men, motives, and sometimes consequences." Edward H. Levi, *Point of View: Talks on Education* (Chicago: University of Chicago Press, 1969), 68.
5. Frederick Schauer, *Thinking Like a Lawyer: A New Introduction to Legal Reasoning* (Cambridge, MA: Harvard University Press, 2009), 211–212.
6. In a similar vein, one major aspect of the legal system, legal reasoning, has been described as "a unique method of dispute resolution. Like science, it follows prescribed rules and procedures, and strives to proceed rationally to a conclusion based on careful observation and thoughtful weighing of evidence. Like art, it is, at least in part, the product of discretionary choices that reflect the hopes, fears, and preferences of its practitioners." Brian L. Porto and Calvin C. Jillson, *The Craft of Legal Reasoning* (Boston: Houghton Mifflin, 1998), 19.
7. *Black's Law Dictionary*, 9th ed., 2009.
8. See chap. 2(A).
9. Richard M. Fischl and Jeremy Paul, *Getting to Maybe: How to Excel on Law School Exams* (Durham: Carolina Academic Press, 1999), 21. "In federal civil procedure, an issue is a single, certain, and material point arising out of the allegations and contentions of the parties; it is matter

affirmed on one side and denied on the other." 35A C. J. S. Federal Civil Procedure § 357, at 541 (1960). One commentator suggests use of a further term, "deep issue," to describe "the ultimate, concrete question that a court needs to answer to decide a point your way... The deep issue is the final question you pose when you can no longer usefully ask the follow-up question, 'And what does *that* turn on?'" Bryan A. Garner, *The Winning Brief: 100 Tips for Persuasive Briefing in Trial and Appellate Court*, 2nd ed. (New York: Oxford University Press, 2004), 56.

10. Rule 401 of the Federal Rules of Evidence, which govern proceedings in federal courts, defines "relevant evidence" as "evidence having any tendency to make the existence of any fact that is of consequence to the determination of the action more probable or less probable than it would be without the evidence." See Kenneth J. Vandevelde, *Thinking Like A Lawyer: An Introduction to Legal Reasoning* (Boulder, CO: Westview Press, 2011), 80, which states, "Evidence is admissible only if it is relevant, that is, it tends to prove or disprove a fact of consequence to the action."
11. The everyday difficulty of distinguishing fact from opinion is explored in Lauryn Axelrod, *TV-Proof Your Kids* (New York: Birch Lane Press, 1997), 178, as follows: "Most of us believe what we see and hear on the news to be true and accurate as reported because the news appears to be up-to-date, authoritative, and run by experts. This is a fallacy. While the news industry rarely fabricates news, it mixes fact with opinions, which can distort the plain unadulterated truth... Learning to distinguish between facts and opinions in the news is crucial for helping children think critically about the news."
12. Legal scholars occasionally differentiate between "rules" and "standards," with "rule" connoting very specific prescriptions and "standard" referring to more general criteria. See Henry M. Hart, Jr. and Albert M. Sacks, *The Legal Process: Basic Problems in the Making and Application of Law*, ed. William N. Eskridge, Jr., and Philip Frickey, (New York: Foundation Press, 1994), 139–141. It has been argued that rules create overly simplistic and artificial classifications and attempt "to govern complex reality through simple binary, yes-or-no categories." From this perspective, there are both benefits and detriments to rules, just as there are for "more-flexible, contextual standards." Peter H. Schuck, *The Limits of Law: Essays on Democratic Governance* (Boulder, CO: Westview, 2000), 428. For present purposes, these distinctions and assessments need not be addressed further. "Standards" is used here to refer broadly to the law, that is, to legal rules, tests, and criteria.
13. Not all legal scholars agree that these distinctions are clear. Cf. Schauer, *Thinking Like a Lawyer*, 204, which observes: "The distinction between questions of law and questions of fact is not without difficulty. A controversy about how to explain the difference between law and fact has generated a substantial body of commentary, even including the view that the distinction is entirely illusory." Schauer puts the controversy

into a functional perspective, related to the overlapping functions of juries and judges: "The confusion comes from the way in which the law has traditionally insisted that facts are for juries and the law is for judges, when in reality many of the things that juries do by way of law application involve making legal determinations, and many of the things that judges do involve making factual ones." (Ibid., 205)

14. M. Ethan Katsh and William Rose, *Taking Sides: Clashing Views on Legal Issues*, 12th ed. (New York: McGraw-Hill, 2006), xix.
15. See US Constitution amendment V, declaring "nor shall any person . . . be deprived of life, liberty, or property, without due process of law"; and amendment XIV, stating "nor shall any State deprive any person of life, liberty, or property without due process of law."
16. Katsh and Rose, *Taking Sides*, xix. See Laurens Walker, E. Allan Lind, and John Thibaut, "The Relation between Procedural and Distributive Justice," *Virginia Law Review* 65 (1979): 141. These authors comment: "For participants, the evidence that an adversary procedure significantly enhances the acceptability of the outcome suggests that civil and criminal processes should be designed to facilitate personal participation by the parties. This participation, the data suggest, will result both in the perception that a comparatively fair procedure was employed and in enhancement of the perception that distributive justice was obtained, regardless of the outcome."
17. Hart and Sacks, *The Legal Process*, 4.
18. Roger Cramton, "Administrative Procedure Reform: The Effects of S. 1663 on the Conduct of Federal Rate Proceedings," *Administrative Law Review* 16 (1964): 111.
19. Henry M. Hart Jr., "Law as a Process (or System of Processes) of Institutional Settlement," quoted in Hart and Sacks, *The Legal Process*, lxxxiv.
20. Hart and Sacks, *The Legal Process*, 154.
21. A similar, but even more pessimistic viewpoint, was expressed in Roscoe Pound, "The Causes of Popular Dissatisfaction with the Administration of Justice," address before the American Bar Association, August 29, 1906, transcript in *Baylor Law Review* 8 (1956): 6. Pound said, "The most important and most constant cause of dissatisfaction with all law at all times is to be found in the necessarily mechanical operation of legal rules."
22. "The basic notion, in a society committed to a representative form of government by and for the citizens, is that private persons should have a meaningful opportunity to participate in government decisions which directly affect their property and activities." Cramton, "Administrative Procedure Reform," 111.
23. Hart and Sacks, *The Legal Process*, 153.
24. "The Law: The Need for Reasons," *Time*, June 21, 1971, 47.
25. 42 U.S.C. §§ 4321 *et seq*. See Daniel P. Selmi and Kenneth A. Manaster, *State Environmental Law* (Eagan, MN: West, 2011), 7:9, stating: "As

in other fields of the law, environmental practitioners in a multiplicity of ways must be sensitive to the benefits and detriments of delay. Whether the delay be on the part of the regulatory agency, the private protagonist, an intervening environmental group, or some other participant in a particular controversy, it is often the case that the economic and strategic significance of delay is substantial, even determinative. Sometimes delay is unavoidable, and sometimes it can be orchestrated. Sometimes it would seem to serve broader public interests and sometimes it would seem to undermine them."

26. Calvert Cliffs' Coordinating Comm., Inc. v. Atomic Energy Comm'n, 449 F.2d 1109, 1128 (D.C. Cir. 1971).
27. Fund for Environmental Defense v. County of Orange, 204 Cal. App. 3d 1538, 1557 n. 1 (1988) (Crosby, J., dissenting), quoting David Shrager and Elizabeth Frost, *The Quotable Lawyer* (New York: Infobase, 1986), 99.
28. Ruggero J. Aldisert, *Logic for Lawyers: A Guide to Clear Legal Thinking*, 3rd ed. (New York: LexisNexis, 1997), 21.
29. Kenneth Culp Davis and Richard Pierce, *Administrative Law Treatise*, 3rd ed. (New York: Little, Brown, 1994), 7.
30. Robert A. Ferguson, *The Trial in American Life* (Chicago: University of Chicago Press, 2007), 49.
31. James B. Stewart, *Tangled Webs: How False Statements are Undermining America* (New York: Penguin, 2011), xviii.
32. Edward J. Sweeney & Sons, Inc. v. Texaco, Inc., 637 F.2d 105, 116 (3d Cir. 1980). See Kevin Jon Heller, "The Cognitive Psychology of Circumstantial Evidence," *Michigan Law Review* 105 (2006): 244. Heller states, "Empirical research into jury decision-making... has consistently found that jurors dramatically undervalue circumstantial evidence and just as dramatically overvalue direct evidence."
33. Ferguson, *The Trial in American Life*, 49.
34. Jessup v. Davis, 115 Neb. 1, 13–14, 211 N.W. 190, 195 (1926).
35. Idaho v. Wright, 497 U.S. 805, 819, 110 S.Ct. 3139 (1990), quoting 5 J. Wigmore, *Evidence* § 1420:251 (J. Chadbourn rev. 1974).
36. Addington v. Texas, 441 U.S. 418, 423 (1978).
37. Rob Atkinson, "A Skeptical Answer to Edmundson's Contextualism: What We Know We Lawyers Know," *Florida State University Law Review* 30 (2002): 37.
38. "When the state tried Simpson for double murder, the jury returned a verdict finding Simpson not guilty. After the verdict, one of the alleged [*sic*] victims' fathers filed suit against Simpson for the wrongful death of his daughter. In the wrongful death civil case, which applied a preponderance of the evidence standard, the jury returned a verdict for the plaintiff, finding it more likely than not that Simpson killed his ex-wife, Nicole Brown Simpson, and Ron Goldman. On its face, these divergent verdicts suggest that juries may have the capacity to distinguish between different burdens of proof." Ryan J. Strasser, "Punitive Damages Caps: A Proposed Middle Ground After Exxon Shipping Co. v. Baker,"

Cornell Journal of Law and Public Policy 19 (2010): 788–789. See Kevin M. Clermont and Emily Sherwin, "A Comparative View of Standards of Proof," *American Journal of Comparative Law* 50 (2002): 263.

39. Legal proceedings often approach issues with the aid of "presumptions," fairly conclusive statements that certain facts or legal implications are to be treated as established. At times a presumption is allowed to be disputed, however, and in those instances "a rebuttable presumption is really just a way of articulating the burden of proof. To say that a letter is presumed delivered is merely to say that the party disputing delivery bears at least the burden of production [of contrary evidence] on the issue of whether the letter was delivered. An irrebuttable presumption states that a presumed fact shall be considered by the trier of fact to be true, regardless of any evidence to the contrary." Vandevelde, *Thinking Like A Lawyer*, 87–88. The best known presumption is the presumption of innocence of the criminal defendant. The prosecution has the burden of rebutting the presumption, that is, of carrying the burden of proving guilt by evidence satisfying the beyond-a-reasonable-doubt standard of proof.
40. Schauer, *Thinking Like a Lawyer*, 219.
41. Tamara Lush, "Loose Ends in Anthony Trial Chafe in Age of TV Drama," *San Jose Mercury News*, July 11, 2011, A4.
42. Industrial Union Department v. Hodgson, 499 F.2d 467, 474 (D.C. Cir. 1974). Reviewing workplace asbestos dust standards promulgated by the Department of Labor, the court also stated, "Some of the questions involved in the promulgation of these standards are on the frontiers of scientific knowledge, and consequently as to them insufficient data is presently available to make a fully informed factual determination."
43. Schauer, *Thinking Like a Lawyer*, 233.
44. See Ruth Beyth-Marom, Shlomith Dekel, Ruth Gombo, and Moshe Shaked, *An Elementary Approach to Thinking Under Uncertainty*, trans. Sarah Lichtenstein, Benny Marom, and Ruth Beyth-Marom (London: Routledge, 1985).
45. See William W. Lowrance, *Of Acceptable Risk: Science and the Determination of Safety* (Los Altos, CA: William Kaufmann, 1976); and Stephen Breyer, *Breaking the Vicious Circle: Toward Effective Risk Regulation* (Cambridge, MA: Harvard University Press, 1993).
46. The meaning of the precautionary principle is a subject of some disagreement, as the following statements suggest: "The Precautionary Principle states that when an activity raises the threat of harm to human health or to the environment, precautionary measures should be taken even if cause and effect relationships are not fully established scientifically." Julian Agyeman, *Sustainable Communities and the Challenge of Environmental Justice* (New York: NYU Press, 2005), 20; "The irreversible nature of much ecological injury drives environmental law to reflect a precautionary principle and to focus, accordingly, on preventing the realization of environmental risks rather than

the redressing of environmental harms." Richard J. Lazarus, *The Making of Environmental Law* (Chicago: University of Chicago Press, 2004), 23; "The Precautionary Principle says that if some course of action carries even a remote chance of irreparable damage to the ecology, then you shouldn't do it, no matter how great the possible advantages of the action may be." Stewart Brand, *Whole Earth Discipline: An Ecopragmatist Manifesto* (New York: Viking Penguin, 2009), 158, quoting Freeman Dyson. There is also disagreement regarding the wisdom of the principle: "The precautionary principle has been so widely recognized as a barrier to progress that... in 2006, the House of Commons select committee on science and technology recommended that the term 'should not be used and should "cease to be included in policy guidance."' (Ibid., 163). See Peter Huber, *Hard Green: Saving the Environment from the Environmentalists: A Conservative Manifesto* (New York: Basic Books, 1999), 189, 191, characterizing the principle as a "theory of ignorance" and a basis for curtailment of technological developments, and stating that "calling it a Precautionary Principle to imply some serious science behind [*sic*] is an outright fraud."

47. "Questions about the environment are particularly prone to uncertainty. Technological man has altered his world in ways never before experienced or anticipated. The health effects of such alterations are often unknown, sometimes unknowable. While a concerned Congress has passed legislation providing for protection of the public health against gross environmental modifications, the regulators entrusted with the enforcement of such laws have not thereby been endowed with a prescience that removes all doubt from their decisionmaking. Rather, speculation, conflicts in evidence, and theoretical extrapolation typify their every action. How else can they act, given a mandate to protect the public health but only a slight or nonexistent data base upon which to draw?... Yet the statutes and common sense demand regulatory action to prevent harm, even if the regulator is less than certain that harm is otherwise inevitable." Ethyl Corp. v. Environmental Protection Agency, 541 F.2d 1, 25 (D.C. Cir. 1976).
48. Coalition for Responsible Regulation v. Environmental Protection Agency, 684 F.3d 102, 121 (D.C. Cir., 2012).
49. See Mary Twitchell, "The Ethical Dilemmas of Lawyers on Teams," *Minnesota Law Review* 72 (1988): 701.
50. Melville v. Southward, 791 P. 2d 383, 387 (Colo. 1990).
51. Persistent concerns and controversies regarding the role of expert witnesses in court are addressed in Jennifer L. Mnookin, "Idealizing Science and Demonizing Experts: An Intellectual History of Expert Evidence," *Villanova Law Review* 52 (2007): 763.
52. US Constitution, art. III, § 2. "Article III of the Constitution confines the federal courts to adjudicating actual 'cases' and 'controversies.'... The 'case or controversy' requirement defines with respect to the Judicial Branch the idea of separation of powers on which the

Federal Government is founded. The several doctrines that have grown up to elaborate that requirement are 'founded in concern about the proper—and properly limited—role of the courts in a democratic society.'" Allen v. Wright, 468 U.S. 737, 750 (1984).

53. Massachusetts v. Environmental Protection Agency, 549 U.S. 497, 517, 127 S.Ct. 1438, 1453 (2007), quoting Baker v. Carr, 369 U.S. 186, 204 (1962).
54. Withrow v. Larkin, 421 U.S. 35, 46–47, 95 S.Ct. 1456, 1464 (1975). See Caperton v. A.T. Massey Coal Co., 566 U.S. 868, 129 S.Ct. 2252, 2259 (2009).
55. A survey of the many meanings of "political," "an equivocal term that must be carefully parsed before it can be usefully applied to judicial behavior," is presented in Richard A. Posner, *How Judges Think* (Cambridge, MA: Harvard University Press, 2008), 9–10. See Terri Jennings Peretti, *In Defense of a Political Court* (Princeton: Princeton University Press, 1999); and Tamanaha, *Beyond the Formalist-Realist Divide.*
56. Vandevelde, *Thinking Like A Lawyer*, 89.
57. Dahlia Lithwick, "The View from the Bench," *Newsweek*, February 8, 2010, 18, quoting Albie Sachs, Justice of the Constitutional Court of South Africa, *The Strange Alchemy of Life and Law* (New York: Oxford University Press, 2009)).
58. In re J. P. Linahan, 138 F.2d 650 (2d Cir. 1943) (Frank, J.).
59. General Provisions Applicable to Courts and Judges, 28 U.S.C. § 455(e) (1982). Although Supreme Court justices are not subject to the same statutory ethics requirements as other federal judges, in January 2011 the citizens organization Common Cause requested the US attorney general to "promptly investigate whether Justices [Clarence] Thomas and [Antonin] Scalia should have recused themselves from the *Citizens United* case under 28 U.S.C. § 455." The group alleged that since that important 2010 decision on corporate and union political spending, "information has come to light that raises serious questions about the impartiality of Justices Thomas and Scalia in the *Citizens United* case. It appears both justices have participated in political strategy sessions, perhaps while the case was pending, with corporate leaders whose political aims were advanced by the decision." "Letter to the Department of Justice re: Conflicts of Interest in the Citizens United Case," Common Cause Holding Power Accountable, accessed Febraury 11, 2012, www.commoncause.org/site/apps/nlnet/content2.aspx?c=dkLNK1MQIwG&b=686043&ct=9039331. See Mike McIntire, "The Justice and the Magnate: Friendship and Museum Project Put Focus on Ethics," *New York Times*, June 19, 2011, 1, discussing activities of Justice Thomas in relation to a private donor of funds to a museum in the justice's hometown.
60. John Paul Stevens, "A Tribute to Justice Byron R. White," *Yale Law Journal* 112 (2003): 971–972, quoting William Shakespeare, "The Taming of the Shrew."

61. Model Code of Judicial Conduct R. 2.8(b).
62. Kimberlianne Podlas, "Please Adjust Your Signal: How Television's Syndicated Courtrooms Bias Our Juror Citizenry," *American Business Law Journal* 39 (2001): 15–16. "What we are seeing is a distorted form of arbitration portrayed as a real trial... One clear distortion of the American judicial system present in the TV reality court shows is the representation of judges... Overall, the women judges, especially Judge Judy, the prototype for the new daytime reality court shows, come off as shrill." See Taunya Lovell Banks, "Will the Real Judge Stand Up: Virtual Integration on TV Reality Court Shows," *Picturing Justice: The On-Line Journal of Law & Popular Culture*, January 16, 2003, accessed February 19, 2013, "http://usf.usfca.edu/pj//realjudge_banks.htm".
63. Fischl and Paul, *Getting to Maybe*, 67.
64. Orley Hood, "On June 3, Soggy's Speech Will Come to Life," *The Clarion-Ledger*, May 25, 2003, "http://orig.clarionledger.com/news/0305/25/oorley.html" (site discontinued).
65. Karl N. Llewellyn, *The Bramble Bush: On Our Law and its Study* (Dobbs Ferry, NY: Oceana Publications, 1960), 107–108.
66. Scholarly analyses of the film, addressing issues such as gender equality and marriage roles, are presented at David Ray Papke, "Cautionary Tales: The Woman as Lawyer in Contemporary Hollywood Cinema," *University of Arkansas Little Rock Law Review* 25 (2003): 485–501. See Rajani Gupta, "Trial And Errors: Comedy's Quest for the Truth," *UCLA Entertainment Law Review* 9 (2001): 129.
67. Frederick Trevor Hill, *Lincoln the Lawyer* (New York: Century Co., 1906), 176. See David Herbert Donald, *Lincoln* (New York: Simon & Schuster, 1995), 106, which states, "Mostly the attorneys had to amuse themselves, and, according to [William] Herndon, they engaged in 'fights—foot and horse races—knock down—wrestling—gambling etc.' 'Whiskey,' he noted, 'was abundant and freely used.'"
68. Doris Kearns Goodwin, *Team of Rivals: The Political Genius of Abraham Lincoln* (New York: Simon & Schuster, 2005), 149.
69. Federal Rules of Evidence 403. Excluding Relevant Evidence for Prejudice, Confusion, Waste of Time, or other Reasons. Lawyers and judges do not always agree, of course, on what amounts to unfair prejudice. In Payne v. Tennessee, 501 U.S. 808, 111 S.Ct. 2597 (1991), a majority of the Supreme Court concluded in a murder case that "victim impact" evidence, relating to the personal characteristics of the victim and the emotional impact of the crimes on the victim's family, was constitutionally permissible for consideration by a sentencing jury. In dissent, Justice Thurgood Marshall wrote: "Admission of victim-impact evidence creates an unacceptable risk of sentencing arbitrariness... The probative value of such evidence is always outweighed by its prejudicial effect because of its inherent capacity to draw the jury's attention away from the character of the defendant and the circumstances of the crime

to such illicit considerations as the eloquence with which family members express their grief and the status of the victim in the community."

70. Charles B. Craver, *Effective Legal Negotiation and Settlement*, 7th ed. (New York: LexisNexis, 2012), 423. See G. M. Filisko, "You're Out of Order: Dealing with the Costs of Incivility in the Legal Profession," *American Bar Association Journal* 99 (2013): 33–40, which states, "It's impossible to say whether incivility in law is escalating or there's simply more grousing about it. But the profession's leaders are calling out what they say is a troubling lack of civility... Courts are also more often sanctioning egregious behavior... Lawyers are also policing their peers."
71. Lee v. American Eagle Airlines, 93 F. Supp.2d 1322, 1336 (S.D. Florida 2000).
72. Ibid.
73. In re Marriage of Davenport, 194 Cal. App. 4th 1507, 1537 (1st Dist. 2011).
74. Craver, *Effective Legal Negotiation and Settlement*, 423.
75. Donald, *Lincoln*, 149.
76. G. Richard Shell, *Bargaining for Advantage: Negotiation Strategies for Reasonable People* (New York: Viking, 1999), 146.
77. Anne-Marie Slaughter, "Thinking Like a Lawyer." Mutual understanding is obviously not a value exclusively endorsed by the legal system. For example, in one of the most conflict-ridden places in the world, the Middle East, an effort was made by an educator and a psychologist to produce "booklets for use in Palestinian and Israeli high schools that force each side to confront a contradictory vision of history. 'The idea is not to legitimize or accept the other's narrative but to recognize it.'" Joanna Chen, "To Get on the Same Page," *Newsweek*, August 13, 2007, 46. See "Requiem for the Right," *Newsweek*, September 7, 2009, 41, which says, "Hannah Arendt identified the ability to listen—to place oneself inside the mind of others—as the essential requirement of democratic statesmanship."
78. Juan Williams, *Thurgood Marshall: American Revolutionary* (New York: Broadway Books, 2000), 111, quoting Herbert Wechsler.
79. Roger Fisher, William L. Ury, and Bruce Patton, *Getting to Yes: Negotiating Agreement without Giving In*, 3rd ed. (New York: Penguin, 2011), xxvii. A similar definition of negotiation, also sometimes called "bargaining," is "a process in which two or more participants attempt to reach a joint decision on matters of common concern in situations where they are in actual or potential disagreement or conflict." Donald G. Gifford, *Legal Negotiation: Theory and Practice*, 2nd ed. (Eagan: Thomson West, 2007), 3.
80. Gifford, *Legal Negotiation*, 1.
81. Craver, *Effective Legal Negotiation and Settlement*, vii.
82. Melissa L. Nelken, *Negotiation: Theory and Practice*, 2nd ed. (New York: LexisNexis, 2007), 1.
83. Shell, *Bargaining for Advantage*, 17.

84. Michael J. Gerhardt, "The Art of Judicial Biography," *Cornell Law Review* 80 (1995): 1634.
85. Joan B. Gottschall, "The Role of Faith in Judging: Fact-finding as a Spiritual Discipline," *University of Saint Thomas Law Journal* 4 (2006): 329–330.
86. Harper Lee, *To Kill a Mockingbird* (New York: Grand Central Publishing, 1982), 314.
87. Vandevelde, *Thinking Like A Lawyer*, 1.
88. For an insightful analysis of "scarcities which make particularly painful choices necessary," and of methods of allotment, including juries, to use in the distribution of scarce goods, see Guido Calabresi and Philip Bobbitt, *Tragic Choices* (New York: Norton, 1978).
89. See William M. Sullivan, Anne Colby, Judith Welch Wegner, Lloyd Bond, and Lee S. Shulman, *Educating Lawyers: Preparation for the Profession of Law* (Hoboken, NJ: Jossey-Bass, 2007), 22, identifying core tasks of professional education, including "enabling students to learn to make judgments under conditions of uncertainty."
90. Aldisert, *Logic for Lawyers*, 18–19.
91. Vandevelde, *Thinking Like A Lawyer*, 3.
92. Lief H. Carter, *Reason in Law* (New York: Little, Brown and Company: 1979), 15.
93. Michael J. Sandel, *Justice: What's the Right Thing to Do* (New York: Farrar, Straus and Giroux, 2009), 207.
94. David H. Souter, "Commencement Speech," May 27, 2010, *Harvard University Gazette*, http://news.harvard.edu/gazette/story/2010/05/text-of-justice-david-souters-speech/ (emphasis added). Even more frequent than the challenge of interpreting constitutional terms is the challenge of interpreting statutory language. "The simplest statute...can become the subject of wildly different interpretations, depending on whom you are talking to: the congressman who sponsored the provision, the staffer who drafted it, the department head whose job it is to enforce it, the lawyer whose client finds it inconvenient, or the judge who may be called upon to apply it." Barack Obama, *The Audacity of Hope: Thoughts on Reclaiming the American Dream* (New York: Crown Publishing Group, 2006), 91.
95. Carter, *Reason in Law*, 21.
96. Describing juries as "aresponsible agencies," two legal scholars wrote: "The aresponsible agency generally has three features: it is representative, decentralized, and it gives no reasons for its decisions...And giving no reasons, it avoids, or at least mitigates, the conflict between the wish to recognize differences and the desire to affirm egalitarianism in all its forms...The jury's representativeness and lack of responsibility have at times been identified as the reason why certain decisions are committed to it. It is the combining of these elements which is the source of the characteristic and powerful way in which the jury operates: Juries apply societal standards without ever telling us what these standards are,

or even that they exist. This is especially important in those situations in which the statement of standards would be terribly destructive," in Calabresi and Bobbitt, *Tragic Choices*, 57–58. A more benign description of the jury's function is the Supreme Court's statement that "it is the jury's function to make the difficult and uniquely human judgments that defy codification and that 'buil[d] discretion, equity, and flexibility into a legal system.'" McCleskey v. Kemp, 481 U.S. 279, 311 (1987).

97. Gerald F. Uelmen, *Lessons from the Trial: The People v. O.J. Simpson* (Riverside, CA: Andrews McMeel Publishing,1996), 175.
98. Carter, *Reason in Law*, 29.
99. Aldisert, *Logic for Lawyers*, 66, quoting Benjamin N. Cardozo, *The Nature of the Judicial Process* (New Haven: Yale University Press, 1921), 19. Discussing "clear legal thinking," Aldisert also states: "We must not establish our conclusions by intense personal desire, keenly felt emotional belief, folklore, superstition, or dogmatic, unquestioning acceptance. Rather we must state grounds for our conclusion...The ability to study law depends upon the power of seeing logical connections in the cases, of recognizing similarities and dissimilarities."
100. Carter, *Reason in Law*, 19.
101. Roscoe Pound, "The Theory of Judicial Decision," *Harvard Law Review* 36 (1923): 946.
102. Porto and Jillson, *The Craft of Legal Reasoning*, 19.
103. Aldisert, *Logic for Lawyers*, 94. See Porto and Jillson, *The Craft of Legal Reasoning*, 2, which comments, "One component of legal reasoning is reasoning by analogy, or, more simply put, reasoning by example."; and Edward H. Levi, *An Introduction to Legal Reasoning* (Chicago: University of Chicago Press: 1949), 1–2: "The basic pattern of legal reasoning is reasoning by example. It is reasoning from case to case. It is a three-step process described by the doctrine of precedent in which a proposition descriptive of the first case is made into a rule of law and then applied to a next similar situation. The steps are these: similarity is seen between cases; next the rule of law inherent in the first case is announced; then the rule of law is made applicable to the second case." A more concise perspective appears in Schauer, *Thinking Like a Lawyer*, 85–102: "Analogies, after all, are a ubiquitous feature of legal argument and judicial opinions. In law, as elsewhere, people argue that because some current situation is like another from the past, then the current one should be dealt with in the same way as the previous one."
104. Highlighting the subtlety of the use of precedents, it has been noted that "cases can often be interpreted as based on several rationales, and these may point in different directions and even conflict with each other." Fischl and Paul, *Getting to Maybe*, 62.
105. Peter H. Schuck, "Court Sense: Analyzing Justices on Ideological Grounds is far too Simplistic," *Los Angeles Times*, July 15, 2009.
106. "The Need for Reasons," *Time*, June 21, 1971, 47, quoting Herbert Wechsler. A more skeptical view of alleged constraints on judging has

been asserted by a prominent and scholarly judge. Speaking of "internal constraints" that are often labeled "judicial method," specifically reasoning by analogy and strict interpretation of statutes and constitutions, Richard Posner says "the first is empty and the second has, despite appearances, a large discretionary element." Posner, *How Judges Think*, 12. He further says, however, "The emphasis that I place on the American judge's extensive (though not complete) freedom from internal and external constraints is not intended to suggest that judicial behavior is random, willful, or political in a partisan sense." Ibid.

107. Roger Parloff, "On History's Stage: Chief Justice John Roberts Jr.," *Fortune*, January 17, 2011, 63, 75. See Bradley W. Joondeph, "Law, Politics, and the Appointments Process," *Santa Clara Law*, Spring 2006, 36, which notes, "Almost every case to reach the Court could defensibly be decided either way."

5 The Citizen as Juror

1. Sebastian Junger, *A Death in Belmont* (New York: W.W. Norton, 2006), 254.
2. Beaver County, Pennsylvania Court of Common Pleas, A Juror's Guide to Jury Duty in Beaver County, 2, www.beavercountycourts.org/JurorsInstructions.htm (site discontinued). See Washington State Courts, A Juror's Guide, accessed February 13, 2013, www.courts.wa.gov/newsinfo/resources/index.cfm, which similarly states, "You do not need special knowledge or ability to do your job."
3. Andrew Guthrie Ferguson, *Why Jury Duty Matters: A Citizen's Guide to Constitutional Action* (New York: NYU Press, 2012), 22, which also relies on the following statement from Henry Kalven Jr. and Hans Zeisel, *The American Jury* (New York: Little, Brown and Company, 1966), 4: "The jury thus represents a deep commitment to the use of laymen in the administration of justice...it opposes the cadre of professional, experienced judges with this transient, ever-changing, ever-inexperienced group of amateurs."
4. Theil v. Southern Pacific Co., 328 U.S. 217, 220 (1946).
5. U.S. v. Luisi, 568 F. Supp.2d 106, 107 (D. Mass. 2008).
6. Michael J. Sandel, *Justice: What's the Right Thing To Do?* (New York: Farrar, Straus and Giroux, 2009), 85.
7. Alexis de Tocqueville, "The Effect of Democracy on Language," in *Democracy in America*, chap. XVI, trans. Henry Reeve (New York: Vintage Books, 1945), 1: 295–296.
8. Ibid., 295.
9. Valerie P. Hans and Neil Vidmar, *Judging the Jury* (New York: Basic Books, 1986), 249. A Supreme Court justice expressed the same perspective: "Juries...are not only a safeguard but through their experience and verdicts they exert tremendous influence on the molding

of the national character." Tom C. Clark, "The American Jury: A Justification," 1 *Valparaiso University Law Review* 1 (1996): 4.

10. John Gastil, E. Pierre Deess, Philip J. Weiser, and Cindy Simmons, *The Jury and Democracy: How Jury Deliberation Promotes Civic Engagement and Political Participation* (New York: Oxford University Press, 2010).
11. Ibid., 4.
12. Ibid., 9.
13. Ibid., 9–10. The study's detailed findings, including distinctions found among "different groups of jurors and different kinds of trials," "add considerable complexity to the generally positive associations between the jury experience and civic and political engagement." Ibid.,128.
14. Ibid., 106. "Most jurors consider it interesting, educational, and an honor to play a part in the fair administration of justice." Judicial Council of California, Jury Service Basics, accessed February 14, 2013, "www.courts.ca.gov/2179.htm".
15. "Estimates are that a full third of US citizens are likely to serve on a jury at some point in their lives." Gastil et al., *The Jury and Democracy*, 4.
16. Administrative Office of the United States Courts, Handbook for Trial Jurors Serving in the United States District Courts, accessed February 14, 2013, www.uscourts.gov/FederalCourts/JuryService.aspx.
17. See Washington State Courts, A Juror's Guide, urging jurors to "keep an open mind, use common sense, concentrate on the evidence presented, and be fair and honest in your deliberations."
18. Judicial Council of California, Jury Service Basics.
19. "To meet their responsibility, jurors must decide the facts and apply the law impartially." Administrative Office of the United States Courts, Handbook for Trial Jurors Serving in the United States District Courts; "You...need to be impartial—in other words, your decisions must not be influenced by personal feelings and biases." Judicial Council of California, Jury Service Basics.
20. U.S. v. Wood, 299 U.S. 177, 185 (1936). "Even the 'state of mind' definition lends itself to different interpretations depending on the particular jurisdiction or the judge or the lawyer." Hans and Vidmar, *Judging the Jury*, 63. Historical and continuing ambivalence about the meaning and value of impartiality in the ideal juror is discussed at Jeffrey Abramson, *We, the Jury: The Jury System and the Ideal of Democracy* (New York: Basic Books, 1994), 17–18, 37–38: "Consider two portraits of the ideal juror. The first and more familiar one highlights the impartiality of the juror and the ignorance that, ironically, makes impartial judgment possible. In this view, the primary qualification of good jurors is that they themselves know nothing beforehand about the case they are about to judge. Precisely because they bring no personal knowledge or opinions to the case, they can judge it with the distance and dispassion that marks impartial justice...In contrast, the second portrait of the ideal juror emphasizes the closeness of the juror to the case on

trial: the juror as peer and neighbor...This so-called local knowledge of the neighborhood qualifies the juror to understand the facts of the case and to pass judgment in ways that a stranger to the community could not...In addition, such jurors can judge cases better than strangers because they know the conscience of the community and can apply the law in ways that resonate with the community's moral values and common sense. Of course, there is considerable tension between these two portraits...The local knowledge model of the jury gradually gave way to the impartial juror ideal."

21. U.S. v. Burr, 25 F.Case 49, 50 (Cir. Ct., D. Va. 1807).
22. Laura Gaston Dooley, "Our Juries, Our Selves: The Power, Perception, and Politics of the Civil Jury," *Cornell Law Review* 80 (1995): 325.
23. Abramson, *We, the Jury*, 1.
24. Robert A. Ferguson, *The Trial in American Life* (Chicago: University of Chicago Press, 2007), 52.
25. Hans and Vidmar, *Judging the Jury*, 245. See Abramson, *We, the Jury*, 3, 91, exploring an alleged "gap between the complexity of modern litigation and the qualifications of jurors" and the suspicion that "jurors do not fathom" the judge's instructions on the law and instead "fall back on their own gut reactions or common sense in deciding how the case should come out."; Joe S. Cecil, Valerie P. Hans and Elizabeth C. Wiggins, "Citizen Comprehension of Difficult Issues: Lessons from Civil Jury Trials," *American University Law Review* 40 (1991): 727; and Valerie P. Hans and Theodore Eisenberg, "The Predictability of Juries," *DePaul Law Review* 60 (2011): 375, 377, which observes, "Another source of the greater perceived unpredictability of juries compared to judges is that jurors are widely presumed to rely on their intuitions, personal biases, and values." An overview of jury dynamics is presented in SunWolf, *Practical Jury Dynamics: From One Juror's Trial Perceptions to the Group's Decision-making Processes* (New York: LexisNexis, 2004).
26. "As the jury in this case, you will be the judges of the facts and you will be the only judges of the facts. You will have to decide what happened. I play no part in judging the facts. That is your responsibility. My role is to be the judge of the law, that is to say, I make whatever legal decisions have to be made during the course of the trial, and I will explain to you the legal principles that must guide you in your decisions on the facts." New Jersey Model Civil Jury Charges, Preliminary Charge., NJ J.I. CIV 1.11A.
27. Massachusetts Superior Court Civil Practice Jury Instructions, General Instructions, CIV JII MA-CLE 1–1.
28. Delaware Online Civil Pattern Jury Instructions, General Instructions, P. J. I. Civ. § 3.2 (2000).
29. Hans and Vidmar, *Judging the Jury*, 149.
30. Neil Vidmar and Valerie P. Hans, *American Juries: The Verdict* (Amherst, NY: Prometheus Books, 2007), 225–226.
31. Tracey Kaplan, "Lynch Acquitted in Priest Beating," *San Jose Mercury News*, July 6, 2012, A1.

32. Scott Herhold, "In Vigilante Case, Jury Was Wrong," *San Jose Mercury News*, July 6, 2012, A1.
33. See chap. 4(C)(1).
34. Judicial Council of California, Civil Jury Instruction 102, Taking Notes During Trial.
35. See chap. 4(D)(2).
36. Federal Pattern Criminal Jury Instructions, 6th Cir., 8.03C (2005); California Jury Instructions Civ. 15.30, Jurors to Deliberate; and California Jury Instructions Civ. 15.60, Deadlocked Jury Admonition.
37. See chap. 4(D)(2).
38. New Jersey Model Civil Jury Charges, General Provision for Standard Charge., NJ J.I. CIV 1.12B.
39. Delaware Online Civil Pattern Jury Instructions, Cautionary Instruction–Sympathy, P. J. I. Civ. § 24.1.
40. Lamb v. State, 251 P.3d 700 (Nev. 2011).
41. See chap. 4(C)(5). "The interest or lack of interest of any witness in the outcome of this case, the bias or prejudice of a witness, if there be any, the appearance, the manner in which the witness gives testimony on the stand, the opportunity that the witness had to observe the facts about which he or she testifies, the probability or improbability of the witness' testimony when considered in the light of all of the other evidence in the case, are all items to be considered by you in deciding how much weight, if any, you will give to that witness' testimony": New York Pattern Jury Instruction Civil, Weighing Testimony, 1:8.
42. See chap. 4(C)(2).
43. California Jury Instructions Civ., 15.60, Deadlocked Jury Admonition; Delaware Pattern Jury Instructions Civ. Sec. 24.6, When Jury Fails to Agree; and New Jersey Jury Instructions Civ. 1.20, Supplemental Instructions as to Further Deliberations by Jury.
44. See discussion of standards and burdens of proof in chapter 4(C)(1).
45. See chap. 4(D)(3).
46. "The [Supreme] Court has stressed the importance of a variety of roles of the jury, beginning with its essential role in citizenship. It has also stated that representative juries instill public confidence that decisions are being made in an unbiased way, and that they inject community values into decisions. These explanations all assume that juries bring to bear community values on their decisions, rather than acting as a mechanical arm of the law," Justin D. Levinson, "Suppressing the Expression of Community Values in Juries: How 'Legal Priming' Systematically Alters the Way People Think," *University of Cincinnati Law Review* 73 (2005): 1063.
47. See chap. 4(B)(1).
48. Ohio Jury Instructions CV 301.05, Orientation for New Jury.
49. Typical admonitions include statements such as these: "I am now going to say a few words about your conduct as jurors. I am going to give you some do's and don'ts, mostly don'ts, which I will call 'The

Admonition.' This admonition is designed to prevent jury tampering and any appearance of jury tampering, something that cannot be tolerated in our system of justice." Arizona Pattern Jury Instructions-Civil, RAJI PI 9, Admonition.

50. Judicial Council of California Civil Jury Instruction 100, Preliminary Admonitions.
51. Illinois Pattern Jury Instruction—Civ. Note 1 (2011 ed.).
52. See chap. 4(B)(1).
53. "Any testimony that I have stricken from the record is not evidence and should not be considered by you in your deliberations. This means that even though you may remember the testimony you are not to use it in your discussions and deliberations." New Jersey Jury Instructions Civ 1.12E, General Provisions for Standard Charge.
54. Tracey Kaplan, "Lynch Acquitted in Priest Beating," A11.
55. Illinois Pattern Jury Instructions—Civ. Note 1 (2011 ed.).
56. See chap. 4(A)(1).
57. See chap. 4(D)(1).
58. See chap. 4(D).
59. Ohio Jury Instructions CV 207.35, Common Closing Remarks. "When you go to the jury room, your first function will be to select one of your number to serve as a foreperson. The person you select to preside over your deliberations does not have any greater power, nor does that person's vote have any more importance, than others." Ohio Jury Instructions CV 207.33, Introduction to Deliberations.
60. Ohio Jury Instructions CV 207.15, Expert Witness.
61. "Although as jurors you are encouraged to use all of your life experiences in analyzing testimony and reaching a fair verdict, you may not communicate any personal professional expertise you might have or other facts not in evidence to the other jurors during deliberations. You must base your discussions and decisions solely on the evidence presented to you during the trial and that evidence alone. You may not consider or speculate on matters not in evidence or matters outside the case." New York Pattern Jury Instructions Civil 1:25A, Juror's Use of Professional Expertise.
62. Beaver County, A Juror's Guide.
63. Illinois Pattern Jury Instructions—Civ. Note 1 (2011 ed.).
64. New Jersey Model Civil Jury Charges, General Provisions for Standard Charge, CIV 1.12W.

6 Inescapable Differences

1. George Lakoff, *The Political Mind* (New York: Viking, 2008), xx.
2. Dan Ariely, *Predictably Irrational: The Hidden Forces That Shape Our Decisions* (New York: Harper, 2009), xxx. Ariely writes, "We are really far less rational than standard economic theory assumes. Moreover,

these irrational behaviors of ours are neither random nor senseless. They are systematic, and since we repeat them again and again, predictable."

3. Jon Hanson, ed., *Ideology, Psychology, and Law* (New York: Oxford University Press, 2012), 11–12.
4. Jonah Lehrer, *How We Decide* (Boston: Houghton Mifflin, 2009), xv.
5. See Michael Shermer, *Why People Believe Weird Things: Pseudoscience, Superstition, and Other Confusions of Our Time* (New York: Holt Paperbacks, 2002), 45, discussing David Hume's "consequent skepticism" approach, "which recognizes the 'consequences' of our fallible senses but corrects them through reason: 'A wise man proportions his belief to the evidence.'"
6. "For most areas of policy concern, it should be assumed that the individual is able to do more than simply order preferences for personal wealth and property. Citizens will be assumed to reason practically, to apply reason to choice." John Martin Gillroy, Breena Holland, and Celia Campbell-Mohn, *A Primer for Law and Policy Design: Understanding the Use of Principle and Argument in Environmental and Natural Resource Law* (Eagen, MN: West, 2008), v.
7. "We live in a culture that's awash in information; it's the age of Google, cable news, and free online encyclopedias. We get anxious whenever we are cut off from all this knowledge... But this abundance comes with some hidden costs. The main problem is that the human brain wasn't designed to deal with such a surfeit of data." Lehrer, *How We Decide*, 158.
8. Michael Specter, *Denialism: How Irrational Thinking Hinders Scientific Progress, Harms the Planet, and Threatens Our Lives* (New York: Penguin, 2009), 46.
9. "Problem schemas, also referred to as 'problem frames,' serve important cognitive functions. They enable us to perform a wide range of problem-solving tasks intuitively, with little expenditure of cognitive resources. But like all knowledge structures, problem frames have a potential downside as well. They can cause us to over-simplify or otherwise misconstrue a problem." Paul Brest and Linda Hamilton Krieger, *Problem Solving, Decision Making, and Professional Judgment* (New York: Oxford University Press, 2010), 34–35. See chapter 2(A), note 13, regarding underlying "frames" on many politicized issues and quoting George Lakoff, *Don't Think of an Elephant: Know Your Values and Frame the Debate* (White River Junction, VT: Chelsea Green, 2005).
10. E. J. Dionne Jr., "End of the Culture Wars," *Santa Clara Magazine*, Fall 2009, 17, 18, discussing "a religious style of politics that [is] dogmatic, partisan, and ideological [,] reflecting a spirit far too certain of itself and far too insistent on the moral depravity of its political adversaries."
11. "Social network studies have long suggested that likes talk to likes; in other words, people tend to selectively expose themselves to people who do not challenge their view of the world." Diana C. Mutz, *Hearing the Other Side: Deliberative versus Participatory Democracy* (Cambridge, England: Cambridge University Press, 2006), 9. Conversely, Mutz

observes: "Exposure to dissimilar views has been deemed a central element—if not the sine qua non—of the kind of political dialogue that is needed to maintain a democratic citizenry: 'Democratic public discourse does not depend on pre-existing harmony or similarity among citizens... but rather on the ability to create meaningful discourses across lines of difference.'" (Ibid., 84)

12. One commentator has emphasized "an anti-intellectualism that periodically rises in the American character... Americans tend to believe common sense the exclusive province of humble folks without sheepskins on the wall or big words in their vocabularies." Leonard Pitts Jr., "The Country Needs Sarah Palin," *San Jose Mercury News*, February 14, 2010, A17. See Sophia Rosenfeld, *Common Sense: A Political History* (Cambridge, MA: Harvard University Press, 2011), 3, which states, "Exponents of democracy everywhere have paid enormous lip service to the epistemological value of the collective, everyday, instinctive judgments of ordinary people."; Sharon Begley, "Red Mind, Blue Mind: The Partisan Divide Over Science," *Newsweek*, December 21, 2009, 32, discussing partisan disagreements over complex scientific issues, and noting political and psychological inclinations to "go with the 'common sense' view" rather than trust scientific experts; and Lehrer, *How We Decide*, 204–206, summarizing research on the influence of partisan identity and bias, such that "voters tend to assimilate only those facts that confirm what they already believe."
13. For an exploration of the dimensions and importance of participation in public conversation, see Robert W. Bennett, *Talking It Through: Puzzles of American Democracy* (Ithaca, NY: Cornell University Press, 2003), 38–40, 45.
14. Dionne, "End of the Culture Wars," 17. See Jack Citrin, "Political Culture," in *Understanding America: The Anatomy of an Exceptional Nation*, ed. Peter H. Schuck and James Q. Wilson (New York: Public Affairs, 2008), 149, describing one consequence of "this quasi-religious conflict of values" as "a party system in which, rather than seeking the political center, warring Red and Blue armies fight to the death over tradition and modernity, faith and science, nationalism and cosmopolitanism, equality of opportunity and equality of results." Citrin also notes, however, that "not everyone accepts this reasoning or agrees that America is breaking apart," for some commentators instead "emphasize the persistence of consensus and moderation."
15. See Howard Fineman, "Sarah, You're No Nixon," *Newsweek*, August 17, 2009, 24, mentioning "the ways in which middle-class exurbanities dread the rise of a polyglot, metropolitan America."
16. Paul Staley, "Our Politics, Our Selves," March 1, 2010, radio broadcast, www.kqed.org/epArchive/R201003010735. Staley said, "And in many debates it becomes a no-man's land because we put our human ability to reason in the employ of our animal instincts, most notably fear... The narrative of extremism... is that somebody else is responsible

for your problems." See Thomas Frank, *What's the Matter with Kansas? How Conservatives Won the Heart of America* (New York: Metropolitan Books, 2004), 159. Frank argues: "Understanding themselves as victims besieged by a hateful world absolves conservatives of responsibility for what goes on around them . . . It allows them, both in politics and in private life, to resolve disputes by pointing their fingers at the outside world and blaming it all on a depraved liberal elite."

17. Amber L. Griffioen, "Truthiness, Self-Deception, and Intuitive Knowledge," in *The Daily Show and Philosophy*, ed. Jason Holt (Hoboken, NJ: Wiley-Blackwell, 2007), 229–230.
18. Leonard Pitts Jr., "Huckabee and I May Disagree, But We Can Find Common Ground," *San Jose Mercury News*, August 22, 2010, A13. See Frank Rich, "The Rage is Not About Health Care," *New York Times*, March 27, 2010, WK10, discussing broader trends, a "kind of national existential reordering," behind "a tsunami of anger," "the current surge of anger—and the accompanying rise in right-wing extremism," ostensibly focused on proposed health care reform legislation; and Jennifer Steinhauer, "Ballot Issues Attest to Anger in California," *New York Times*, January 10, 2010, A1 (surveying voters' "mounting disgust over California's fiscal meltdown and deteriorating services").
19. Roben Torosyan, "Public Discourse and the Stewart Mode of Critical Thinking," in *The Daily Show and Philosophy*, 108.
20. Dan M. Kahan, "Fixing the Communications Failure," *Nature* 463 (2010): 296. Kahan states: "A growing body of work has suggested that ordinary citizens react to scientific evidence on societal risks by endorsing whichever position reinforces their connection to others with whom they share important commitments. As a result, public debate about science is strikingly polarized. The same groups who disagree on 'cultural issues'—abortion, same-sex marriage and school prayer—also disagree on whether climate change is real and on whether underground disposal of nuclear waste is safe." "The ability of democratic societies to protect the welfare of their citizens depends on finding a way to counteract this culture war over empirical data." Kahan and other scholars are part of the Cultural Cognition Project, which studies "how cultural values shape the public's risk perceptions and related policy beliefs" and which also has "an explicit normative objective: to identify democratic procedures that enable society to resolve culturally grounded differences in belief in a manner that is both congenial to people of diverse cultural outlooks and consistent with sound public policymaking." See Dan M. Kahan, Donald Braman, Paul Slovic, John Gastil, and Geoffrey L. Cohen, "The Second National Risk and Culture Study: Making Sense of—and Progress In—the American Culture War of Fact," *The Cognition Project at Yale Law School* (2007), accessed February 15, 2013, http://research/yale.edu/culturalcognition/; and Dan M. Kahan and Donald Braman, "Cultural Cognition and Public Policy," *Yale Journal of Law and Public Policy* 24 (2006): 147.

21. Shermer, *Why People Believe Weird Things*, 46–60. Shermer categorizes the fallacies into four groups: problems in scientific thinking, problems in pseudoscientific thinking, logical problems in thinking, and psychological problems in thinking.
22. Ibid., 59, quoting Alfred Mander, *Logic for the Millions* (New York: Philosophical Library, 1947), vii.
23. George F. Will, "The Left's Demonization is Faulty Rationalization," *San Jose Mercury News*, January 12, 2011, A9.
24. Gene Weingarten, *The Fiddler in the Subway* (New York: Simon & Schuster, 2010), 251, quoting Garry Trudeau.
25. Azar Nafisi, *Reading Lolita in Tehran: A Memoir in Books* (New York: Random House, 2003), 268.
26. "Trusting one's emotions requires constant vigilance; intelligent intuition is the result of deliberative practice." Lehrer, *How We Decide*, 49. See Daniel Kahneman, *Thinking, Fast and Slow* (New York: Farrar, Straus and Giroux, 2011), 13, 21, contrasting "the automatic and often unconscious processes that underlie intuitive thinking" with "the conscious, reasoning self that has beliefs, make choices, and decides what to think about and what to do"; and Dan Ariely, *The Upside of Irrationality: The Unexpected Benefits of Defying Logic* (New York: Harper, 2010), 294. Ariely declares: "Some of the ways in which we are irrational are also what makes us wonderfully human (our ability to find meaning in work, our ability to fall in love with our creations and ideas, our willingness to trust others, our ability to adapt to new circumstances, our ability to care about others, and so on)...We need to appreciate those imperfections that benefit us, recognize the ones we would like to overcome, and design the world around us in a way that takes advantage of our incredible abilities while overcoming some of our limitations."
27. See John T. Noonan, Jr., *Persons and Masks of the Law* (New York: Farrar, Straus, and Giroux, 1975), vii. Noonan emphasizes "the central place of the human person in any account of law" and that "neglect of persons...had led to the worst sins for which American lawyers were accountable." He states: "Little or no attention is given to the persons in whose minds and in whose interaction the rules [of law] have lived—to the persons whose difficulties have occasioned the articulation of the rule, to the lawyers who have tried the case, to the judges who have decided it."
28. Thomas C. Galligan, Phoebe A. Haddon, Frank L. Maraist, Frank M. McClellan, Michael Rustad, Nicolas P. Terry, and Stephanie M. Wildman, *Tort Law: Cases, Perspectives, and Problems*, 4th ed. (Dayton: LexisNexis, 2007), 12.
29. Stephanie M. Wildman, *Privilege Revealed: How Invisible Preference Undermines America* (New York: New York University Press, 1996), 140.
30. Paul West, "Voters Ask Who Can Top Obama," *San Jose Mercury News*, January 2, 2012, A1.

31. Elizabeth S. Smith and Alison Bressler, "Who Taught You to Talk Like That? A Comparative Analysis of Civility and Identity in Online Political Discourse," paper delivered at Midwest Political Science Association, Chicago, Illinois, April 14, 2012, 30.
32. See Krishna K. Ladha, "The Condorcet Jury Theorem, Free Speech, and Correlated Votes," *American Journal of Political Science* 36 (1992): 621, questioning the assumption that individuals make independent voting decisions, uninfluenced by "opinion leaders" and lacking "common information, culture, religion, beliefs, or other elements that could lead to correlated votes." "Much of the time, groups of people end up thinking and doing things that group members would never think or do on their own…Some of the best and worst developments in social life are a product of group dynamics, in which members of organizations, both small and large, move one another in new directions." Cass R. Sunstein, *Going to Extremes: How Like Minds Unite and Divide* (New York: Oxford University Press, 2009), 2. See Richard H. Thaler and Cass R. Sunstein, *Nudge: Improving Decisions about Health, Wealth, and Happiness* (New Haven, CT: Yale University Press, 2008), 53, which summarizes, "Humans are not exactly lemmings, but they are easily influenced by the statements and deeds of others."
33. Christine Barbour and Gerald C. Wright, *Keeping the Republic: Power and Citizenship in American Politics*, 4th ed. (Washington, DC: CQ Press, 2009), 519.
34. Laurie Goodstein, "Illinois Bishops Drop Program Over Bias Rule," *New York Times*, December 29, 2011, A1. One scholar commented as follows on the "problem of defining issues" in matters voters face: "There may be some governing direction, but aside from that possibility, there is no natural definition of an "issue"…The definition of what is an issue may well have an effect on outcomes. Focusing on issue definition suggests additional ambiguities. One reason that majority voting may yield different results depending on how issues are framed is that voters may care about matters differentially." Bennett, *Talking It Through*, 11.
35. John Coates and Taylor Lincoln, *Fulfilling Kennedy's Promise: Why the SEC Should Mandate Disclosure of Corporate Political Activity*, report published by Harvard Law School and Public Citizen, September 2011, 6.
36. See Steven Harmon, "State Sues for Names of Donors to PAC," *San Jose Mercury News*, October 26, 2012, A1; and Steven Harmon, "Judge Okays Probe of Shadowy Group," *San Jose Mercury News*, October 31, 2012, B2.
37. Nicholas Confessore and Michael Luo, "Secrecy Shrouds 'Super PAC' Funds in Latest Filings," *New York Times*, February 1, 2012, which reported, "Groups supportive of each party employed a technique that allows them to cloak the identities of many of their donors." The impact of the Supreme Court's decision on campaign spending in Citizens United v. Federal Election Commission, 558 U.S. 310, 130 S. Ct. 876 (2010), is reflected, for example, at Mike McIntire and Nicholas Confessore, "Corporations' Influence Isn't Always Clear: Tax-exempt

Groups Shield Donations to Political Campaigns," *San Jose Mercury News*, July 8, 2012, A6, which comments, "The secrecy surrounding these groups makes a full accounting of corporate influence in the electoral process impossible." For discussion of the arguable benefits of anonymous—as distinguished from secret—political donations, see Lawrence Lessig, *Republic, Lost: How Money Corrupts Congress—and a Plan to Stop It* (New York: Twelve, 2011), 260–263.

38. Steven Harmon, "State Sues for Names of Donors to PAC," A13, quoting Tracy Westen, Center for Governmental Studies.
39. Bennett, *Talking It Through*, 39–40.
40. Bush v. Gore, 531 U.S. 98 (December 12, 2000).
41. Sheehan v. Franken (In re Contest of General Election), 767 N.W.2d 453 (Minn. June 30, 2009).
42. See Mark Lane, *My Indictment of the CIA in the Murder of JFK* (New York: Skyhorse Publishing, 2011); Gerald Blaine, *The Kennedy Detail: JFK's Secret Service Agents Break Their Silence* (New York: Gallery Books, 2010); and Barry Ernest, *The Girl on the Stairs: My Search for a Missing Witness to the Assassination of John F. Kennedy* (CreateSpace Independent Publishing Platform, 2011).
43. See "*JFK: Three Shots That Changed America*," directed by Nicole Rittenmeyer and Seth Skundrick (A&E Home Video, 2010); and "JFK: The Lost Bullet" (National Geographic Video, 2011).
44. Michael Isikoff, "Haunted by the Dean of Watergate," *Newsweek*, June 22, 2009, 19. See Bill Mears, "Judge Orders the Release of Nixon's Watergate Grand Jury Testimony," July 29, 2011, accessed on February 15, 2013, http://articles.cnn.com/2011-07-29/politics/nixon.watergate.testimony_1_grand-jury-judge-orders-testimony?_s=PM:POLITICS; Brian Stelter, "Watergate Reporting, the Second Draft," *New York Times*, April 2, 2012, which notes "enduring news media fascination with the scandal, which seems to inspire a new television special every 5 to 10 years [and] "many questions about the scandal remain unresolved"; and Jessica Gresko, "Sealed Watergate Papers May Be Released," *San Jose Mercury News*, June 3, 2012, A2.
45. See Chad Flanders, "Bush v. Gore and the Uses of 'Limiting,'" *Yale Law Journal* 116 (2007): 1159; Richard L. Hansen, "The Untimely Death of Bush v. Gore," *Stanford Law Review* 60 (2007): 1; and Gerald L. Neuman and Nicholas Hatzis, "Was Bush v. Gore a Human Rights Case?" *Constitutional Commentary* 25 (2008): 215.

7 GUIDANCE FROM THE LAW

1. Dan Ariely, *Predictably Irrational: The Hidden Forces that Shape Our Decisions* (New York: HarperCollins, 2009), 43–44. "The ability to supervise itself, to exercise authority over its own decision-making process, is one of the most mysterious talents of the human brain. Such

a mental maneuver is known as executive control, since thoughts are directed from the top down, like a CEO issuing orders." Jonah Lehrer, *How We Decide* (New York: Mariner Books, 2009), 116.

2. As explained in chapter 4(A)(1), the word "issue" is used here in two different ways. Public "issues" means questions and concerns of broad public significance and interest. In contrast, "legal issues" or the "issues in a case" connotes more specific points of disagreement that must be resolved in order to decide a case. A public "issue" is, in effect, the broad problem or "case" to be resolved. Legal "issues" are the more focused points of dispute which bear on resolution of the case.
3. Michael S. Wald, "Same-Sex Couple Marriage: A Family Policy Perspective," *Virginia Journal of Social Policy and Law* 9 (2001): 299. On June 26, 2013, the US Supreme Court decided two cases concerning same-sex marriage. Hollingsworth v. Perry, 570 U.S.___(2013), and U.S. v. Windsor, 570 U.S.___(2013). *Hollingsworth* was resolved solely on procedural grounds. *Windsor*, which held the federal Defense of Marriage Act unconstitutional, did not definitively or comprehensively declare legal principles to resolve the broader same-sex marriage debate. The Court's decision, however, did contain statements about equality. For example, the Court said that the Act demonstrated "interference with the equal dignity of same-sex marriages" and that its "principal effect is to identify a subset of state-sanctioned marriages and make them unequal."
4. Adam Lamparello, "Incorporating the Supreme Court's Eighth Amendment Framework into Substantive Due Process Jurisprudence through the Introduction of a Contingent-based and Legislatively-driven Theory," *Nebraska Law Review* 88 (2010): 747. See Andrew H. Friedman, "Same-Sex Marriage and the Right to Privacy," *Howard Law Journal* 35 (1992): 195.
5. "The Slippery Slope of Same-Sex 'Marriage,'" Family Research Council, accessed February 20, 2013, http://www.frc.org/get.cfm?i=bc04c02.
6. Richard M. Fischl and Jeremy Paul, *Getting to Maybe: How to Excel on Law School Exams* (Durham: Carolina Academic Press, 1999), 21. See Chap. 4(A) n9.
7. Adam Liptak, "Health Ruling Hinges on How Justices Frame the Core Issue," *New York Times*, March 27, 2012, accessed February 20, 2013, http://www.nytimes.com/2012/03/28/us/supreme-court-hears-arguments-to-health-care-law.html?scp=1&sq=&st=nyt.
8. National Federation of Independent Business v. Sebelius, 132 S. Ct. 2566, 2600 (2012).
9. "A growing number of Americans doubt the existence of climate change. A poll from late 2009 found fifty-one percent, down from seventy-one percent in 2007, of American adults believe carbon dioxide will lead to global warming." Nathaniel Gronewold et al., "Rising Partisanship Sharply Erodes U.S. Public's Belief in Global Warming," *New York Times*, December 3, 2009, accessed February 20, 2013, http://www

.nytimes.com/cwire/2009/12/03/03climatewire-rising-partisanship-sharply-erodes-us-public-47381.html.

10. John Hart, "The Poor of the Planet and the Planet of the Poor: Ecological Ethics and Economic Liberation," *University of Saint Thomas Law Journal* 5 (2008): 146, describing the view that "global warming does not exist, or, when evidence of its impact proves irrefutable, it is just part of a 'natural' cycle, a temporary global 'climate change' not related to human industrial activity or auto emissions."
11. For a discussion of divergent views, see William D. Nordhaus, "Why the Global Warming Skeptics are Wrong," *The New York Review of Books*, March 22, 2012, accessed February 20, 2013, http://www.nybooks.com/articles/archives/2012/mar/22/why-global-warming-skeptics-are-wrong/?pagination=false; and David G. Victor, *Climate Change: Debating America's Policy Options* (New York: Council on Foreign Relations Press, 2004), v, noting: "In the United States, climate change has become a lightning rod. On one side a sizable minority that dismisses most or all of the science. There are as well those who view the threats of climate change with such seriousness that nothing less is required than a prompt and complete reorganization of the modern industrial economy—away from the use of fossil fuels...and toward some alternative energy future."
12. Dan M. Kahan, "The Gun Control Debate: A Culture-Theory Manifesto," *Washington and Lee Law Review* 60 (2003): 3.
13. Ibid., 4, 6. Kahan juxtaposes a "more egalitarian and communitarian" outlook in favor of more gun regulation with a "more hierarchical and individualistic" perspective in opposition. Ibid., 8.
14. See Joan Jacobs Brumberg, *The Body Project: An Intimate History of American Girls* (New York: Random House, 1997), 201–205, presenting different views on causes of teen pregnancy; Megan Weinstein, "The Teenage Pregnancy 'Problem': Welfare Reform and the Personal Responsibility and Work Opportunity Reconciliation Act of 1996," *Berkeley Women's Law Journal* 13 (1998): 117; and Douglas Kirby, *Emerging Answers: Research Findings on Programs to Reduce Teen Pregnancy* (Washington, DC: The National Campaign to Reduce Teen and Unplanned Pregnancy, 2007), 2, accessed February 20, 2013, http://www.thenationalcampaign.org/resources/pdf/pubs/EA2007_FINAL.pdf.
15. See Michael L. Radelet and Ronald L. Akers, "Deterrence and the Death Penalty: The Views of the Experts," *Journal of Criminal Law and Criminology* 87 (1996): 1; and Paul A. Winters, ed., *The Death Penalty: Opposing Viewpoints*, 3rd ed. (San Diego: Greenhaven Press, 1997).
16. Ron Briggs, "State Voters Must Repeal Capital Punishment Law," *San Jose Mercury News*, February 15, 2012, A15.
17. See Chap. 4(B)(1).
18. Massachusetts v. EPA, 549 U.S. 497 (2007).
19. Ibid., 511.
20. The Clean Air Act's provisions on the enactment of regulations are found in Section 307(d), 42 U.S.C. §7607(d).

21. Chap. 4(C)(1).
22. Announcements and details of three of the EPA's major actions can be found at US Environmental Protection Agency, Endangerment and Cause or Contribute Findings for Greenhouse Gases Under Section 202(a) of the Clean Air Act, 74 Federal Register, December 15, 2009, 66496; US Environmental Protection Agency, Light-Duty Vehicle Greenhouse Gas Emission Standards and Corporate Average Fuel Economy Standards, 75 Federal Register, May 7, 2010, 25324; and US Environmental Protection Agency, Prevention of Significant Deterioration and Title V Greenhouse Gas Tailoring Rule, 75 Federal Register, June 3, 2010, 31514.
23. Rufo v. Simpson, 86 Cal.App.4th 573 (2001).
24. Standards of proof are discussed above at chapter 4(C) (1).
25. 539 U.S. 607, 123 S. Ct. 2446.
26. Charlie Goodyear and Pamela J. Podger, "California Molestation Law Struck Down: Lifting of Statute of Limitations for Prosecution Ruled Unconstitutional," *San Francisco Chronicle*, June 27, 2003, A1, which commented, "Thursday's decision came as a deep disappointment to prosecutors and crime victims, who have argued that molested children need years to come to terms with the abuse and report it to police"; and Don Munsch, "High Court Strikes Down Law on Statutes of Limitations," *Amarillo Globe-News*, June 27, 2003, accessed February 20, 2013, http://amarillo.com/stories/062703/usn_highcourt.shtml, which asserted, "[The ruling] affects future victims because the sex offenders have been given a pass and they will not face prosecution until caught again, putting countless children at risk."
27. 539 U.S. at 652 (Kennedy, J., dissenting).
28. 539 U.S. at 601.
29. Chap. 7(C)(3)–(4).
30. Eric Klinenberg, "One's a Crowd," *New York Times*, February 5, 2012, SR4.
31. Even judges can be subject to deadlines for how soon they must render a decision after the conclusion of a case. For example, the California Constitution declares that a judge shall not receive her salary while a case "remains pending and undetermined for 90 days after it has been submitted for decision." Cal. Const., art. VI, § 19.
32. See Chap. 6(G).
33. Lawyers, of course, frequently seek and are granted continuances, extensions of allowable time, when deadlines become problematic for any number of reasons. Lawyers' relief when they secure continuances is usually considerable.
34. See Alex Altman, "The Unpredictable Candidacy of Herman Cain Takes Its Final Turn," *Time*, November 30, 2011, accessed February 20, 2013, http://swampland.time.com/2011/11/30/the-unpredictable-candidacy-of-herman-cain-takes-its-last-dramatic-turn/. This article reported on the conclusion of a presidential candidacy after a former Republican "frontrunner" was beset by "reports of sexual harassment

and startling knowledge gaps revealed under the scrutiny of national attention"; and Jim McGee, Tom Fiedler, and James Savage, "The Gary Hart Story: How It Happened," *Miami Herald*, May 10, 1987, accessed February 20, 2013, http://www.unc.edu/~pmeyer/Hart/hartarticle.html. This article described the investigation of marital infidelity of 1988 frontrunner Democratic presidential candidate Gary Hart, which resulted in his withdrawal from the race).

35. Sheryl Gay Stolberg, "Firing Blows Up in Face of Feds, Fox," *San Jose Mercury News*, July 22, 2010, A1.
36. See Chap. 6(G).
37. See Chap. 4(A)(1), 4(C)(1).
38. Ruggero J. Aldisert, *Logic for Lawyers: A Guide to Clear Legal Thinking*, 3rd ed. (New York: LexisNexis, 1997), 21.
39. "Modern Anglo-American law, of course, does not view circumstantial evidence as inferior to direct evidence...Empirical research into jury decision-making, however...has consistently found that jurors dramatically undervalue circumstantial evidence and just as dramatically overvalue direct evidence." Kevin Jon Heller, "The Cognitive Psychology of Circumstantial Evidence," *Michigan Law Review* 105 (2006), 243–244.
40. Claude Allegre, J. Scott Armstrong, Jan Breslow, Roger Cohen, Edward David, William Happer, Michael Kelly, William Kininmonth, Richard Lindzen, James McGrath, Rodney Nichols, Burt Rutan, Harrison H. Schmitt, Nir Shaviv, Henk Tennekes, and Antonio Zichichi, "No Need to Panic About Global Warming: There's No Compelling Scientific Argument for Drastic Action to 'Decarbonize' the World's Economy," *Wall Street Journal*, January 27, 2012, accessed February 20, 2013, http://online.wsj.com/article/SB10001424052970204301404577171531838421366.html.
41. William D. Nordhaus, "Why the Global Warming Skeptics Are Wrong," *The New York Review of Books*, March 22, 2012.
42. Kenneth A. Manaster, "Law and the Dignity of Nature: Foundations of Environmental Law," *DePaul Law Review* 26 (1977): 764.
43. Wald, "Same-Sex Couple Marriage," 229.
44. See District of Columbia v. Heller, 554 U.S. 570, 128 S.Ct. 2783 (2008); and McDonald v. City of Chicago, 130 S.Ct. 3020 (2010).
45. See chap. 5(D).
46. See chap. 4(C)(2).
47. See chap. 1 and chap. 6(A).
48. John Houghton, *Global Warming: The Complete Briefing*, 4th ed. (Cambridge: Cambridge University Press, 2009), 15–16.
49. Robert J. Spitzer, *The Politics of Gun Control*, 2nd ed. (New York: Chatham House, 1998), 64.
50. William J. Krouse, *Gun Control Legislation* (Congressional Research Service Report for Congress, 2008), 3.
51. For discussion of proposed changes in California's three strikes law, see *A Primer: Three Strikes—The Impact After More Than a Decade*

(California Legislative Analyst's Office, 2005); and Julia Reynolds, "The Hidden Impact of Three Strikes," *Monterey County Herald* (Monterey, CA), November 30, 2011, accessed February 20, 2013, http://www.montereyherald.com/news/ci_19420585.

52. See chap. 4(C)(3).
53. Alexis de Tocqueville, *Democracy in America*, ed. Richard D. Heffner (New York: Penguin, 1956), 147.
54. See chap. 3(C), (F).
55. See chap. 4(C)(4).
56. Fed. R. Evid. 702.
57. Daubert v. Merrell Dow Pharmaceuticals, Inc., 509 U.S. 579, 593 (1993).
58. Ibid., 589.
59. See chap. 4(C)(5).
60. Adam Liptak, "Supreme Court Rejects Judge-Drawn Maps in Texas Redistricting Case," *New York Times*, January 20, 2012, accessed February 20, 2013, http://thecaucus.blogs.nytimes.com/2012/01/20/supreme-court-rejects-judge-drawn-maps-in-texas-redistricting-case/.
61. "In 1986 retention elections in California, business and insurance interests made large campaign contributions to oust Chief Justice Rose Bird, who was known for her pro-consumer and pro-tenant decisions. Significantly, the groups used advertisements not to point out Bird's anti-business decisions, but rather to point out her opposition to the death penalty, a punishment supported by a majority of Californians." Richard L. Hasen, "High Court Wrongly Elected: A Public Choice Model of Judging and Its Implications for the Voting Rights Act," *North Carolina Law Review* 75 (1997): 1321. See Erwin Chemerinsky, "Evaluating Judicial Candidates," *Southern California Law Review* 61 (1988): 1986, which stated, "The media campaign against the justices received heavy contributions from big business interests that were angry with the court's decisions protecting consumers', tenants', and employees' rights."
62. "ExxonSecrets," Greenpeace, accessed February 19, 2013, www.greenpeace.org/usa/en/campaigns/global-warming-and-energy/exxon-secrets/.
63. Richard A. Muller, "The Conversion of a Climate-Change Skeptic," *New York Times*, July 28, 2012, accessed February 20, 2013, http://www.nytimes.com/2012/07/30/opinion/the-conversion-of-a-climate-change-skeptic.html?_r=1&.
64. Neela Banerjee, "Prominent Climate Change Denier Now Admits He Was Wrong," *The Christian Science Monitor*, July 30, 2012, accessed February 20, 2013, www.csmonitor.com/Science/2012/0730/Prominent-climate-change-denier-now-admits-he-was-wrong-video.
65. The History Channel, *Events That Shaped Our Lives*, Audio CD (Cedar Knolls, NJ: Radio Spirits, 2004), Disk 1, Track 8.
66. Learned Hand, *The Spirit of Liberty*, ed. Irving Dilliard (New York: Vintage Books, 1959), 144.
67. See chap. 4(D)(1).
68. Lehrer, *How We Decide*, 217.

69. The dubious behavior of the "judges" in television courtroom shows is discussed above at chap. 4(D)(1).
70. Ann Coulter, *Slander: Liberal Lies about the American Right* (New York: Crown Publishing, 2002), 10, quoted in chap. 2(C).
71. See Joe Stumpe and Monica Davey, "Abortion Doctor Shot to Death in Kansas Church," *New York Times*, June 1, 2009, A1; and Richard C. Paddock and Maria L. La Ganga, "Officials Decry Attacks on UC Staff," *Los Angeles Times*, August 5, 2008, accessed February 20, 2013, http://articles.latimes.com/print/2008/aug/05/local/me-attacks5. The latter article stated, "Firebombs that struck the home and car of two UC Santa Cruz scientists this weekend were part of an increasingly aggressive campaign by animal rights activists against animal researchers at University of California campuses."
72. Gabrielle Levy, January 10, 2013 (10:12 a.m.), "Piers Morgan Deportation Petition: White House Responds," UPI.com Blog, accessed February 20, 2013, http://www.upi.com/blog/2013/01/10/Piers-Morgan-deportation-petition-White-House-responds/7141357830406/. The White House's response, denying the petition, included the following statement: "Let's not let arguments over the Constitution's Second Amendment violate the spirit of its First [Amendment]."
73. Carrie Lukas, "Using Children to Pass Gun Laws is Grotesque and Childish," *Forbes*, January 18, 2013, accessed February 20, 2013, www.forbes.com/sites/carrielukas/2013/01/18/using-children-to-pass-gun-laws-is-grotesque-and-childish/.
74. Jon Meacham, "What He's Like Now," *Newsweek*, May 25, 2009, 36, 39.
75. See chap. 5(D). In chapter 5's discussion of jurors' listening skills, it was noted that strictly speaking jurors are not conducting negotiations, even though the cooperative and open-minded search for agreement in jury deliberations is similar to the negotiation process. Similarly, the ordinary citizen's discussions with others for the purpose of developing her own conclusions on public issues usually does not involve the kind of concrete give-and-take and compromise which is characteristic of negotiation.
76. David H. Souter, "Commencement Speech," May 27, 2010, transcript, *Harvard University Gazette*, http://news.harvard.edu/gazette/story/2010/05/text-of-justice-david-souters-speech/ (emphasis added), quoted in chapter 4(D)(3).
77. Hinton v. Monsanto Company, 813 So. 2d 817, 830–831 (Ala. 2001).
78. For a review of these competing considerations and experiences under California's 1990 term limits law, see Mike Zapler, "Many One-time Backers Now See Term Limits as Big Mistake," *San Jose Mercury News*, August 1, 2010, 1.
79. Harry L. Wilson, *Guns, Gun Control, and Elections: The Politics and Policy of Firearms* (Lanham, MD: Rowman & Littlefield, 2007), 239.
80. Krouse, *Gun Control Legislation*, 3.
81. Kelo v. City of New London, 545 U.S. 469, 125 S.Ct. 2655.
82. Ibid., 477 (Stevens, J.).

83. Ibid., 494 (O'Connor, J., dissenting).
84. See chap. 4(D)(3).
85. Karl N. Llewellyn, *The Bramble Bush: On Our Law and Its Study* (Dobbs Ferry, NY: Oceana Publications, 1960), 71.
86. John Paul Stevens, "Judicial Predilections," *Nevada Law Journal* 6 (2005): 3.
87. See Keith E. Whittington, "Bill Clinton Was No Andrew Johnson: Comparing Two Impeachments," *University of Pennsylvania Journal of Constitutional Law* 2 (2000); Wes Allison, "Election 2000 Much Like Election 1876," *St. Petersburg Times*, November 17, 2000, http://www.sptimes.com/News/111700/news_pf/Election2000/Election_2000_much_li.shtml (site discontinued); and Adam Cohen, "Justice Rehnquist Writes on Hayes vs. Tilden, With His Mind on Bush v. Gore," *New York Times*, March 21, 2004, accessed February 20, 2013, http://www.nytimes.com/2004/03/21/opinion/editorial-observer-justice-rehnquist-writes-hayes-vs-tilden-with-his-mind-bush-v.html?pagewanted=all&src=pm. ("The presidential elections of 1876 and 2000 have the sort of eerie parallels that make amateur historians' pulses race. Both ended in a deadlock, with Florida holding the key.")
88. See Ed O'Keefe, "Bush Accepts Iraq-Vietnam Comparison," *ABC News*, October 18, 2006, accessed February 20, 2013, http://abcnews.go.com/WNT/story?id=2583579#.T1vC02C4K_E; John Harwood, "Obama Rejects Afghanistan-Vietnam Comparison," *New York Times*, September 15, 2009, A5; and Sanjeev Miglani, "Afghanistan Neither Vietnam nor Iraq, but Closer Home Perhaps," *Afghan Journal*, November 11, 2009, accessed February 20, 2013, http://blogs.reuters.com/afghanistan/2009/11/11/afghanistan-neither-vietnam-nor-iraq-but-closer-home-perhaps/. See Frank Rich, *The Greatest Story Ever Sold: The Decline and Fall of Truth in Bush's America* (New York: Penguin [USA], 2007), 66, 113, 160, discussing "Vietnam analogies" and "Vietnam parallel" to war in Iraq.

8 CONCLUSION: ABOUT RESPONSIBILITY

1. The National Task Force on Civic Learning and Democratic Engagement, *A Crucible Moment: College Learning and Democracy's Future* (Washington, DC: Association of American Colleges and Universities, 2012), 69.
2. In re Discipline of Laprath, 670 N.W. 2d 41 (S.D. 2003), quoting Matter of Chamley, 349 N.W.2d 56, 58 (S.D. 1984).
3. MGIC Indemnity Corporation v. Weisman, 803 F.2d 500, 504 (9th Cir. 1986).
4. Kriegsman v. Kriegsman, 150 N.J. Super. 474, 375 A.2d 1253, 1256 (App. Div. 1977).
5. Thompson v. Seligman, 863 N.Y.S.2d 285, 286 (N.Y. App. 2008), quoting Brady v. Bisogno & Meyerson, 819 N.Y.S.2d 558, 558 (2006).

6. American Bar Association, Model Rules of Professional Conduct, Rule 1.3 cmt. 1.
7. Beaver County, Pennsylvania Court of Common Pleas, *A Juror's Guide to Jury Duty in Beaver County*, 2, www.beavercountycourts.org/JurorsInstructions.htm (site discontinued); Michael J. Sandel, *Justice: What's the Right Thing To Do?* (New York: Farrar, Straus and Giroux, 2009), 85; and Administrative Office of the United States Courts, *Handbook for Trial Jurors Serving in the United States District Courts*, 13, accessed February 17, 2013, "www.uscourts.gov/FederalCourts/JuryService.aspx".

Index

CPSIA information can be obtained at www.ICGtesting.com
Printed in the USA
LVOW10*1510300414

383886LV00013B/379/P

9 781137 344816